# Been There, Done That, and Now This

by
**Arbutus E. Focht**

PublishAmerica
Baltimore

First printing

ISBN: 1-4137-5852-5
PUBLISHED BY PUBLISHAMERICA, LLLP
www.publishamerica.com
Baltimore

Printed in the United States of America

# DEDICATION

This book is dedicated to my departed husband, Herbert O. Focht, and to our caring and spunky children, Dianne Fisher, Debra Takach, and twins, Keith and Kevin Focht, who at first thought I, their Mom, was deserting them. Their thoughts were, *No place could be as lovely as pictured in a retirement community, and no place could offer so much to its residents. Was I certain it wasn't operated by a cult, and I would be programmed into being submissive like the women in the movie, The Stepford Wives? Before moving so far away, I should check things out more thoroughly.*

I have and am pleased my offspring are now content in the knowledge that I, their mom, am safely and happily settled in a retirement community, and though each day is met with anticipation, they still, and will forever, remain dear and close in my heart.

# ACKNOWLEDGMENTS

Special warm and glowing thanks go to my decorator, Natalie, and also neighbors, Daphine Kent, Jo and Lu Crochetiere, and our neighborhood helper, John Kuledge, and wife, Joan. All have touched my life, and continue to make it joyful since my April 1, 2002 residency here in this retirement community, The Villages in Florida.

I particularly wish to thank my dear Florida chums, Jane and Bob Stem, who took me under wing and shoved me into joining a once-a-month breakfast club called The Village Idiots. All Village residents are welcomed. There are no dues, no roll call, no elections or committee reports, no redeeming social value whatsoever, only fun and getting to know other Villagers

More recently, others I wish to thank are: Richard Matwyshen, our 2005 president of our singles' club, who so freely volunteered to salvage some of my manuscript I presumed lost.

Very importantly, my humble thanks to Carl Bell, my Computer Professor, who not only shopped and helped update my computer and printer system, but steadfastly assisted with the technical jargon I lacked, and needed to help finalize my dream.

To Dee J. Hartman, my dear niece, an artist, teacher, author, songwriter and performer in Altoona, PA, I send my grateful thanks and appreciation for your devoted time and efforts in preparing the cover for my book. I am well pleased.

Last, but never the least, my most personal and heartfelt thanks reaches out to embrace Publish America, my publisher, for allowing me to share with the many seniors who wish and dare to uproot and move into a retirement community. Extra special thanks and hugs go out to their Author's Support Group: Meg Phillips, my first leader, and Acquisition Editor; and to Natalie Batovsky, Editor; Patricia A. Barto, Cover Design Producton Manager; Lilly and Patrice; and all who, via e-mail, assisted me in requiring all acquisitions needed for publication. Again, my humble and heartfelt thanks!

# Chapter 1
## The Good News

The phone jangled here in my Camp Hill, Pennsylvania, home and I continued with leg-swings, my every other morning exercises done in a prone position on my office floor. *Let it ring,* I told myself. *Only twenty more swings, then knee bends and I'll be through. If the message is important the party will call again. But...suppose it's one of my children? Suppose one of them needs me?*

I live alone. Herb Focht, nicknamed Bill, a wonderful man, my husband of thirty-eight great years, is gone now, following a bout with lung cancer. I can still hear his, "Darling, I love you too damn much to die." Faith and love kept us together two and a half years more than doctors predicted. Though out of sight, he still lives on in many hearts, especially mine, and our four children: I see his slow mischievous grin in our twin son, Kevin; his sturdy, sensible ways in twin brother, Keith; his sweet thoughtfulness in Dianne and his firm determination in Debra. They are grown now, either tied up raising their own or involved with outside activities. Though precious to me, I see them only occasionally. Usually holidays and birthdays are tied together to exchange gifts. I've heard many senior parents out there are experiencing this same scenario, and I'm not really bemoaning the situation, just realizing I must look after *me*.

7

I jumped to my feet, checked the caller ID box only to read "Unavailable". Usually they are telemarketing calls, with someone selling something. Then I remembered once I refused to answer, then changed my mind to find Doctor Binder on the other end. So here I was changing my mind again.

The voice said, "Bootsy...?"

As a toddler I couldn't pronounce 'Arbutus', and liked to wear white boots, so came the nickname...

"This is your Pennsylvania stockbroker, here in Florida." He and his wife had recently moved to The Villages, Florida's Retirement Community where he would set up an office. "Bootsy, Saturday night when I see the people here dancing in the Square, I think of you. You would love it. The people are friendly and nice, and you can live 100 % cheaper than you are there in Camp Hill."

I remembered this month of March, with all the rain, and how it cost $200 to just have my lawn mowed. I wanted to hear more about the Villages, considered a little slice of paradise on earth, and also "Florida's Friendliest Hometown", which won *Better Homes and Gardens Magazine's* prestigious "Best in American Living Award" for affordable housing.

"Hold on, I'm getting a lady from the office to talk to you." Introductions were made, and we had a three- way conversation. She informed me there would absolutely be no sales pressure to buy when I came for a visit to sample one's lifestyle. She would send a Preview Plan with lengths of stay, cost, etcetera.

"Come down," she said. "Compare prices, and you're going to discover The Villages is very friendly to your fixed retirement budget. Monthly costs vary, depending on the size of the home and its usage, as well as the type and size of the homesite it occupies."

She continued to tell me the standard 5,400 sqare foot homesites are 60 feet by 90 feet and come completely developed with wide, paved streets, sod and landscaping, sewer and water, street lights and all street signage, curbs, gutters, storm sewers and underground utilities. "Home styles vary. There's the Patio Villas, Courtyard Villas, Ranch Homes and Designer Homes, which range from $63,000 to $400,000. Estimated average monthly cost is $515, and that includes amenity fee, sewer, water, electric, trash collection, telephone, cable television, insurance and average taxes and Development District

Assessment." She surprised me when she added, "The Villages has a twenty-four hour Neighborhood Patrol, its own television station and newspaper."

I was thinking perhaps I could also write for this newspaper, but told her, "It all sounds too good to be true. I like the idea of a neighborhood watch. I wouldn't have further need for a security alarm, as I do here in my Pennsylvania home. So tell me, how close is the hospital?"

"About fifteen minutes away, but one is under construction in the Villages, along with a Lutheran church, which will add to the three existing, including a Catholic."

"I like everything I've heard."

"Yes, it is a fine place for seniors, 55 and over. It includes everything your stockbroker has mentioned. Use of our nine swimming pools, and automatically becoming a member of three country clubs. The center of activity is the charming, old-fashioned Town Square, designed by the creative team which designed much of Florida's Universal Studios."

That sounded nice.

Another office rep got on the line. She would be glad to send me a video, plus brochures picturing the various style of homes.

They arrived in a week, and I immediately called my sister, Kathy, in Manhattan. "Hey, Kathy! How would you like to take a trip to Florida and check out a retirement community?"

"Are you actually thinking of moving? I thought you loved it there in Pennsylvania."

"Oh, I do! But it's been hard. Without my Bill, I'm very much on my own, and I'm tired of it. Though I have a lawn man to mow my grass, and love to plant flowers and see them blossom, I'm tired of weeding, raking leaves, shoveling snow, and…the long cold winters."

"I don't blame you. I could never keep up with all of that. I'm happy here in my studio apartment. Alright! Okay! I'll go along. It sounds like fun. Where shall we meet?"

"I'll fly out of Harrisburg on Delta, into the Orlando Airport."

"That sounds good. I'll check Delta, and take a flight which arrives near the time you do, and meet you there."

Everything went even better than planned. When I alighted, a man wearing a green jacket stood amidst the crowd and held up a sign

9

reading "FOCHT". I thought, *Gee, there's another Focht around here.* The Villages had sent him. He was there actually looking for me!

We found Kathy downstairs where the Village limousine waited to scoop us up and off to The Villages. Once we arrived at The Village Sales' office, I was told, "Bootsy, someone is waiting to greet you," and out walked my smiling stockbroker and his wife.

Later, following dinner at the La Hacienda Country Club, we four drove into town to watch people dance in the square. Kathy and I decided to stay awhile longer just as a lanky, comical-looking mime, the first I had ever seen, came strutting toward us. I threw him a kiss, expecting a smile, but his arm jerked skyward and a finger pointed to his cheek. Standing on tip toes, I went to kiss it, but his head jerked sideways and his lips brushed mine. I laughed, and when he motioned for me to dance with him, Kathy said, "Go ahead," and sat watching as we joined the many others in a fox trot.

Then Kathy and I hopped a cab which took us to our two bedroom, two bath courtyard villa where we would spend the next three days. During our stay we took advantage of the complimentary continental breakfasts in the sales building.

The second day, a village rep snapped our picture beneath street signs which read FOCHT, and DAVIN, and we were taken on a splendid trolley ride to tour the villages. In the afternoon a sales rep took us around town to view villas.

Our third day, a hot ninety-two degrees with a slight breeze in the Villages...ninety-five back home in Pennsylvania...Kathy and I traveled via cab to the La Hacienda Country Club. There, we leisurely enjoyed a tasty lunch. Two hours later, again with another realtor, we toured different sections of The Villages. We viewed, compared prices of more villas, and I sighed over each. Then, it was back to the country club, where I took a quick dip, and joined Kathy under a large beach umbrella by the pool.

A lady, carrying two margaritas breezed by. "You girls should try these. They're absolutely wonderful."

"We just might," I said. "By the way, do you live here in The Villages?"

"Yes, and I love it. It's Heaven before you reach the real thing."

"Where did you live before you moved here?"

"York, Pennsylvania."

A feeling of warmth swept through me. "It truly is a small world. I live in Camp Hill, and my twin son, Keith, lives in York Haven, just fifteen minutes away."

She commenced to say, "The Village has numerous clubs. There's a Pennsylvania, New York and Ohio and many more. If you wish to do more than relax, the Villages has two hundred organized activities per week through their Recreation Department. Everything you desire to suit your taste: Golf, tennis, softball, horseshoe, water volleyball, water basketball, shuffleboard, dance clubs & classes, etcetera."

When she left, another lady arrived with her swimming paraphernalia, and pulled her chair up beside ours.

Though neither Kathy nor I are golfers, she enthusiastically told us, "Yes, the Villages has a lot to offer. This is a golf-cart community. We can use our own cart for a nominal trail fee and play unlimited free golf on their nine executive courses." She went on to say, "We also have three private fishing lakes, three lakefront parks, and nine swimming pools, all covered by a monthly amenity fee."

She left to take a dip in the pool and I told Kathy, "I'm going to move my chaise out into the sunlight and work on a tan."

"Good idea. I, myself, can't tolerate the sun."

"I'm careful. This brimmed hat will protect my face." While absorbing Florida's glorious sunshine, I resumed a quiet pose and daydreamed about the wonders of it all.

Later, when it was again time to seek shelter under the umbrella, I stood up and tried to step into my Zorros, but they were so beastly hot, I flipped them from my feet, and bounced up and down on the hot pavement. A nice man from one of the pro shops stopped to chat and saw my predicament.

"I'll take care of that for you," he said. Bending, he picked them up, walked over to the pool, dipped them in and with a broad smile handed them to me. "There, that should do the trick."

"Thank you, kind sir." I could tell he got a kick out of the 'kind sir' bit, and chuckled as I added, "You are a true gentleman."

I wiggled my toes into what are called flipflops here. Suddenly, a lovely Monarch butterfly came skirting across the azure blue skies, and headed for the pool area. All eyes watched as it came closer and closer. Now, just a few feet above, and to my right, I gasped with delight as I watched it zero in and so gracefully light on the skirt of my floral printed swimsuit.

"I can't believe this. It's so beautiful. Why do you suppose it picked me?"

Several commented, "It thinks you're a flower."

Kathy laughed. "That's amazing. This is an omen, saying you should move here."

Later that afternoon we did go house-hunting, with still another agent. I became smitten with the last home shown. Only two-tenths of a mile from downtown, and located close to a shopping center, I would also have free access to a swimming pool, snack bar and club house.

Kathy urged, "Grab it. Place a bid," and I did. That evening, the last realtor showed us around town, and we ended at the club house. Once inside the door, a man marched up to me.

"How soon we forget?" He was the young gentleman from the Pro Shop. "Come, I want you to meet Jenny, my wife." He took my hand, led me to a table, and introduced me to a little petite, brown-eyed miss. The band struck up a familiar tune, "Under the Boardwalk", and he turned to Jenny. "If you don't mind, I'm going to dance with Bootsy."

I floated on air in the arms of this young man who was saying, "You're a great dancer. My father lives in upper New York State and loves to dance. Move here, I'll have him come visit and he can be your dance partner."

I thanked him for the compliment. "It's not me, it's you, the excellent leader." For that I received both a big smile and a hug.

The following morning at the airport, before Kathy and I parted, I told her, "While here, there's not an aching bone in my body."

She grinned. "Not mine, either."

Upon returning to Camp Hill, I called my lawyer, and he said, "Don't sign the contract yet. You're moving too fast. Get your children involved. Return to The Villages and spend a couple months before uprooting and selling your lovely home."

I tried calling a family conference, but everyone was occupied with pre-arranged weekend plans. Regarding moving, Kevin advised, "Check around here first. The Villages is so far away. But, if that's what you want to do, do it. I'll always love you wherever you go.

We'll all miss you. I know you'll be happier down there, though I'm concerned because you'll be swinging with the sharks. (Not really). As to what you should take with you? Pick what you cherish. Be smart money-wise, you can't afford to lose it. Remember decisions change your life. You have my blessings."

Keith told me, "In the hot months come visit the family. A week here, there, and end with a party before you return. We're here for you. If it brings you a lot of joy, go for it. It's growth. You're the matriarch of the family and have always come through. It's the wise thing to do, and you have my blessings."

Daughter Debra couldn't be reached, and the oldest, Dianne, told me, "Mom, I'm envious. We'll come and visit, and probably see each other more. You've done a fine job in raising us, teaching us to be independent and stand on our own two feet, like you have since Dad died. You have my blessings. But, Mom, why not wait until the fall? Maybe by then, I'll be able to take time off from work and go with you. Maybe you can rent a place for three months and see whether it's what you want."

That sounded like a wise idea. I shared pleasing stories I had heard while I visited The Villages. Neighbors helped neighbors. Chain gangs were formed to assist new neighbors moving in. Neighbors took ill neighbors to the hospital or to see their local physician. Evening neighborhood gatherings were again the "in-thing", like in the olden days. Though one must be at least 55 in age, or more, to live in the Villages, I was surprised no one appeared old. Happy hearts glowed on smiling faces. Undoubtedly, because many followed the golden rule, "Do unto others as you would have them do unto you." Like a framed saying on one of my bathroom walls claims, "Those who bring sunshine to the hearts of others cannot keep it from themselves."

Over the next two months, while making mental notes regarding my future, I learned since the time for me to leave grew near, my children felt I was deserting them. I didn't see their line of reasoning, but did assure them I would look into a three-month rental and not make any hasty decisions.

It wasn't until the middle of August when I decided to write and tell my plans to Janie Major, a friend of thirty-eight years who lived in

Berwick. The morning Janie opened my letter, her brother, Bob, from Florida unexpectedly walked into her home, and she said, "Listen to Bootsy's letter. Can you believe this?"

Unknown to me, they had visited The Villages last year, and she had planned to return again.

We began to jot notes back and forth, and decided to fly down together. I called The Villages Sales Office and made arrangements for a month-long stay. The Villages Shuttle would be at the Orlando airport on the lower level and pick us up on September 1, 1999, at 1:43 PM. Including The Villages Office discounts, a month's cost for each would amount to $692.20.

With plans underway, I felt it necessary to jot them off to my one twin son, Kevin, my strongest opposition.

Hi, there, Kevin, Lynna, too,

This is your Mother speaking. Isn't this great, sending messages on AOL? Not as scary as I presumed.

Just want you to know Janie Major will leave her home in Berwick, arrive here by Greyhound August 31, and spend the night with me here in Camp Hill. Friday morning at 8:30, Bill Winfendale, my handyman, will take us to the airport where we'll board US Airways, fly to Orlando and take the shuttle bus to The Villages. Plans are to stay until September 29, return on flight 1600 from Orlando, change to flight 315 in Pittsburgh, and arrive home at 3:15 PM.

The reason I chose to leave now is The Villages has a special offer and we can rent a villa for $1,099 a month, plus $250 for security and $25 for cleaning. We will receive $400 Villages Dollars for meals, and be reimbursed the $250 upon completion of our stay.

Please don't worry about me, I have a sensible head upon my shoulders. I've learned my former Lutheran minister from here, Pastor Bill and wife, Louise Slees, live there in The Villages. Plus Carol and Bob Furlong, a church couple from Lemoyne, and of course you met my stockbroker, who, with his wife, will return to their home there in The Villages on October 11.

Janie hopes to find a nice rental for permanent residency, and there's the possibility she may buy a little villa, and not return when I do. If I enjoy my stay, I may move into another villa and spend the month of October. Never fear, I shall not forget any of you dear brats, and don't want you to think unkindly toward me. I'm not deserting anyone. If I buy it would be sometime next year, after I sell my home here.

However, if I can get ADM Milling Company to quiet the noise which comes from their motors which run, twenty-four hours, seven days a week, and invades my home and nearby neighbors, (they're still trying...I think) and too, Penn Dot to put up sound barriers over on the highway as promised, I might consider just renting a villa at The Villages for three months in the winters. I would like to keep one month open to spend time in Hawaii, when Ginny or friend Del invite me, as they have over the past six years. (Hawaii is my favorite place but it's located twelve-and-a-halfhours away from here.) We shall see. I shall cross the bridges as I come to them. How I wish your dad could be here to walk over them with me. Like our Aunt Straw and Uncle Charlie did in later years, when it became cold, and their winters were spent in Daytona.

Over the past twelve years, I've tried to get along the best I could by myself. But in The Villages, it amazed me how all the ladies I spoke to, even singles, claimed I wouldn't be alone while there. Everyone looks after the others as they're in the same boat. I'm tired of being alone and feel I have fifteen good years left. I don't need a man, physically, just someone to care, to call daily to see I haven't fallen down stairs, with a broken hip, etcetera. It has happened to others. Even friend, Janie, but she had her hubby there. Yes, while alone, I'm careful and do hang onto railings.

So, I hope you see where I'm coming from and where I'm going. The phone is ringing. Gee, I hope this doesn't destroy my writings. I will try to close without a spell check. So honey, children of mine, I shall sign off with...

Much love and many hugs,
from Mom

I felt it imperative Janie know of my plans, and sent an e-mail message to her, regarding costs. It reaped the following letter:

Hi, Bootsy, congratulations, you figured right. This sure seems to be a good deal and I'm looking forward to it. Arriving in Harrisburg via bus 4:45 on Friday. See you then. Jane.

# Chapter 2
## 30 Arrival

August 31, 2000, while Bill Winfendale and I sat on a bench inside the Harrisburg Bus Terminal awaiting Janie's arrival, I anxiously observed the travelers who zipped past the windows on the opposite side of the room.

"How long have you known each other?" Bill asked.

"For thirty-eight years. Twenty two of which we palled around together and our children grew up and attended the same schools in Berwick, PA, then sixteen more after we moved away, here into the Harrisburg area. Though we kept in touch, we haven't seen each other over the past twelve years. Not since her husband, Glenn, passed away. Oh! There she is." I jumped to my feet. "That looks like Janie over there. She hasn't changed, except for her white hair."

We eased through the crowd, reached the other side, and rushed to catch up to her. "Janie!" I called out three times. Bill tried, also, but she didn't look our way. I called her name again. She paused, quickly turned, gave me a hurried smile, a quick hug and said, "Watch my luggage. I have to pee so bad," and off she went in the direction of the lady's room.

Bill pulled her luggage out to his car, returned shortly, and soon we three were headed through town, down the highway to my Camp

Hill home, and yakking our fool heads off. Janie shared her surprisingly nice trip. "I didn't mind it at all. It's grand to be here, and together, again. Like old times. I looked forward to it."

When we parked in front of my yellow brick rancher with white shutters, she smiled. "It's nice. I like it." Admittedly, I was thrilled my bushes and flowers were still profusely in bloom. Especially the mums, alternating in color and scalloping the border of my front lawn. Inside, once we stepped over the doorsill, a woman of few words, she said, "It's cozy." However, when we reached the master bedroom, we laughed, when her eyes nearly popped out at the sight of my opened suitcase. Prior to her arrival I had packed, emptied and re-packed three times.

"Tell me you're not going to take all of those clothes. You did say the villa has a laundry room, didn't you?"

"Yes, I know, and I keep promising myself I'll do better when packing the next time, but for some incomprehensible reason, I don't seem to succeed. I matched up tops and bottoms, and listed everything on this tablet." I reached over, grabbed it from the nearby stand and handed it to her. She studied it a moment.

"You don't need three pairs of white slacks. Take one."

Janie always had a sensible head upon her shoulders, and here she was, doing the sensible thing. I now slid my two arms beneath a pile of clothes, near an unnecessary garment, and told her, "Okay, when I lift, you yank."

The suitcase ended minus an arm-load. Still, it proved to be quite heavy when I pulled it through the local airport the following day. Once we disembarked in Orlando, we had an hour and twenty minute wait before the shuttle bus arrived to take us to The Villages. It too, proved a pleasant trip for both Janie and me. As we rambled down the highways, we commented on the shopping centers, restaurants, and the wide open spaces as we whizzed by, and I was particularly smitten with palm trees reaching to the high heavens. We enjoyed chatting with a single lady and two married couples, who, also, were anxious to check out The Villages and their new living quarters.

Once there, a gentleman named Leonard escorted us to the dining area in the sales building, where we enjoyed an early afternoon snack, compliments of The Villages. When presented with a gate pass, keys to our Villa, and a garage door opener, we scooted off via cab, to home away from home, on 926 Midera Drive. Here, we opened the door and stood inside, and stared with mouths opened. "It's all anyone would desire." I gasped. "If my children could see this, they'd be happy for me."

We admired the homey kitchen, the little drop-leaf oak table and chairs. Beyond an opened doorway, a dining-room stretched into an ample size living-room. We reached the first bedroom and bath. I gave Janie first choice and was pleased she wanted the one without the walk-in closet. One more part of our September home to see, and we were in for still another surprise. As I slid back large plate glass doors, I remarked, "This reminds me of a favorite TV show of mine...*The Golden Girls*. I've always wanted to live in Florida in a snazzy place like theirs, and...here we are. So, I'll tell you what. Today, let's pretend we're the Golden Girls. I want to be Rue McClanahan...worldly, peppy and sexy. Who do you wish to be? Bea Arthur? Dorothy, the sensible school teacher?"

"That'll be fine with me."

So, while putting on a pretentious *la de dah* air, I smiled sweetly, and said, "Come on, Dorothy, follow me," and ever so gracefully, we stepped over the doorsill into a carpeted and glass enclosed lanai. All inhibitions were abandoned and we giggled like school girls. Never had I felt such sheer happiness in being so downright silly. Especially with my friend, Janie.

"This is living," she sighed as she plopped herself into the closest rattan chair and stretched out her legs.

"My sentiments exactly." I occupied my own chair directly opposite hers, and gleefully looked out onto a somewhat small, though well-landscaped, verdant green lawn. Both sides were embraced by coral stucco walls. In the middle, a concrete walkway led to a white picket fence, where directly beyond, a family of white Egrets gracefully strutted across a golf course. "Isn't this lovely, Janie?"

"Yes, and did you notice the Crepe Myrtle tree with fluffy red blooms? Over near the wall on the right? It's loaded with buds, I hope they bloom before we leave."

"Me, too. Back home, just around the corner from me, one becomes covered with beautiful lavender flowers, similar to those on my seven

19

lilac bushes which border the edge of my property. Though my lilacs are quite healthy, the nursery man says not to even think of planting Crepe Myrtle. They're not supposed to survive in our cold climate. Speaking of home, I'm happy we're located here on a golf course. Aren't you? It gives me a pleasant feeling to have people around in case a problem should arise."

A frown creased Janie's brow. "I'd just as soon have more privacy."

I studied her a moment. We'd be together a complete month. In the past, the most we had been together was a weekend. That was fifteen years ago.

Later in the evening, we decided to walked into town and eat dinner at Katie Belles Restaurant. On our trek home, we came to a wooden bench on the left of the sidewalk.

I plopped down, and looked up at Janie. "My left knee hurts, and I'm going to rest a bit."

Before coming to The Villages, fate hadn't been too kind to me. Since I fell on a wet floor in a Harrisburg restaurant, and my left knee had to be arthroscoped twice, sometimes it proved troublesome if I walked quite a distance, or danced too long. Along with this, at times, sciatica nerve damage was near to intolerable since last week when I simply turned to pick up a boombox in my basement. At the time, pain so fierce shot from my hip, on down my leg, and I screamed, and grabbed onto a table to fight from collapsing on the floor.

Plans were to give the radio to the painter, who for three days left his car radio blaring outside my window while painting the porch railing on the home of the dentist who lived caddy-corner from me on the hill. With the hip pain, I had changed my mind. Thoughts were, I wasn't supposed to stick my nose into somebody else's business, or along with my sore hip, my feelings could be hurt. Yet, now when I'm troubled with quick spasms of hot pain shooting down my right leg, and I baby that leg, the left knee aches. I remembered as a child, when I said I hurt, I was told, "It's just growing pains," and I accepted that. Usually, I now attempt to hide pain until it's ironed out and in the past. Even the bladder infection which cropped up prior to climbing into bed last night. Seeking help at the Camp Hill Emergency Room would have gobbled the night away, and I wouldn't have been a perky traveling companion.

"You can't sit there!" came from Janie.

"I'm tired."

"Come on!" she ordered. "This is a cab pick-up. See the sign?"

So I was on my feet again, to slowly mosey home to our villa. All in all it had been an interesting first day.

At 9:00, Jane yawned.

"Sleepy?" I asked.

"Yes, it's my bedtime."

Would this cause a problem? Usually, I read, watch television or am busy at the computer until 12, and sometimes 1:00 AM, to finish a story for the Middletown Press and Journal, a senior citizen's Newspaper for Kids over 50. Here, since I have no computer I must pen everything.

When Janie retired, I busied myself, unpacked and admired my nice big bedroom. All in all, the complete villa was tastefully decorated. I remembered to take my Premarin tablet, and on my way to the kitchen, paused in the living room to admire the fourteen-inch fish ornament on the shelf beneath the television set. Black and classic, it undoubtedly was molded out of heavy metal. Curious, I walked over, picked it up, and blinked in surprise. According to the tag on the bottom, it had been purchased at a Pier 1 store. A touch of nostalgia swept over me. Camp Hill has a Pier 1 store close to my home, and I frequently shop there.

"Hey, Janie!" I called.

"What?"

I hurried to her room and stood outside the opened door. "May I come in?"

"Sure!" She was closing her drapes.

"Look at this." I pulled the fish from behind my back. "Here, lift it." I held it out to her.

She shrieked "Get that thing out of here!"

"No. Just lift it. It's made out of wood."

"I said 'get that thing away from me'." Anger shook her voice, arms trembled as she reached as if to shove me away.

"What's wrong with you? Janie. Tell me." I backed out of the room, and under my voice muttered, "You're weird."

I returned to my room, lay in bed, and wondered why had she acted so strangely? Did the self-assured, strong-willed Jane I once knew, change so much?

Come morning, stirring in the kitchen awakened me. I blinked until the numbers on the clock remained stable. 6:00 AM. I silently groaned, rolled over, reached for the box on my night stand, removed earplugs and after placing them in my ear, dozed off until 8:00.

Later, I moseyed out on the lanai with my cup of tea. Janie lowered the morning paper, looked up, smiled and said, "Good morning." Gesturing with her cup, she added, "My third cup of coffee. Boy, did I sleep!"

I told her, "Me, too," and refrained from saying more.

"I already had breakfast, I used the items from the complimentary welcoming bag The Villages left us."

"Great. Did you eat out here on the lanai?"

"Yes, I still think it will be nice to have breakfast here every morning."

"Me, too. But don't you feel strange in your PJ's and robe? With golfers whacking away out there on the course?"

I thought of how each morning before breakfast, I must exercise, make up my bed, as well as my face. Am I too regimented to change? Could I become more like Janie? Calm, never rushed? So sure of myself? I secretly envied her lovely peaches and cream complexion. She sat there with face stark bare of make-up, looking calm, cool, and pretty. Years ago, when our family lived in Baltimore, I took a housewife's beauty course at Miss Walter's Modeling Academy, and was advised to never even open the door to let the maid in without first applying my lipstick. I smiled to myself and thought I never had a maid. Except a two week loan of one sent by a Montrose heart doctor to help with our two year old twins when, for awhile, my heartbeat had been irregular. I did have a weekly cleaning lady, but that didn't count. Still, down through the years, I prided myself and followed Walter's advice. Janie didn't have to.

She brought me back to the present with a light chuckle. "Nah, the golfers aren't bothering me any. I was here this morning before they were. It's lovely out here."

I agreed, and said, "Less I forget, I must tell you when something troubles me, to have peace of mind I have to get it out in the open. Especially if we're going to get along with each other. So, I'm going to do that, now. What was wrong with you last night? Why did you go bananas when I showed you that fish? It looks expensive. Like heavy metal, but is actually light simulated wood. That's what I was trying to tell you."

"It's a long story, and I don't care to get into it, now."

"I can't accept that."

"Alright, if you insist. It started a long time ago." Her eyes clouded. "I was 12 at the time, and one day my brother chased me all around the house with a yellow plastic fish, and he wouldn't let up until he caught me. Ever since, I have this phobia when it comes to fish. I hate them. I know it sounds silly, but it's one thing that I've never been able to overcome. Call me paranoid."

"No, not that. Last night I wanted to call you 'Whacko', but now, I understand. Yet, if it troubled me that much over the years, I would have sought help."

"I never thought about it, because it didn't bother me until last night when you came at me with that darn fish."

"I'm sorry. I had no idea what was going on in your mind. By the way, did you notice I replaced the fish with a basket of flowers from in my bedroom? The fish is in my room."

"Yes, I noticed. Thanks, I appreciate that."

Following breakfast, we walked to Publix Super market, and picked up essentials. From there we visited the golf cart store, and rented a golf cart for the month of September. Cost: $114.

"Have you ever driven one?" Larry, the clerk, asked.

Jane and I both gave our heads a negative shake.

"It's easy." He gave a slow smile. "I'll take you over to the Plaza's large parking lot for a lesson, and in a little time you'll get the hang of it."

"Is that a promise?" I asked. "At this stage in life, anything new has me wondering."

"Believe me. It's easy."

Since Janie wasn't game to learn right away, off Larry drove, with me by his side. Out in the parking lot, when he first showed me how to operate the controls and I took over, I felt a tad intimidated. But later when I manned the wheels and drove back to the shop to pick up Janie I told her, "I feel like a frontier woman. It proved daring and quite adventuresome." Together we laughed and sort of formed a camaraderie as we whizzed along, back to our villa, at a daring speed of thirty miles an hour. When I pulled into our garage, I flicked off the ignition, looked over at her and said, "Tomorrow, it's your turn."

"Oh, sure!" She rolled her eyes heavenward.

# Chapter 3
# Company's Coming

Day three, I still wondered about Janie. Since she didn't drive, perhaps it wouldn't be wise to push her into manning the golf cart? In time she would come around. Staid, surefooted in everything, she'd get the hang of it in no time.

With me at the wheel, since the Lutheran Church still wasn't constructed, we set off in search of the Hacienda Center, where the services would be held the following day. Yes, on Sunday, we made it to church on time. However, on our way home, I zoomed out on the highway, crossed to swing left, when a car came barreling toward us, and I breathlessly swerved over to the extreme right on the diamond marked golf cart section.

"Whew!" I told Janie, "We both just learned a lesson, today. Our little caddy can't travel nearly as fast as a car."

Back at our villa, we bounced around and spiffed up the place. Our first company, Janie's brother, Bob, and wife, Marge, from an hour away, would arrive at 4:00 to spend the evening with us. Later, we would meet their cousin, Linda and mate, Bud, in town, and together attend the Sunday night concert in The Church on The Square.

Janie's relatives were nice. Linda and her husband, I had known in Berwick. Though much thinner and taller than his sister, Janie, Bob, with his calculated grin, reminded me of her in many ways. Steady, sure of himself, and unlikely to skip through life and err as I'm prone to do. I should someday like to find a suitable mate kind of like him. He's caring like my darling Bill, except my Bill could be a tease, and a sweet romantic. Yes, frivolous like me at times. Ah, yes, this romantic senior lady yearns for someone to walk by her side. Someone to care about, someone to laugh with when things go wrong.

Once inside The Church on the Square, we found six excellent seats together. While filled with anticipation, I learned Janie, last year, had already attended concerts there with her brother. Alas, the lady singer had excellent voice control; nothing more. We, and numerous others left during intermission, and headed for Katie Belles restaurant for dinner. By the time we arrived, we were given a 'clicker' and advised of a twenty minute wait for a table. It seemed unique, quite enjoyable, seated outside on benches, beneath blue, blue skies, as we listened to music floating from the nearby gazebo. Time seemed to swiftly pass, and at one point, a gentle breeze caressed my cheeks, a wisp of hair floated before my eyes, and I thought of my Bill. It was at that precise moment, we were ushered indoors where chatter picked up with an excited pace as we hovered over menus.

"This sounds interesting," Janie pointed. "Kitchen Sink Salad."

I glanced over her shoulder, and gave my head a negative shake. "I thought the same thing, years ago when I ordered Garbage Salad in a restaurant back home, and ended with horrible stomach cramps."

Bob folded his menu and placed it by his plate. "This is different. It's not the same. Marge and I come here frequently on weekends, and it's good."

So, that was that. We all ordered Kitchen Sink Salad, and iced tea. Though too ample in size, the salad, with all the rough stuff one's supposed to eat daily, along with olives, and mushrooms, it was topped with tender strips of chicken, and proved quite tasty, just like Bob said it would be.

After our stomachs were satisfied, Linda said, "Yes, we'd like to see your villa." So off we went, to Janie's and my September home. There, together, we flitted from room to room, and Linda showed genuine enthusiasm. "This is really nice. I'm impressed." Of course, I smiled in agreement. Janie and I had really lucked out. Though, to this day, I can't understand the terminology, 'lucked out'. In this case, I genuinely believe we had 'lucked in.'

Monday, following breakfast, Janie surprised me with, "Today, I'm going to try my hand at driving our golf cart. I mean our caddy, the Cadillac."

"That's great! I'll take you over to the Plaza parking lot, and you can practice there. Like I did."

She did remarkably well. I sensed her delight. From there, I took the wheel and we dashed all over the place. First to the drugstore for glucosomine tablets. On to the furniture store to find it closed. Next, we browsed through a novelty shop where we found many unusual items. Included was a seated mustachioed male mannequin with hands folded behind his head and an I-could-care-less-expression on his face. Here, we laughed, and a customer snapped our picture with him.

I winked at the lady photographer and teased, "I'm going back home and tell everyone Janie and I shared him."

Janie blushed, then snapped, "You can have him. You're the one looking for a man. Not me. I'm never going to marry again. I've been there and done that."

"So have I. But I want to do it again. Only if I can find someone as nice as my Bill. In time, you might change your mind."

"Wanna bet?"

"Nope. Not yet."

Janie bought an alarm clock, and we debated over a $45 vase of silk flowers for on our kitchen table. We passed it by and drove over to Winn Dixie where we purchased some toiletries and a $4 pretty, hot pink Gloxinia plant. Outside, as I placed it in our golf cart I told her, "A bargain, magnifioso." Janie at the wheel, agreed, and straightened her hat. I mimicked, straightening my own. Yes, since we must get around in our carts, to keep our hair somewhat tidy, (my bangs out of my eyes) we wear our brimmed chapeau's. Janie's this day was coral, matching her coral silk blouse. Mine? Beige, trimmed in a lime green silk scarf to match my blouse. I've always loved hats, and wherever our family moved over the past forty-four years, I became known as 'the hat lady.' Janie is now a 'hat lady', also.

"Where to now?" she asked.

"Off to the golf cart shop, to see if we can do something to get rid of the gas fumes which infiltrate our pad each time we pull into our garage."

Larry, the regular clerk, said, "Leave the cart cool off in the driveway, then push it inside."

"No can do, regarding the pushing, " I told him.

"That's more of a man's job," said Janie. "We'll leave the garage door open for awhile, and see if that will help."

Our next stop, since we were in town, was the Sales Office where we grabbed an enjoyable snack including lemonade, a baggo for Janie, a sweet roll and hot chocolate for me. I shared the sweet roll with Janie so I'm not guilty of downing the whole thing. When we walked outside into the sunlight and headed for our golf cart, I asked, "Do you want to ride around and explore the place? Want to visit different villages and see the villa I nearly bought in June?

"Sure! We may as well. Sounds good to me." We found a 'for sale' sign still posted in the front yard, and climbed out of our cart and stood outside and peeked in all the windows. "I like it," she said. From there, we passed several other nice looking villas, one on a lake, an ideal location, and jotted down each house number.

Back home, when I reached to remove our Gloxinia plant from the caddy, Janie groaned. "Look what you did. You knocked its head off." Sure enough, I looked down to see the one pink bloom at my feet. "Never mind," she said. "It still will look nice on our table." It did. The greens showed up nicely in the container covered with pink aluminum.

Quite tired, we both kicked off our shoes and zonked off a bit. She, in front of the TV, and I, in the solitude of my room. Later, with vim and vigor restored, I whipped up a tasty fruit salad, soup and toasted cheese sandwiches for dinner.

Once Janie tidied the kitchen, we were raring to 'be on the go again.' This time, we would walk into town. It was Fiesta Night and we wondered what treasures the venders would have on display on the many tables circling the square's perimeter? We were nearing the square, and straight ahead, leaning against one table, we could see lovely white doors with inserts of cut glass. On one side of the street, cars were parked bumper to bumper. We passed one, and I caught a handsome man's eyes following me. I smiled to myself, not daring to point this out to Janie. Perhaps he was lonely? I wanted to turn around and tell him to get out and join the dancers who were jiving' to the band music in the square.

Soon, we stopped at a table to admire turquoise jewelry. I caught myself gently swinging shoulders in tune to the music, as was the lady vendor behind the table. She looked up and grinned.

Then I pointed to a necklace and said, "Isn't this beautiful, Janie?" and turned, only to find I was talking to myself. Janie was already three tables ahead of me. I swallowed hard, and hurried to catch up...I'm prone to get lost in crowded new places and when I do, become somewhat panicky. I attribute this to living in the country as a child and it wasn't until I turned eighteen, and accepted an office position in the city, that I was permitted to go in alone...Now, storm clouds hovered overhead. Thunder rumbled across the sky. The crowd suddenly began to thin. Venders gathered their wares, and finally, quite breathlessly, I reached Janie's side.

It proved to be an exciting half hour spent, with my purchase consisting of a lovely persona watch with a minute hand, and Janie had picked out a pretty blue flowered plant, for on our kitchen table. A few drops of splattering rain and I said, "It's time we head for home."

The spot where the handsome man sat behind the wheel was now vacant. We passed the big clock on the corner and continued down Del Mar, heading for the gate. A clap of thunder, and our steps hastened. A car stopped. The male driver asked if he could take us home. "No, thanks. We only have a few blocks to go," we both told him. Soon a couple pulled alongside, and asked if we wanted a ride, and our response was the same. Then another couple stopped, saying they didn't want us to get wet. Such nice people! No, we didn't get wet. Only a few drops had fallen.

Shortly, after our return home, I received a call from Nancy, our repair person who fished out our kitchen sink plug I had put in incorrectly, and I learned our villa hadn't been rented for the month of October. I would look into this, in case we decided to stay another month.

Then, I called the president of The Singles' Club, and learned the dates of their monthly meetings.

Next, since I have been a thirty-four year member of Beta Sigma Phi, an international sorority, not college affiliated, but founded in 1930 by Walter Ross, and built on friendship, culture and service to the community, I phoned Faye Fountaine, the head representative in this area. I have only one more year to receive my Masters Degree, in learning how to live the beautiful life. Prior to my Camp Hill departure, Faye and I had chatted at length via phone, and she knew I would be arriving in town, with wishes to establish contact here, and see if I'd fit in.

My final call was to my daughter, Dianne, in the Reading, Pennsylvania area.

"Honey," I told her, "I feel I've been living in the wrong place all of my life."

As I now write, when it comes to the villas I've seen, none can compare to the one I'm in now. Yes, I'm content here. Janie must be, too. It's 10:50 PM and she sleeps in her chair. I too, am becoming somewhat droopy-eyed and must soon hit the sack. So I'll close now with "Good night, World, and thanks, God, for another fantastic day."

# Chapter 4
# A Walking Disaster

Tuesday, September 5: Some say this is the closest place to Heaven without being there. While others smile and claim this is God's waiting room. As I rolled over in bed, slowly peeped through slit eyelids, and stretched this sunny morning, my thoughts were 'God, I'm not ready yet!'

While I dressed, I realized here you don't see anyone sitting or lying around, waiting, agonizing over aches and pains. Instead, you'll find them in golf carts, going here, going there, golfing, shopping, dancing nightly in the square, or in Kate Belles. Or, like Janie and me, checking out vender's wares in the town square on Monday and Thursday evenings.

Today, Janie would drive, and we would take off and have fun checking out the stores in town. We found the furniture store doors open, and went inside where I browsed around and mentally updated the furnishings in our villa. If it were mine!

Our next stop, Darlene's, where we had fun trying on clothes.

"How do you like this blouse?" Janie asked, turning this way and that.

"Fine, the blue in the plaid matches your blue slacks." So, she bought the blouse for eighteen dollars. Me? A cute three piece ensemble, slacks, top and blue and white striped matching shorts. "The slacks and shorts are large," I told her. "But, I hope, since they're thirty-five percent cotton and rayon, they'll shrink."

On to Winn Dixie, where I selected a roasted chicken, fruit and vegetable salad, macaroni and milk. When I removed a box of macaroni from the shelf, Jane asked "What are we going to do with it?"

"Make baked macaroni and cheese. But tonight, we'll have this roasted chicken, with baked potatoes, asparagus, veggie salad, and fruit." It had already been established that, since she didn't cook, I would gladly prepare the meals. She in turn, would be in charge of clean-up.

"I don't like asparagus," she said.

"That's okay. I'm not fond of it. It makes my urine smell for two days."

"Mine, too."

"So...," I said, as I rested my arms on the cart and wheeled around the corner back to the veggie section, "I'll put this back. Now, how about peas?"

"I never realized until now, how many things I don't like. Yes, I like peas. You're spoiling me." I didn't really think this. I love to fuss in the kitchen, and in sharing straight down-the-middle money-wise, it's sensible to prepare food we both enjoy.

On our trip home to the villa, she asked about my infection. I hesitated to say anything, because when I finally got around to tell her I couldn't walk fast like she does, or I'd have a knee problem, she told me, "My, you are a walking disaster." Then, when she told me she couldn't walk as slowly as I, because her bunion would hurt, I had to laugh, but kept quiet. I did share the fact my bladder problem flared up again, and I was most uncomfortable.

"Don't fool around with this." she scolded. "Nip it in the bud, or you'll end with a kidney infection. When we get home, call the Urgent Care Clinic, and hire a cab since golf carts aren't permitted to cross over highway 441."

I felt a sense of peace, in sharing, and it put my mind to rest a bit. For years, since my Bill's departure, I've had no one to even suggest what I should do. I've handled all problems alone. I had made this trip to show myself and my family I could still do it.

And so it was. I called a cab and had the driver drop me off at the Urgent Care Center. There, Terry, the pleasant receptionist, had me fill out a questionnaire. Next, an obese nurse escorted me past a lengthy semi-circled desk, behind which sat an immense mustachioed doctor, a thin doctor and several nurses. I was placed in a room with a curtain-covered, sliding glass door. The nurse took my temperature, 98.4 and my blood pressure 71/80 and left. I read a magazine for forty-five minutes. Tired and cold, I escaped, walked past the desk, still occupied by the same crew as before. The only difference, the mustachioed doc was rattling the ice in his glass, and sipping water. No one spoke to me. Out front, at the admission desk, I told Terry "I'm freezing," and together we walked back to my room where she removed a white blanket from a closet for me. Nice! Finally the heavy set doctor entered the room, introduced himself and I told him, "I have a bladder infection."

"Yes, I know." He wrote a prescription for 2 Tequin tablets. "Take one today, and the other tomorrow." This amazed me. Back home if I had a bladder infection, I was put on antibiotics for fourteen days, and told the importance of taking them all.

Terry called a cab for me, and my watch said I had been there a total of four hours. I understand the clinic has seven rooms to accommodate people with problems, and they are cared for according to the urgency of their needs. Yet, four hours for a bladder infection? Still, it was worth it. It rained during the time I had been there, and as I climb into the cab, I could still hear it furiously pelting the building, grateful the driver had parked beneath the portico. Five minutes later, he dropped me off in front of the drugstore. Here, the pharmacist needed to call my doctor. The tablet strength he ordered was not available. Instead, I received 2 pills of double strength and was advised to cut them in two, and take one half daily. Cost? $17.11.

During the night, the medicine played hop-scotch with my heart. Five beats, and stop. Seventeen, and stop. Five beats and stop. I didn't feel too perky when I climbed out of bed in the morning. I told myself I'd be fine.

Following breakfast of green tea, OJ, Grapenuts and banana downed on the lanai, the world seemed rosier, and Janie and I took off in our golf cart. We drove into different villages, up and down streets, in search of 'Sale by Owner' signs. We rang doorbells, and the owners were congenial, downright nice and anxious to take us on tours of their homes. One wanted $121,000, another $139,000 and the last, $149,000. And, of course, we ended again parked in front of my supposed villa. The one on which I previously put a $500 deposit and my lawyer had it returned.

Home again, and we found three messages on our answering machine. Nancy called, again. Yes, this villa is still available for the month of October. I phoned the rental office and learned October is considered a prime time month, and the going rate would be $1,600. That didn't include a golf cart. We'd think about it.

Our second call came from my stockbroker, who said we shouldn't have to put up with gas fumes. "Return the golf cart to Sales and Rentals and have it replaced with an electric." We would do that.

Our third call was the sales rep. She can't take us through my villa, the dream house. Instead, Joe, a male realtor will pick us up at 10:30 tomorrow morning, and besides, show us others which are available. My hopes are we'll discover one I'll fall madly in love with. Yet, I must get myself in gear, shove myself out, and check more thoroughly to make absolutely certain this is where I wish to be, forever and forever.

Tonight, due to torrential rains, our plans to walk to the square and listen to a popular band with a fabulous singer fell along the wayside. Instead, we stayed in. I prepared dinner of left-over macaroni and cheese, doctored with tomato soup, (quite tasty) plus yummy chicken sandwiches, (using the rest of the chicken) with Vidalia onions, lettuce, mayonnaise, and topped the meal with fruit salad. Jane and I both shampooed our hair, and washed three batches of laundry. Then I wrote letters. On this happy and tired note, I'll say, "Good night, World."

Following breakfast the next morning, I stretched and told Janie, "I'm going to lie down a little bit."

"At 8:30 in the morning?"

"Yes, until the realtor comes. I stayed up until twenty after one, jotting down notes, keeping up to date, and ended with a miserable headache in the middle of the night."

"I had a terrible headache, too. Did you take anything?"

"No. I eventually forced myself out of bed, drank a glass of water, burped a few times and it settled. It's from all that cheese we ate yesterday. We went hog-wild you know, during our afternoon snacktime. Cheese and crackers. Remember, we nearly emptied the new container of pimento? Then we had cheese in the macaroni. Yes, it had to be the cheese."

"Really? I never heard that."

"Cheese and also chocolate. I have to be careful, especially when it comes to chocolate. Back home I hide my chocolates beneath my sofa."

"Why?"

"If I see it, I eat it, and this way I must get on my knees to get a piece."

"That's funny."

"Yes, others think so, too. Especially my youngest grandkids, my only grandson, Aaron 9, and his sister, Caralie Elizabeth 10. Last year, when I was in Hawaii, Keith took them along to check on my Camp Hill home, and asked if they wanted to know Grandmom's secret. Of course they giggled over this, and the three got down on the floor and had a party. The last time I saw them they asked, 'Grandmom, if you move to Florida will you still hide your candy beneath the sofa?' I told them 'Of course, and you can find it there when you come to visit.'"

To this, Janie said, matter of fact like, "I don't have a sweet tooth. Rarely do I desire a piece of candy."

"I wish I could say the same. Someone else must be aware of my sweet tooth, because every Christmas, for the past two years, I've received a three pound box of Hershey's chocolate in the mail. I have no idea who sends it."

"It could be a secret admirer. So, tell me, what happens if you eat too much chocolate?"

"Let's see." I looked back on that troublesome time. "It was last fall when my left breast gave me a fit. It felt hot to the touch, all the time, and the pain was excruciating. So much so, I informed Dr. Soto Hamlin, my surgeon, I was willing to have it removed. But, thank the dear Lord, I didn't have to."

"What did they find?" Jane leaned forward, an inquisitive look on her face.

"A clogged milk duct. Remember, many long years ago when our children were born, we were told chocolate milk and tea would help make a good milk supply? Nursing was the 'in' thing back then. Were you told this?"

"No, but then I didn't nurse Brian nor Mark."

"I nursed Dianne and Debbie. Only two months. I didn't Keith and Kevin. The doctors advised me not to even try. Their birth left me too exhausted. With the exception of an ounce, they weighed sixteen pounds In one day, I dropped from one hundred thirty-nine to ninety-seven pounds. I was kept in the hospital two weeks, and fed four meals a day, until I became strong enough to go home with my babies. Admittedly, I felt badly because I couldn't nurse them. Especially since it was considered the ultimate in establishing a strong and loving bond between mother and child."

"I never heard that, either."

"Truthfully, Janie, I discovered it made no difference. I loved the twins and still do, every bit as much as I do my daughters."

"I've always felt close to my Brian and Mark." I yawned, and she told me, "Okay, you go take a nap. I never do."

I longed to say, The Lord is my shepherd, I shall not want, he maketh me to lie down when I'm tired. Instead, I moseyed out of the room and, when my head hit the pillow, I snuggled down and quietly said, "This feels so good, thanks, God."

Following my short nap, we were off again, ready to house search with Joe. No luck this time, either. Janie and I both agreed, my dream house I had first picked, though updated and pretty, was entirely too large, too bothersome for one person to keep clean. No others impressed me, so the search continued.

# Chapter 5
# Things to Consider

Today, as we zoomed up and down streets, Janie tossed around excellent tips to follow. "First, you must decide whether you want a vinyl or a block building."

"Block! My children are concerned about hurricanes, though I assured them the most I've ever seen were spunky winds and swaying trees. But," I continued, "block are generally ten thousand more."

"If you can swing it, get what you want. Most importantly, decide where you wish to locate. Remember, you can change the inside, but you can't the location."

Janie and I discussed everything imaginable. We continually compared notes after enjoyable chats with new people we met in stores, restaurants and also in the square. My exploring mind worked overtime. I believe Janie's did, also.

This evening, we decided to walk into town, where we grabbed one of the green chairs in the square and sat down to watch people dance. Line dancing was definitely in. This was great, since women outnumbered the men fifteen to one, so I'd been told. Regarding line dancing, Janie wasn't interested. As for me? I had two lessons in a room full of hopefuls at Katie Belles. Though fun and a tad confusing, due to my sore knee, I hobbled off the floor and called it quits.

"We won't have to hurry home when the street lights go on," Janie was saying. "We'll be able to stay in town a while longer."

I agreed. Over the past months since it got dark earlier, we had to constantly be aware of TIME. Golf carts without lights were not permitted on the street after dark. It was surprising, how many times you'd sit there in the square, chatting, commenting on dances, or your tasty hot dog served from the nearby wagon, and accompanied with a cold, zesty drink, just having plain fun, when suddenly, street lights were on. One had to scurry on home or be picked up by the police and receive a fine of ninety dollars. Here, time flew away so fast.

Though we didn't line dance, this night we felt fortunate when a tall gentleman with red hair came over and sat beside us. After introductions, Janie and I took turns dancing the fox trot with him. When the dance ended at 9:00, we three ended at Perkins, where we enjoyed a piece of their blueberry pie he had been raving about. While there he asked if we would go to Outback for steak with him the following night. Janie said that would be nice, but I kicked her beneath the table. I wasn't about to go to Outback with a near stranger. Still, the date was made, and on our homeward hike, I chewed her out. Here, she thought he would be a nice man for me and I told her I would know the right man when he showed up. Previously, I had been warned quite a few men were looking for a 'nurse with a purse'. Could he be one of them? He limped, due to a hip replacement, had a heart problem and was diabetic.

Later, back at the villa, after a soothing bubble bath, I lay in bed and mentally tried to finagle a way to get out of that date. Maybe, Janie could go alone?

Come morning our phone jangled. The man with the red hair was on the line. When I hung up, I walked out into the lanai, near hysterics with laughter.

Janie looked up from her paper and asked, "What's so funny?"

"Our date cancelled out."

"Thank God for that! What was his excuse?"

"Someone saw him with us, told his girlfriend, and she didn't like it one bit."

Sunday, as always, with hats upon our heads, we drove into town to The Church on The Square. Non-denominational services began at 12:00 AM, and, if the snow-birds were there, and we were not outside in line by 11:30 AM, it would be difficult to find two seats together. Snow birds are people from up North, who come South to escape the cold weather, and since they hadn't arrived yet, we had no problem.

Five o'clock in the afternoon, it was off to church again. This time to attend Oscar Feliu's concert. Just wonderful! His voice, like Jimmy Vale's, smooth as silk and sweet as syrup had me wishing I were much younger with my head upon his shoulder on a moonlight night. This concert was free, as most were.

Late evenings were Janie's and mine to enjoy. This was a my time to take pen in hand, while Janie had her nose in a book, or retired early, as she was an early riser. You've heard the old, expression— Early to bed, early to rise, makes a person healthy wealthy and wise? I guess I'll never reach that stage. I'm nocturnal, a night owl. Admittedly, a happy one!

The following day was ours to *goof off*. In our humble caddy, our golf cart, we lumbered over many golf cart paths, through an underground tunnel, and gobbled up twenty minutes of traveling to the new El Santiago Club. Here, we enjoyed a delectable lunch, and I specifically enjoyed the airy Florida Keys atmosphere, and the happy looks on faces of other diners. A fun day!

**Me and Janie dining at the El Santiago Club**

# Chapter 6
# Love Bugs and Golf Carts

The end of our time in this September rental was nearing. Life had been enjoyable in this cozy villa, with its down-to-earth warmth. Especially mornings, when we sat at the table in our lanai, chatted over breakfast, looked out over the expansive golf greens and watched golfers at play. I would have loved to call this villa my own. I even finagled a way to contact the owner, a doctor, who said, "It's an investment. Why don't you come look over some of my property here, in Daytona?"

Then one morning when I looked out our front window, I called to Janie. "Hey! Come! Look! There's a rental sign on the villa caddy-cornered across the street. I'm going to look into it and see how much they want."

She said, "Smart lady!"

I called the listed telephone number, and yes, that particular villa would be ours for the month of October.

Our last three days on Midera had been the busiest. Sorting, cleaning, and packing. When we ran out of boxes, I told Janie, "I'll hop in our golf cart, head into town, stop at Eckerd's and see if they have any empties, and hurry right back."

At Eckerd's, I stood in line behind a lady who handed the pharmacist two prescription slips.

"How long will it take to have them filled?" she asked.

"Fifteen minutes," he said.

There was a lull, and I jumped in. "Excuse me? Do you have any empty boxes?"

"I'll look and see," and he vanished.

The lady turned around and I received a thorough tongue lashing. "That was rude, interrupting like that. You should know better."

"I'm sorry, I'm in a hurry, it's raining and I'm in my golf cart." This fell on deaf ears. Saying nothing, she walked away. When I quickly made it over to the tooth brush section, I happened to glance back in the direction of the counter, and saw she had returned. Truly, I can't stand to have people angry with me, so I hurried over and touched her shoulder. She stared at me, with a questioning look.

"Please forgive me for being insensitive," I said. "I didn't mean to be rude."

She surprised me, with "Oh, I'm the one humiliated. I was rude. Forgive me, I don't know what got into me. After the words were out of my mouth I felt terrible. I'm really sorry."

"Please, you needn't be. I was the rude one."

"No, I was, and have no excuse for it. I'm sorry."

"Don't be." To end it all, I smiled and told her, "I'm one of God's angels and he doesn't want you to be unhappy."

"Thank you, my dear. Now I feel better." And that was that. We ended with a hug, and I, too, felt better.

Our new villa was pretty. Definitely modern, charmingly decorated, in peach and green, and nearly took my breath away each time I stepped over the doorsill. Because it's owned by a private party, and there's no middle-man, or woman, we are saving a hefty ninety-five dollars, monthly. This place truly is everything I would wish for except a den, yet, because of location, within walking distance to the square, if on the market, I would buy.

I felt I was getting, not only closer to what I was looking for in a home, but also a place to fit in, socially. Particularly, since this last Monday, Pat Beers, the president of Laureate Epsilon Kappa, chapter of Beta Sigma Phi Sorority, called and invited me to come visit their group of ladies, the group in which Faye belonged. Before, my days were filled. Now, it was great fun, as I bounce head-on with this peppy group, who had taken me under wing, twice monthly, being my chauffeur, picking me up to help with exciting Ways and Means projects, such as painting pretty flowers on containers in which bread can be baked, and bringing me home again. Janie wasn't hep about such things. She was more into books. While my life seemed more complete, more meaningful, sort of what peanut butter and jam does for a bare piece of bread.

One evening, while with this group, I became overwhelmed with awe, about everything in general: First, we enjoyed a scrumptious dinner at the Orange Blossom Country Club. Then there was an entourage of cars, which headed for the home of sister Mary Lee McClure, where we were served a yummy hot chocolate desert. I shall never forget that night nor the delightful younger miss, Lucy Sower, who sat next to me. She was into computer programming.

I confided, "I miss my computer. Back home in Pennsylvania, sometimes I'm up until one o'clock, typing an article for a local newspaper. Since my computer isn't here, in the evenings I'm scribbling my latest story with pen. "

"What's it titled?"

I took the last yummy bite of gooey chocolate cake, smacked my lips and grinned. *"Love Bugs and Golf Carts."*

Brows raised, she looked up and asked, "And who are the love bugs that will drive your golf cart?"

I fought to control a giggle, then soberly said, "I'm not referring to 'people love-bugs', but Florida's real honest-to-goodness genuine insects: their Love-bugs."

"Oh!" She grinned, somewhat sheepishly.

I told her, "When my friend, Janie, and I arrived here, we weren't aware such critters as Love-bugs existed. I heard they're troublesome two months out of the year. Four weeks in May and four in September. When the males fly in swarms."

"I didn't know that."

"They remind me somewhat of our lightning bugs up North," I added. "If you're up for a lesson, I'll tell you Florida Love-bugs are thinner and smaller, and they mate differently. During mating season the female climbs to the top of a blade of grass, readying herself for the swarm. Imagine this! Then a male flies over, attaches himself to her, and their 60-80 hour lives are spent in mid-air, mating." I grinned, adding, "So comes the name 'Love-bugs'. It's their honey-moon, so to speak...with the female doing the driving. I also learned after they mate, she deposits 100-350 eggs on the ground, beneath decaying vegetation."

"I didn't know that, either."

"Oh, I'm learning so much, since here. I'll take you a step further. Are you aware love bugs are attracted to the reflection of sunlight on gasoline and diesel fumes, and are often seen around gas stations and highways?"

"No." She gave her head a negative shake.

"Also, just last week, my friend, Janie, and I discovered they're attracted to light colors, especially white. Our golf cart was parked outside of Walgreens and we had to whisk off a slew before we could begin our trip home. You should have seen us zoom out of that parking lot. Quite hurriedly, I must say. Then along the way, we came upon an irate man, standing by his white Cadillac. It was supposed to be white, but was actually polka-dotted black with love bugs. We had never seen anything like it. There he stood, swatting them off with a heavy terry cloth towel. "They're a terrible nuisance," he growled. I noticed he even had a bug-guard fastened to the front of his car. I had also seen guards on golf carts. Not my rental.

"I don't have any on mine, either. So, tell me, did you have any bugs on your golf cart by the time you arrived home at your villa?"

"No, I traveled as fast as I could, and imagine the wind must have whipped them away. But, when I pulled into the garage, and climbed out of the cart, Janie sighed, 'Ah, no. There are black stains on the back of your pretty, new, white shorts.'"

"Were you able to remove the stains?"

"With difficulty. I tried Shout it Out, Tide, and Clorox, giving the areas a thorough rubbing. Eventually, the stains totally vanished after several washings, and each time, placing the shorts outside in the sun. But hear this! Last weekend, when we were at the Village Life Style Festival on the polo grounds, I came across a salesman advertising a commercial bug remover. It's called 'Blast Off' and he said it really works. So, remember this, if you're ever troubled with these buggers, called Love-bugs."

"Thanks! I'll remember."

"By the way, Florida's most popular bug isn't the Love -bug. Before coming here, I spoke with a water aerobic teacher and she clued me in on what to expect. One must look out for not only alligators in swampy areas, but Florida roaches which are called Palmetto bugs.' You see, Lucy, because of your climate here, the abundance of water and foliage, this particular bug has been in existence thousands of years. I was advised not to spread tan bark directly next to my villa or home, if I moved here, because the Palmetto female lays her eggs on the underside of bark."

It proved to be one of my most enjoyable evenings, visiting and chatting with these new sorority sisters, who made me feel at home. We ended the meeting with some exchanging of sisterly hugs and telephone numbers.

Two days later, when I drove to our Ace Hardware store for bug spray, a nice salesman, formerly from Hershey, Pennyslvania, said, "Don't worry too much about these Palmetto bugs. Most are content to stay outdoors in decaying leaves which help aerate the soil." When he told me one fertilized female can produce ten million in 3.4 generations, I told him about the bug I came face to face with in our former villa.

"He was caramel color, rather big, like a June bug up North, and that morning he came scooting across my bedroom carpet, headed directly for the opening beneath the dresser, and I went game-hunting. It was imperative I outfox him. Otherwise, not only would I have to live with him in my room for the full month, he might start a generation of offspring. So, I grabbed a newspaper, stood it up against the dresser, in his path, and he hiked straight upward, giving me a chance to fold the paper with him in it, and I swatted him off into the toilet bowl. My friend, Janie, and I stood looking down at him before I flushed him away. 'Gee!' she said. 'They're ugly things, aren't they?'"

The salesman agreed, saying, "Don't get me wrong. Seasonal sprayings are compulsory to keep all bugs under control . With all homes, whether stick built or stucco, special care is taken before construction, with the ground sprayed, and covered with a sheet of vinyl. Here, bugs are simply a part of Florida we must endure in order to enjoy all of its other attractive benefits."

**Picking the last of my gardenias to share**

# Chapter 7
## Another Villa Change

No, we couldn't rent this second villa for another month. It had already been booked for the month of November. However, one day I stopped to talk to a pretty mite of a lady in our neighborhood. Her name was Pat Dungan and she was out for an afternoon stroll with Bunny, her little dog. During our chat, she told me, "No, I'm sorry. I don't know of any available rentals in this area." She paused a moment and continued. "My widowed mother is in a nursing home, and her villa has been vacant now for three years. My husband and I are keeping it up. Despite the fact we're certain she will never return, we can't find it in our hearts to part with it."

"Oh, I'm so sorry, Pat. But would you please consider renting to my friend, Janie, and me? Please? Pretty please with sugar on it?" Together we laughed.

Then, for a brief moment, sadness swept her beautiful face, and I sensed an emotional struggle. "I'll talk it over with Ron and see what he thinks. For the rest of the week, he's tied up with his baseball team, and two out-of-town games." I crossed my fingers, and sensed I had one foot in the door, yet, there was still another to go.

Three days later, Pat called. "Yes, Ron says it's alright. He'll get together and work out a suitable agreement with you."

So, after two months here, we were now about to begin our third, just two streets over, and at The Villages normal seasonal rate. Our landlord, Pat's husband, Ron, a retired policeman, a likable chap, agreed to loan us his electric golf cart.

When he drove it over, he said, "Bootsy, this golf cart has been souped up, geared to soar past every other golf cart."

Janie never would think of doing such a thing. I did! Only once. The trickiest part is backing out of the garage without running into the neighbor's flower bed. The cart seems inclined to fly. Undoubtedly, as its master had.

Yes, all in all, this pro was now in control, even when I drove across the steep, up and down, million dollar golf cart bridge. It reminded me of a roller coaster, and took me over route 441, to the post office. My first drive there, proved 'the pits'. Determined not to have an accident, I grasped the wheel tightly, gunned it at the bottom, zoomed to the top, and with eyes straight ahead, held on for dear life, and to all who called out and waved as they passed by, this time all I could muster was a quick smile, and a high pitched "good morning" screech. The bottom was coming up fast. In order not to go off the path and hit a tree to the left, I swiftly swerved into the wooded area, jerked to a stop, proudly rested my head on the wheel, took a deep breath and, lifting my face to the Heavens, I said, "Thanks, God! We did it." Then I nearly giggled my fool head off, and I imagined He did, too!

Daily, I ran into more surprises. Here, I felt at home, safe and confident because it was a gated community, with a twenty-four hour crime watch.

Here, The Villages also cares about its people. One afternoon as I pushed my shopping cart up the aisles of the Publix Super Market, music I had been listening to suddenly stopped. An announcement came over the intercom, and ended with, "If this message wasn't clear, those listening should consult their family physician." The store was actually giving a hearing test. Amazing?

Another time, on a moonlit night, while Jane and I sat in the square listening to the band, and watching people dance, I turned to her and said, "I'm hungry for ice cream."

She responded with, "Me, too!"

"Okay! Janie, let's hike over to Publix and get your peanut butter parlor and some of my black moose, vanilla with streaks of peanut butter and chocolate."

While in the store we enjoyed looking at different items most super markets don't carry. My nose led me to a counter with bags of cinnamon scented pine cones. We became carried away with it all, when a lady clerk walked by. Jane looked at her watch.

"What time do you close?" she asked. It's 8:30."

"Eight o'clock."

"Oh!" Jane and I both groaned. "Why didn't you tell us?"

"Oh, that's okay. Don't worry. Take your time."

Now tell me, in what country; in what store in the whole wide world have you ever heard of this happening?

# Chapter 8
# A Return to PA and Home

Time, as usual, whisked by much too fast. Though I still hadn't found a villa to call my own, here I was, packing my bags, and gathering everything of mine to take along on my December 16 flight home to Pennsylvania. I would be spending the holidays, especially Christmas, with my children. Janie, on the other-hand, wished to stay in our rental until January, and spend the holidays with relatives in Ocala, before returning to her home in Berwick.

Then, there I was, sitting in a window seat on the plane, daydreaming above the clouds, wondering what awaited me upon my return home? This had been my second time away for so long. There was no need to worry. When I stepped into my tidy home, I breathed deeply of the warmth, the genuine feeling of belonging. Windows sparkled, the kitchen floor shone, and my plants were alive and hardy. Grace Peterson, not only my 'in a pinch' cleaning lady, but friend, and sister-in-law of Bill Winfendale, caretaker of my lawn and car while I was away, had done a magnificent job.

Christmas came and soon we were into January. Ah, yes, if I could wish January to simply fly away, I would have done so at the end of December.

Four days into the new year as I hurried into the kitchen to answer the phone, I whacked my foot on the rung of a white, wrought iron chair. I screamed and wobbled the chair close enough to sit down. From past experience, I knew the cartilage in the left knee had torn...the same knee that became fracture seven years ago when I slipped on a wet restaurant floor in Harrisburg. That time X-rays showed the problem and several months later the first arthroscopy was performed. The surgeon drilled holes in the knee, went in and shaved off sharp edges of bone and smoothed the cartilage. For eight months, off and on, pain was still my companion, as was a cane. Finally, I sought the help of Dr. David Joyner, Penn State football team's surgeon, and following still another arthroscopy, in a month I was in fine shape. Until that Thanksgiving, when I climbed over a farmer's fence to get a shock of corn for around my front lamp post, and my pant leg caught onto the bottom wire and I fell right smack on that knee. TLC took care of it after giving up a few months of my favorite past time, dancing.

Ah, yes. This time, I would care for myself for awhile, and not run to a doctor right away. In time, I finally weakened, and ran to Joyner's Orthopedic Group, on Trindle Road, not far from my home, only to learn Joyner was no longer there. I relied on one of his former associates, Dr. Kalenak, and received a shot of cortisone. "This should help you for six weeks," he said..

Wrong! Four weeks later, I returned. "What about collagen shots?" I asked.

"We could try them. They come in a series of three. They're beneficial to fifty percent and for fifty percent they're not."

So, I left after my first shot, which wasn't nearly as painful as cortisone. Sis Kathy, in New York, read everything she could regarding collagen, and our phone wires burned as she kept me up to date.

"Did you know they can get collagen from chicken's combs?" she asked.

I laughed about this and said, "Then I'm going to come to New York, and chase all the chickens down Broadway, until I catch one."

That week, game to try anything to prevent the necessity of another arthroscopy, I began taking Glucosimine Chondroiton. I read it builds cartilage. After a week, with no improvement, I decided to search for Dr. Joyner again, in hopes he would come to my rescue. I called Penn State and learned I could find him in his Hershey office every other Thursday. I left word for him to call.

One busy day, when my phone jangled, a voice asked to speak to Arbutus Focht. (He, as do all the doctors and my friends, always call me by my nick-name.)

Somewhat agitated, thinking a telemarketer was on the line, about to drink up my time, in a huffy voice, I asked, "What are you selling?"

"This is Dr. Joyner," the surprised voice said.

I had erred, explained and emitted a chuckle. Because of my previous surgery, I had become smitten with Joyner's office crew, and also his easy going doctor-to-patient manner. So much so, with each visit, I carried in a plate of my homemade peanut butter fudge. It got to the point where, after months slipped by, his girls began to check the list of incoming patients, and said "It's time for Bootsy. I'm hungry for some of her homemade candy." The epitome of social etiquette, after receiving the fudge, Joyner, himself, would send a personal *thank you*. One mentioned he had gone tail-gating to a Penn State game and shared my fudge with friends, and everyone enjoyed it. Then, when he discharged me as a patient, he said 'drop in any time, just to chat', and I laughed, "I know you. You just want some more of my fudge."

Now, he was saying, "I can see you this Thursday."

On my way to his office, I was unfamiliar with Hershey's traffic pattern, and became lost during my search for Chocolate Avenue. I made a wrong turn, but breezed into his waiting room only five minutes late and discovered he still had another patient in his examining room.

He greeted me with a friendly handshake and we discussed my predicament. "We'll see how you feel after the next two shots. Be patient regarding Glucosimine. Keep on it at least six weeks, and Bootsy, I'm not able to operate since carpal tunnel surgery on both wrists." With fingers upward, I noted the scars. "Don't worry. If surgery is needed, there's an excellent colleague of mine who will take good care of you."

For weeks, I lived with pain. I could sit, then suddenly with a sickening sharp stab in that knee, I would grimace and bite back a sob. My screams in the night would awaken me. The leg couldn't be

straightened unless I slipped my right leg beneath and pulled it along
. Nor could I roll over in bed unless I manually lifted the troubled leg
and turned it.

Finally I ran back to Joyner. "How long has it been now?" he asked.

"Eighteen weeks, and I've had it!"

"You've been in pain too long. It's time to go see a fine colleague of
mine, Dr. Kalenak."

Since I'm a member of RWA (Romance Writers of America), I
smiled and asked "Is he cute?" He described him. and I said "But, I
never kissed a man with a mustache."

"He'll probably shave it off for you."

Dr. Kalenak proved to be quite personable and the doctor who
gave me the collagen injection. Upon checking X-rays, he said,
"Arbutus, you and I are scheduled for a rendezvous on May 25, at
12:30."

"A midnight rendezvous? How nice!" I laughed. Though I had
wanted Joyner to operate, it wasn't until later I learned that in 1973,
Kalenak had been Joyner's professor in medical school.

Prior to this arthroscopy, I caught up on everything. Thoughts
were to sit back, read, and relax during recovery. Groceries were
purchased, including a few TV dinners, enough milk, OJ, and bread,
for two weeks. I also whipped up a pot of chicken rice soup, baked a
meatloaf, breezed through my home with the vacuum, caught up
with the laundry, and cleaned off the patio. I even managed to pick
flowers and place them on my husband's grave.

Then May 25th arrived. For the many, who, in time may have knee
problems, warranting arthroscopies, I would keep a day to day diary.

Today, while seated on one of the beds in the inner-waiting room,
with its rainbow colored curtains, at Grandview Surgery and Laser
Center, apprehension rode high as I conversed with the
anesthesiologist. He promised he'd monitor me, and I wouldn't be
deathly ill as I had been following a umbilical hernia repair nearly
two years earlier.

Nurse Jill spoke up. "I'm your OR nurse. You can have local
anesthesia instead of general, if you like. With local, you'll be sedated,
weave in and out of consciousness, may hear people talking, but you
won't feel, or remember a thing. It cuts down on swelling, the chance
of a blood clot, and there's no need for breathing apparatus."

"I'll take the local." She left to check with Kalenak, returned, and soon nurses ganged up, one on each side of me. "This will be a slight pinch," the one on my right said.

"There, that didn't hurt much, now did it?" said the one on my left.

Kalenak entered, masked in white, clothed in burgundy, and asked if I was ready. "First, I need a hug." A congenial fellow, I received his and gave mine, and he left. Nurses wheeled me into OR. I was asked if, at the count of three, would I help them roll me onto the table. I was mid-air and thoughts vanished. I didn't remember a thing.

I awakened in the room, with the striped curtains now pulled. Nurse Gwen asked, "Bootsy, from one to ten, how would you rate your pain?"

"Eight and a half." She would give me slightly more morphine.

Kalenak breezed in, smiled, now in crisp suit, white shirt, tie, gleaming shoes, and my eyes reeled him in and released him. He was dressed to kill, and not a Mockingbird!

"Bootsy, your leg was in bad shape. The cartilage was like shredded coconut. I cleaned and smoothed it all out for you. You'll be fine. You'll be able to dance again."

"That's wonderful news. I'm glad it's over. Only you shouldn't have mentioned coconut. I love coconut Easter eggs."

I left the clinic with my good friend, Norma, who, dear that she was, volunteered to spend the first twenty-four hours with me. I carried the clinic's little pink tray, just per chance my stomach decided to do hand-springs. It did! Three times Norma had to pull to the side of the highway. We reached home at five o'clock, six hours after I had arrived at the clinic. I hurriedly called there, and talked to a Dr. Yucha.

"I'm deathly sick, now with the dry heaves. They won't stop. Once I start, you can hear me all over the world."

"Yes, I'm out here in my garden in Lemoyne, and can hear you way down here." Laughter. A prescription of Phenergan was called into a local drug store. Charlie, a good church friend, would go for them. Six suppositories, $38.59. One sufficed. My stomach settled.

One big problem remained upon my return home. My ice bag, which I applied to my repaired knee, kept springing a leak. One night, you could find me at 11:30 PM, on crutches with a hair dryer in hand, drying the bottom sheet on my bed. Then the blasted drier shut off. I would sleep on the other side of the bed. First, I would watch the hilarious Golden Girls on Channel 42. While laughing my fool head off, it finally dawned. The dryer probably had a shut-off valve and had simply overheated. That was the case and I ended up sleeping in a dry bed.

During all of this, I couldn't help wondering, will I ever be able to return to Florida, to the lovely villages? Will I ever be able to be alone, again, and so far away from family? I would concentrate on that later, when I felt better.

# Chapter 9
# Recuperating

Four days following the arthroscopy procedure, while still in nightclothes, I stood propped on a crutch and glanced out my bedroom window to see a cardinal splashing in the birdbath. Directly beyond, a rabbit nibbled on blades of grass. Nearby, pecking at seeds tossed out for him, was "My Friend", a homing pigeon with a magnificent purple stripe around his neck, and a banded leg, numbered 3527. Seven weeks ago he unexpectedly showed up in my driveway, and has been vacationing on my property ever since. I named him 'My Friend', because twice he ate out of my hand, once he flew onto the patio and perched himself on my shoulder, and he is always there for me. Today, my knee aches, even without pressure on it, and more than a little disillusioned, I turned away from natures' tranquil scene.

Yes, I've been adjusting. Especially my body movements in ways to alleviate pain. My children, who came to check on me, claimed I am doing remarkably well. At first, I thought so, too. However, my first few trips to the bathroom were the 'pits'. The only way I could sit without emitting a scream was to slowly wiggle toes forward on the carpet, until the sore leg straightened. Getting off was easy. With both hands between my knees and resting on the seat, at the count of three, I lunged forward. To climb into bed, I sat far back in the middle, swung up my good leg, then with both hands, lifted the left.

On my fifth day, since Dr. Kalenak convinced me therapy would be beneficial, I attended my first of three weekly sessions with José, a nice therapist, at the Joyner Sports Medicine Institute. Though tiring, surprisingly, the exercising didn't hurt as much as I had expected.

At the clinic, I was hooked up to an H-electronic machine, the same used on the Lakers and the76ers players. This stimulates muscles, and helps cut down on edema...swelling...and is so relaxing. Next, came the manual exercises, thirty of each: leg lifts, knee bends, knee flatteners (pretending you're squashing an egg beneath your repaired knee), thirty toe slides, standing on the left foot three times, holding for thirty seconds, thirty up and down on toes, thirty with heel raised high, and ending with fanny squats. Then, the therapist gently mobilizes the knee cap by moving it up and down. No, the latter doesn't hurt. In fact, it's rather soothing.

The sixth day: Along with exercising, I put a sign "House For Sale by Owner", on my front lawn, and hobbled on crutches, struggling with yard care and also keeping the inside of my home tidied. (It received attention from one prospective buyer who called but never arrived.)

Regarding leg progress: This night, I climbed in bed by first placing my right knee in the middle, and swung up the repaired, without using hands.

The seventh day: I overdid it here at my home, hobbling around my flower bed, weeding for two hours.

The eighth day: Yesterday's accomplishments have taken their toll. My crutches have become my companion today. I've changed my mind. I will sell my home after my knee is mended. Then I'll move to a Villa in The Villages, Florida, where there's no lawn care, nor snow to shovel. This day, I lay low.

The ninth day: Still babied my leg. It was packed in ice and elevated on a little bench, while daughter Debbie's 16-year-young, Erica, with shearers in hand, trimmed the back of my hair, and she and her friend, Sherry, hovered over me, teaching me how to e-mail my writings. Later, since Debbie expressed wishes for some of her baby pictures, not only did I begin to make up an album for her, I put some of my own stashed away vacation pictures in albums.

The tenth day: I managed to paint my kitchen door, while I leaned on one crutch. No repercussions, and the door looked lovely. On this day, as I reminisced through all of this. I've learned: (1) never plan surgeries on holiday weekends. Friends and families have already made reservations to escape to the mountains or seashore. If single, you'll have to pretty much 'hoof it' alone. (2) Crutches are quite useful. They shut off TV's, close closet and cupboard doors, move dishes across counters and can reach beneath sofas where chocolates are hidden. (I'm deserving.)

This evening, my first bath in a tub, and my thoughts were, *I feel almost back to my normal self. Thanks, God, I don't want to ever get out.* It was sheer heaven to leisurely stretch out in soft, lilac scented bubbles which caressed my shoulders, and reached to my chin. Until then, only showers had been permitted. As I glanced at my cane propped against the bathroom wall, and wiggled toes amidst the bubbles, I couldn't help but smile and think, *That cane, too, will soon be gone.*

During my next appointment with Kalenak, I asked, "Why am I still in such pain when I curl up into a fetal position?"

"You're not supposed to be able to do that, yet." (A Reader's Digest book recommends this sleeping position to prevent a.m. back aches.) Kalenak added, "And no, you can't go tubing down the Shawnee on the Delaware with your children and friends as you do every Fourth of July. During a three hour trip, you might hit a rock and undo all the repair I've done."

My eleventh day: Really had a therapy workout. Returned home to eat lunch, and view *The Young and the Restless* and *The Bold and the Beautiful*. That's me, (giggle). When handicapped, everything takes so long. During commercials I watered flowers on my patio, then hobbled out to put water in the birdbath. Grabbed onto bushes to get there with the hose in my hand. Napped, E-mailed friends and wrote four overdue letters.

The twelfth day: Sometimes, in between therapy sessions, when I first begin to exercise here at home, a miserable charlie horse comes galloping in. These muscular cramps are extremely painful. I rid myself of one today by deeply massaging my leg, then hurriedly bounced up and down. Such cramps, occurring during sleeping hours, will vanish if you try Dear Abby's suggestion. Slip a cake of soap beneath your sheet. It works! Recently, I read leg cramps may be caused from not drinking enough water.

The thirteenth day: Pain in sore knee has lessened considerably. I walked around the kitchen with no cane, nor crutches. Even tried a few dance steps. Hurriedly stopped.

The fourteenth day: Noticed an ugly protruding lump on the outer part of my repaired knee. Son, Keith's thoughts? "Perhaps the surgeon forgot to remove a wad of gauze?"

The fifteenth day: I called the doctor's office and a nurse put my mind at ease. "It's undoubtedly just a formation of scar tissue, not to worry."

The sixteenth day: At therapy session, I learned in trying to cut down the swelling, I'm not to leave the ice pack on my knee more than twenty minutes. I am to remove it and wait forty minutes before starting again. During the night, I've been leaving it on for two hours. "It could cause hypothermia, and damage tissues," therapist, Chris, warned. Therapist, José, added, "Keep an eye on the lump on your knee. Make certain it doesn't become infected." Tired, today.

The seventeenth day: During the night, each time I felt a compelling urgency to roll into a fetal position, a flash of searing pain swept through my knee, as it had prior to surgery. Too tired to take Tylenol. (Prescribed pain medicine causes hallucinating and talking in my sleep.)

The eighteenth day: Last night, I felt a tug as if something pulled loose. Today, the lump is way down. The knee appears almost normal .Walked a few steps without crutches. I find a cane works best on carpeting. However, when propped, they easily topple. Mine has three times, now, on three occasions, causing a slightly bruised right foot.

The nineteenth day: The inside of knee hurts when I walk. A cane helps somewhat. Went grocery shopping. It nearly did me in. The knee hurt so much I felt like crying, but held back the tears.

The twentieth day: I awakened, lay still for a moment, and wondered which leg had been operated on? Later, it was great to simply hobble downstairs and wash two loads of laundry. I hoped to stay on the lower level until the job was finished. The doorbell rang. I climbed the stairs to find no one there. Learned it had been the neighbor boy, Michael, the dentist's son, who pitches in and mows my lawn.

The twenty-fifth day: During therapy, a few more exercises have been added: Five minutes on the bicycle, thirty walking sessions, up and down a step, and three, balancing on the repaired leg, hopefully for thirty seconds. I learned I'm scheduled for therapy sessions until July 20.

The twenty-sixth day: a check-up with surgeon, Doctor A. Kalenak. He's pleased with my progress.

The twenty-seventh day: With the refrains from my radio urging, *I wanna dance with you,* I began to slowly sweep across the room. I thought of the get well greetings signed by sixty members of the Metropolitan Singles Dance Group. One gentleman had written, "George, your dance partner." At first, I couldn't help smiling, wondering which man was George? Then I remembered. He was the one who had been dancing since the age of three, and when we jitterbugged together, he was velvet-in-motion on the dance floor. Though no pain whatsoever, while I danced alone, later when I applied eye make-up a terrifying flash caught me off-guard. My hand jerked and my brow resembled a clown's. A few moments later, I could feel the pain slowly ebb, leaving behind a dull ache.

When I hobbled into the clinic, two women said their arthroscopies were far more painful than their recent knee replacements. I must remember Kalenak said my leg had been in bad shape.

Today, as I stand before my window, and look out, I sadly note "My Friend", the pigeon, has been missing now, for seven days. I pray he has safely winged his way home and is alright. I will be. I'm still trying to shift into low gear and set a slower pace. Yes, I know, there's an old saying: "You can't teach an old dog new tricks." But I'm more like a young-at-heart feline with her leg caught in an *age trap.* Once I'm completely released, I won't fly away. I'll simply reach out and once again pounce...on life. Preferably in The Villages. Yes, I'll bide my time, and be patient.

The following day, as I pulled into my driveway, I happened to glance down over the sloping lawn, and saw something pink propped against the lilac bushes. My umbrella! Yesterday, I had placed it on the patio to dry and high winds had blown it away. Hopes were it hadn't torn in its journey. I walked the full length of the patio, passed my car, cautiously walked sideways down the leaf-covered slope, and found the opened umbrella still in perfect condition. Extremely tired, I wouldn't go the same route I had come to get to it. Instead, my patio was straight ahead, and I figured if I used the spoke of the umbrella, jammed it hard into the patio's concrete surface, took hold of a limb from that tree over there, I could lunge forward and hoist myself up. Yes! I would do this. Only in the attempt, I was air born, inches from my goal, and without enough leverage, felt myself falling backward. Thoughts of my poor knee whizzed through my mind, and I protectively turned sideways, when *Thud,* I ended on my back and rolled in a fetal position. With the wind knocked from my sails, I lay there, eyes closed. *You're okay, just breathe deeply,* I told myself.

When I opened my eyes I pondered the situation. Had I been knocked out, with broken bones, when would anyone have found me? Would the family across the field be able to see me? No, I wouldn't be visible through the bushes. What about the people across the street? No, the sloping ground was too high. I lay on a pile of leaves, and looked down at myself. What would people think if they did find me? Well, they would say, "she's wearing a pretty, white lace-trimmed petticoat. Legs aren't bad." I got to giggling, and told myself it was time to think sensibly and get up on my own. So, ever so slowly, I pulled myself up into a sitting position, then with feet firmly settled on the soil, brushed off leaves and dirt from my clothing and hair, and realized my body still felt intact. Yes, for a moment, on my return walk to the back door, I had to wonder if the dear Lord was trying to tell me something? That I'm to remain 'put' and not move so far away? No, it wouldn't matter where I would be, everyone was too far away or too busy. With the knee arthroscopy, and now this, I'd proven to myself, I could conquer anything. I'm moving to The Villages. Not part time, but all the way. I can, and will do this.

# Chapter 10
## Preparing to Head South Again

Summer breezed in, and off and on I limped through most of it. No, my knee wasn't coming along as well as I expected. Dr. Kalenak kept telling me, "It will take time. Be patient, Bootsy." I really tried to be.

On October 19, I awakened early in the morning, around 6:12, and lay there and pondered which route to go. Should I spend the winter in Pennsylvania? Because of our recent chilly weather, with high blustering winds, and the weatherman's prediction, it would go down to 38° at night, I had a strong urge to head for The Villages, but first I wanted to sell my home.

So far, four people called and dropped by to go through, and each time, I kept telling myself, *This is it. They love it and will want to buy.* One young fellow, employed just two blocks away, requested I wait until spring to sell. Yet, I can't. Years are spinning by so fast, and every year counts at this tender age of 76. One couple came twice, and the complete family, including their two daughters, were truly enthused. Then Papa finally called to say his wife and the girls talked everything over, and decided the bedrooms weren't as large as they wished them to be. Next, came an interesting couple, in their sixties. They had met on the Christian Internet. He was from Erie, she was a local gal from Camp Hill. When they first met, they took an immediate liking to each other. After dating a year, they were certain they were in love. He sold his home, and she was going to place hers on the market. Both loved mine, but it had been three weeks and neither called again.

Over breakfast, I decided I'm not waiting anymore. I picked up the phone and called the Dungans, Pat and Ron, Janie's and my former landlords, in The Villages.

"Our rental is available for forty days, beginning on October 31, at The Villages' going rate of $2,000," Ron said. "Since you left, I've been keeping my eyes and ears open, looking for a place in this area, where you said you wish to locate. Last week, there was one for sale, down the road, but I checked it out, found it needed a lot of work, was priced too high, and had a swimming pool, which I don't think you would want to be bothered with. Why trouble yourself with the upkeep, when there're nine free Village pools you can use?"

"You're right, Ron. Thanks a million for your help. God be willing, I'll see you on the thirty-first."

When I hung up, I called the Middletown Airport and purchased my flight ticket. I would be flying to Florida on October 31. Then I got to thinking — suppose I find a place to buy and haven't yet sold my home, here? Later, when I stood before the filled bookcase, stretching across the entire family-room wall, I asked myself, *Why couldn't my children come and pick books they may like? Is the world whirling too fast for everyone to take time, sit down and read? It seems to be that way for me. Also, why can't my kids come to help clean out my place? And, what will I do if a buyer comes along, and I'll have to vacate sooner than anticipated? Do I place everything in storage here in our Camp Hill area, or hire a mover to transport it to a storage place in Florida? I will be returning to Camp Hill on December 9, hopefully, if the airports are open and there's no more bomb or anthrax threats as there have been lately.* Two days earlier, our airport had closed for five hours and travelers were transported to Gettysburg. White powder which had been found in a blanket handed to a stewardess was checked. It proved to be just that, powder, yet all precautions had to be taken.

Tentative plans were to leave now, and return to spend Christmas with my children. Yet, if my home sold, and I flew to Florida, when I returned, what then? Where would I go? None of my four children said, "Mom, you know you're welcome to stay with us." Perhaps they felt if they didn't think or talk about it, my plans wouldn't materialize.

I cleared off the table, removed the phone from the hook and dialed Ron and Pat Dungan, my again, soon-to-be landlords. This time, I would make certain I received the correct address and phone number in the Villages, so friends and relatives would be able to reach me there. Last year, The Villages gave us an incorrect phone number and an irate gent became more than a little miffed with so many calls coming in asking for "Bootsy." Once the number was corrected, I called and left an apologetic message.

Ron was on the line. "No, Pat's not in. She's out having our new dog, Bunny, groomed. Bunny, the 16-year-old dog you were familiar with, died eight months ago. Bunny, the first dog was named during the Easter holiday, on the day of delivery, and the second Bunny simply carried on the name."

I chuckled, surprised to hear Ron, a rather quiet dignified man, with a slow smile, now talk so randomly. I decided not to cut our conversation short. I yearned for a man's input, regarding my big astronomical move, uprooting from old familiar grounds and shoving off into new territory.

"No, Pat's not in," he reiterated. "But, yes, I can help you."

I received the numbers for both the telephone and my mail box, and said, "I needed these. I'm transferring some funds to my bank account there, in hopes to buy a villa during my forty-day stay."

"Your best bet is to first find the location you wish to be in."

"It's the Hacienda, where you and Pat are."

"Then your best bet is, if you have plenty of time, start looking around. Knock on doors. Say you live down the street and you're looking to buy. People may sell. That's how we got our place. The folks were looking for a bigger villa. This one they had lived in, never went on the sales market."

"Thanks, Ron. It's nice to get ideas as to what to do and expect. I miss this, talking to a man. Men are so sensible, and can look ahead, solving problems, sometimes before they arise. My confidante, the doctor I grew fond of, was always there for me, but I no longer am so fortunate. I used to call and say, 'The lawn man is next door on his mower, but my grass isn't that high.' Then he would say, 'Tell him to come back next week.' Another time I called to say my dentist claimed I needed twenty-eight hundred dollars worth of work done on my teeth. Two crowns should be replaced, a tooth was about to crumble and a rough spot between my teeth was the beginning of a cavity, and it should be filled."

"What did the doctor say to this?"

"Have the cavity filled, and wait for the tooth to crumble."

"Did the tooth crumble?"

"Nope!"

A chuckle, then, "Well, once you're here, I'll help you as much as possible. First, if it were me, I'd get the movers to transport your furniture down here, to store and lock in a dry, clean place."

"I'm not bringing that much, in case I should purchase a furnished villa, like I nearly did last fall. All I'm going to take with me is one bedroom suite, filing cabinets, computer, a white, wrought iron kitchen set, a small wicker love seat and chair, and my patio furniture, plus some pictures. "

"In that case, I'd rent a truck and have someone bring everything down. Someone strong enough to handle the furniture."

"My handyman wanted the job, but he's 70."

"No, you'll need someone younger. Here's another idea. You may want to store and lock up everything there in your area. You don't want to cross a bridge, and not be able to get back a decision which had been made too hastily. Something may happen along the way."

"Like the airport situation, the way it is today?"

"No, I don't let that bother me. I was thinking about your idea of handling the sale of your home by yourself. It may take too long. I'd find a reputable realtor, someone who sells property a lot, rely on him to look after your home and do a good job."

To me this sounded the most logical and sensible route to go. Under lock-box, my home would be in the hands of a realtor, and it would be his duty to check and make certain there were no frozen pipes or water problems of any sort. It wouldn't be necessary to rely on my friends, as I had last year, during Janie's and my four-month stay in The Villages.

"Once you're here, Bootsy, something is going to pop up. You'll know it's the right time, the right villa. Start looking around."

"I shall do that." I was thinking about my handyman and his sister-in-law, Grace, keeping an eye on my home, here, to make certain it would be suitable for showing at all times. Especially have the walks clear, if it should snow."

"Upkeep can be a pain." Then he added "Here, I don't find warm weather objectionable."

"I, myself, didn't while there. So, if all goes well, I'll see you on October thirty-first. I'll hold the happy thought."

The following day, I called my stock broker in The Villages, hoping to get his thoughts regarding Florida, now that he and his wife had been there a year. She answered. I asked, "Tell me truthfully? Are you happier there in Florida than you were here, in Pennsylvania? Do you have any regrets having moved there?"

"Truthfully, Bootsy, I'm happier here than any other place I've lived. It simply is a way of life."

We spoke about my plans. "If I sell my home within the next ten days, I'll store everything I want to bring along. My children still haven't come to sort through a large amount of items."

"I'd issue a deadline."

"I'll e-mail them."

"Good idea."

"Regarding your crystal chandelier you bought in Paris, if you want to take it along with you, I'd leave it hanging over the dining room table when you show your home, but stipulate it's not included in the sale of your home. Regarding the electric fireplace in the family room, does it throw off heat?"

"Yes, and it's also a fan. Though it's vivid orange in color, last year it would have been nice to have when Janie and I were down there. It was so cold, and to keep warm, we ended up buying wool sweaters at a garage sale."

"Orange is an old color."

"I know, but I've always liked it. Yet, I now agree. The fireplace isn't really necessary." I spoke about the eight boxes of items stored in my shed, and perhaps I should have another patio sale, yet time seemed so short.

"If there's nothing you really want or need, give them to the Salvation Army. Or, Goodwill. Get an itemized statement as to the value and declare it on your income tax."

That sounded like a smart idea, one I would surely follow. We spoke regarding The Village Shuttle Bus. Their free number to call was 877-255-8756. The bus left the airport at stations, B-17 at 3:30, and A at 3:45. The next bus didn't leave until around 5:45. The cost was twenty dollars, and she always paid a gratuity. Rates for people living in The Villages were five dollars cheaper, and one must show their community member card.

"How's the weather?" I asked.

"Pleasant, though it looks like rain, and before it comes, we're going swimming over at the Orange Blossom Country Club. I'm slipping into my bathing suit as we're talking."

"Well, run along. Take a dip for me. I appreciate your briefing me as to what to expect. Only now, I feel I'm not making a mistake in selling my home here and moving there."

"You're not, Bootsy." I hung up, breathed a sigh of relief and told myself,.*Without a doubt, I'm headed in the right direction.*

# Chapter 11

# Decisions! Decisions!

The following morning, Kathy in New York called. "Bootsy, you can't buy a villa in Florida without first selling your Camp Hill home. You'll be hit with a big Capital Gains Tax."

I told her, "Thanks. I'll look into this."

It didn't happen that day, as the morning slipped by and in the late afternoon, following their working hours, daughter, Dianne and her husband surprised me with a visit.

"We're here! We're here! We came to help," Dianne squealed as she gave me a big hug. I couldn't believe it. What a nice surprise that was.

While Eric carted boxes of items from the shed, and stacked them on the patio for Goodwill to pick up the first thing tomorrow morning, Dianne and I cleaned out part of the basement.

"I haven't had time to even touch this section of the house," I told her. "I've been so caught up with everything."

"I can understand where you're coming from, Mom. That's why we're here."

So, together, she and I packed boxes of items I wanted to keep, and neatly stacked them along the full length of the basement wall. "I want the room to look open and spacious," I told her.

"Good idea, Mom."

Next, we had fun emptying a big trunk. She would take it along home with her. Bags and bags of blankets, pillow, and bedspreads. I sighed when I removed the last spread, a cotton knit, with apple green squares on white, and a red flower centered in the middle. "I bought this fifty years ago, in Sears where I worked in the credit office. Ah, yes, I loved it. It was our first bedspread, when we lived in your grandmom, Ninnie Focht's home, where we stayed a while with her and Pop Pop Smith, her dad. Mom and I had wallpapered one wall of your dad's and my room, in green, patterned with blossoms of white dogwood. I can still see it. Green leaves matched the green in this spread."

"Don't throw it away, Mom! I don't know what I'll do with it, but I want it." With the last bag dragged up the stairs, a coughing spell overtook me. "Nerves!" I said as I headed out the door.

When Dianne and Eric left, I stood in my driveway and we tossed kisses back and forth, until their truck vanished around the corner. A moment of sadness swept through me, like an echo in the distance. Just then, I looked up the street and recognized the car coming toward me. Twin son, Keith, and wife, Marsha, had arrived to help clean out my china closet. China and crystal I planned on taking to Florida had already been packed by yours truly.

Alone in the early evening, the house seemed so quiet. I would phone my Realtor, Bill Zody, and get some in-put regarding the big capital gains, and, once and for all, put my mind to rest.

"If the property you buy and sell doesn't exceed $250,000, It doesn't need to be reported."

"It won't, Bill. When I buy a villa in Florida, my goal is not to exceed the amount I'll receive from the sale of my property here."

"Then you'll be fine."

October thirty-first, the morning of my departure arrived. What a morning! I looked out the back door to discover my handyman, Bill, had come in from the country an hour and forty minutes before we were to leave for the airport.

Already, he busied himself shifting boxes, from one end of the patio to the other, closer to the driveway; better accessible for the Goodwill driver's truck. I opened the door and called,"Good morning, over there! Hey, Bill? Why so early?"

A silly grin. "So I'd be on time."

"Well, don't bother me, I'm on a tight schedule. Do whatever you want. If you haven't eaten, come get some cereal. Pour some for me, too." He did, and I'd take a bite, flit into my bedroom, comb my hair, flit out for another bite, etcetera. The doorbell rang. "Answer that, for me, will you Bill?"

Realtor, Bill Zody, with two new keys he had made for my house. The bell rang again, this time, the Goodwill man.

That hour passed too swiftly. At 9:30 AM, Bill sat at the wheel of my white Chrysler, and with me as a passenger, we were on our way down the street, heading for the airport. One block from my home and I yelled, "Bill, turn around! I don't have anything warm to wear. I forgot to grab a sweater or a coat, and it will be cold December tenth when I return."

He pleased me, with, "Don't worry, Miss Bootsy. I'll find a warm jacket in your hall closet for you, and bring it along when I pick you up at the airport."

Twelve hours later, in the alcove entranceway of the Dungan's home in The Villages, I stood in the darkness and rang their doorbell. Neither Ron, nor Pat answered. I turned away, and wearily began my walk down the driveway, wondering what to do, now. Suddenly, I heard a noise, lights flared on, and I quietly whispered, "Thanks, God!"

When I turned, Ron threw open the door. "There you are! We thought you would be here much earlier. We were about to turn in for the night."

While we walked up the street to my rental, at 1218 Fernando Lane, I rattled on, and told him I had forgotten The Villages Shuttle Bus phone number. "Also, my plane landed at 3:15, and by the time I picked up my luggage and reached terminal number 1, at 3:45, the shuttle had left."

"That's too bad."

"Admittedly, I felt extremely uncomfortable. Frightened, would be a more suitable word. There I was, stranded at an airport in which I wasn't too familiar, and all these drivers, men, and some women, white, black and yellow, stood by their vans, and kept hounding me to be a passenger. One man, and supposedly his wife, approached me, and said for $75 they could take me to The Villages. I wasn't about to trust any of them. Then, to top it off, a woman outside, who waited for her passengers to arrive, told me, 'If you're waiting for The Villages Shuttle, you should be at station 17.'"

"From one to seventeen is a long hike." Ron said.

"When my eyes followed to where she pointed, they were my sentiments. Yet, with cane in one hand, and pulling my luggage with the other, I began to hobble back to where I had originally sat. Midway, my carrying case fell off the top of my main luggage, and items spewed all around my feet. When I bent to retrieve everything, my cane slid from my hand and clattered noisily on the concrete. Exhausted and sweating, now feeling utterly ridiculous, I looked up and hoped the people who stood there watching, and those who stopped to stare, would come to my aid. No one did, Ron. Perhaps the most were simply tired travelers, like myself, and not the polite Southerners as I, at first, imagined."

"One never knows," Ron stated, a half smile curling his lips. "Well, you're here, now. How did you finally get here?"

"After sitting there in the shuttle bus area, for two and a half hours, I finally hopped a ride on a Limo Shuttle. The driver told me, "The Villages is out of my jurisdiction, yet, I can take you there and see that you arrive safely." True to his word, he did, after getting lost in an unfamiliar section. His fee was only $38, and with my ten dollar tip, it proved considerably cheaper than expected."

We finally reached my villa. Ron unlocked the door and I walked inside, looked around and uttered a sigh of relief. "Boy, it looks the same, and it's great to finally be here, but I'm famished. On the plane, all they gave me to eat were two bags of dried chips, a glass of milk, and OJ."

Ron said, "There's some Boost drinks in the fridge. Help yourself."

He left, and I nearly made a mad dash for a drink, even though I was near to certain I wouldn't care for it. I was shocked to find nothing could have been so refreshing. Nor could Carol Furlong's message on my answering machine have been more welcoming. I pushed the blinking button.

"Boootsy. Welcome! I'm glad you are here. I received your letter yesterday, but knew you would be out running around. If I don't hear from you by four o'clock, I'll catch up with you later."

# Chapter 12
# Wow! I Really Did It

On the first night in my villa, after the exhausting twelve hour trip, I was content to do nothing but dress for bed and slide in between cool, crisp white cotton sheets. Then I flicked on the eleven o'clock news on TV and finally ended my day as usual, by switching over to The Golden Girls, and laughing myself silly. When I finally turned off the bedroom light, I immediately drifted away in slumber.

Eight o'clock the next morning, I opened my eyes to a bright new day, and drank in the peaceful surroundings. As I looked around, I told myself...Wow! I really did it! I'm here...in The Villages.

For breakfast, I drank a half can of Boost, to give enough *boost* for me to take off for the Publix Supermarket, where I would purchase enough groceries for a week. I'd leave now! I opened the door, which led into the garage, pushed a wall button, watched the door roll upward, hopped aboard my cream colored golf cart, and said, "Well, my Lord, here we go, off to see if I remember how to operate this thing. Will I find my way? Yes! We can do it!"

Traffic was light. I reached midtown, to find a lot of construction going on and detour signs everywhere. Janie had informed me, via phone, about office buildings and quite a few magnificent homes which had already been constructed. They were for sale, beginning at $325,000, I had heard. *Out of my league*, I told myself as I rounded a corner, certain I was now headed in the correct direction. Thinking I could eat a horse, I was that hungry, I slowed a bit, to get my bearings. Janie always said I was terrible when it came to directions. Especially remembering them. I would prove her wrong. A horn honked behind me. An impatient male, and as usual, in a hurry? I pulled my golf cart to a stop sign, climbed out and moseyed back to tell him to go around me. Instead, a lady behind the wheel smiled up at me.

"No, I'm not an impatient man. I saw you slow down, and thought you were lost and I could help you find your way."

"Thank you. That's very kind of you."

Her name was Natalie, a rather fancy dresser. Lime green linen playsuit, a crop of freckles, blonde hair, shoulder length, and fashionably styled, page-boy. I was more than a little impressed, and to think she went out of her way for me?

I continued on. Riding my golf cart seemed like *old hat*. If a cat, it would purr. I rather enjoyed being at the wheel again. Shopping, too, proved to be fun.

I used the grocery cart as a crutch, and no one could tell I babied my knee. Grocery cost? $80.24. I shot my wad, so to speak, and would not go hungry.

Second day, and shortly after I climbed out of bed, the phone jangled. Carol, who had left the nice welcoming message on my answering machine, greeted me with," Good-mornin', did I get you up? Are you awake?"

"Yes, I'm awake, and just finished with my morning exercises."

We caught up to date regarding my trip, and she asked me to check my calendar and see if November 29 was clear.

"I don't have a calendar."

"Then you're free. Remember Romaine Harry, from our Lemoyne Church?"

"Umhmm."

"She moved down, not in The Villages, but in Leesburg. I thought it would be nice if we got together with Pastor Bill and wife, Louise, for lunch."

"Sounds grand to me."

"Okay, get a pen and paper and mark it down."

Later, while I prepared an omelet, I remembered Pat's husband was away, and perhaps she might enjoy coming for breakfast? While onions were nicely sizzling in the pan on the stove, permeating my kitchen with their delightful odor, I dialed her number.

"No, I have already eaten, but thanks, that was nice of you to invite me. Oh, someone called here, asking for you. The name was Martin. His credit card said Glenn. His number is 751-5190.

"It's undoubtedly a realtor"

Breakfast was over and I dialed the number, and recognized the voice, Natalie's. "What a nice surprise," I said. "You never gave me your last name, and I didn't think to check your number."

She told me, "I've been thinking of a good bank you may want to contact in case you wished to file for a loan. It's the Sun Trust, directly across from Eckerd's. Go there, tell them the worth of your PA home. The bank is on US Highway 441."

"I'm not permitted to cross the highway in my golf cart, and there's no way to cross over the Golf Cart Bridge to reach that bank."

"I would be glad to take you. First, look around for the villa you want. Go to the 3 A's and get a map. They cost only $2.00.

"Thanks for the suggestions. I'll do that."

"Tomorrow, I must go to Orlando, but I'm free today, if you want, I can go look at some villas with you now. Remember, resales go fast. I would call the Resale office and have my regular sales rep pull up the listings."

She found a house up the street and around the corner, on Medira, the street on which Janie and I first lived, and told me, "It has just been put on the market. I'll meet you there in five minutes."

We pulled up in front of the courtyard villa at the same time. It proved to be a dream, all I would ever long for. At $174,000 it cost more than I wished to pay, and also I would have no use for a three car garage. Yet, the furniture was beautiful, and had it been for sale, I would have bought it and put it in storage until I found a villa in which it could be placed.

We looked at another villa, in another section. No comparison. I sighed, and said, "I don't think any will satisfy me after going through the first one."

I was dropped off here at my rental, and Natalie's thoughts were, "If it should go on the market, it could be fixed up, taking a room at a time, and somehow, put back the walk-in closet that had been done away with to make a small and private hallway which led to the master bedroom."

After her departure, I sacked out for two hours, then decided to drive into town and go shopping at Winn Dixie. There, I purchased apples, apricots and suntan lotion. I got caught in the rain when I exited. It soon began to pour, and just this side of the Del Mar gate, I hurriedly climbed out of the golf cart to pull down the flaps. I arrived home in dripping wet shorts, but when I entered my villa, it seemed extra post-toasty cozy to me. I ate left-overs for dinner; pea soup, salad, and watermelon. Good, though it would have been more enjoyable eating with someone...man or woman.

At loose ends, after the dishes were washed and put away, I called to chat with Pastor Bill. He laughed, when I played Carol's pleasant welcoming message on my answering machine. "I'm thinking of taping it, to play when I feel alone, away from my children."

"That's a fine idea," he said.

I asked, "Is your honey there?"

"Yes, she's on the other line."

"Hi, there, Louise," I said.

"Hi, Bootsy. I picked up when the phone rang. Welcome to The Villages."

"Thanks. So far I love it here, but after a two hour layover, a four hour flight, it took another six hours for transportation from the airport. Did you know the Village Shuttle bus number isn't listed amongst other buses listed on the rotating cylinder in the airport?"

"Maybe it's listed as *The Villages Sales Office*."

"Perhaps, I never thought of that." I spoke of my villa search. "My landlord Ron, and his wife, Pat, have been looking for one in their neighborhood. Because villas there are within walking distance to the square, they're rarely put on the market. Once they are, they're gobbled up quickly. Even the latest Ron had seen, and didn't think suitable for me, sold the day I arrived."

"Don't be discouraged, there will be others."

"I'll hold the good thought. Pat's husband said, perhaps in time, she will sell the one I'm in now. It's cozy, though lacks closet space. Stop in sometime and I'll show you around. Maybe I'll cook and invite you for dinner when I have time."

The pastor's voice raised two octaves. "You COOK? We'll stop by to see you before the twenty-ninth."

A chuckle from Louise, then..., "But we'll call first."

# Chapter 13
# An Ideal Villa For Me?

Another week slipped by, and tonight I called, Bill, my handyman, in Pennsylvania.

"No, your house hasn't been sold, yet. But," he added, "A lot of realtors have gone through, and they left a pile of business cards on your dining room table."

In hearing this, I became more than a tad disappointed, because this morning I had already called my bank in Pittsburgh, and received a loan. Hopes were to use it, along with other funds, and have a substantial sum to pay on a villa, also for furniture, and still have a cushion for any emergencies, should they arise.

Now, more determined than ever, I would strongly push ahead in my search. The following day I subscribed to a newspaper. No ads were listed. Another day, while in the local bank, I sat and read their newspaper, The Daily Sun, and jotted off resale villas, those located close to the square. With map in hand, I visited them all, to find none satisfactory. One was too far away. Another, too close to the curb. Another, roomy, but too dark because of tinted windows. Yet, I sensed I was getting a bit closer to my dreams. Then one morning I discovered three ads in the newspaper. Listed with a young realtor, they all sounded promising. In checking with him, they weren't, yet he would keep me in mind, and call if anything became available.

One day, while out scanning neighborhoods, I found myself in the De La Mesa Village, and there, straight ahead, was a sharp looking villa, with a sign in the front yard. It read, "For Sale, by Owner". Thrilled with thoughts this could be mine, I brought my golf cart to a sudden halt. In checking around the neighborhood, I learned the villa was owned by a lady lawyer, in New York. A male resident, across the street, had the key.

That week, we went through twice, and I still found it enticing, exquisitely furnished, with even a Murphy bed in the lanai, along with two lovely boudoir chairs and a white corner desk. All I would need. The last time through, I told the gentleman, "I want this villa!" The courtyard in back, was artistically landscaped with bushes circling a kidney-shaped court of white stones, bordered in brown. Maintenance free. I liked that.

I was so smitten, I called the owner, in New York.

"I love your villa. It's tastefully decorated, and the price is right. I want it."

"Thank you. The Villages sent pictures of what they've done to make it a rental. I imagine it's nice. I don't go in for much chats: Plants, flowers and such. I'm glad you like it, but I must tell you, a brother and sister, from the Bronx, are coming down on Thanksgiving to look it over, with intentions of buying."

I groaned. "There goes my lovely villa."

"Not necessarily," Barbara retorted. "What will be, will be, my dear."

No sooner did I hang, up when the phone rang again. Marti Rowland, a new friend with sparkling eyes and a captivating smile was on the line. I met her at the new sorority chapter's two functions which I had been invited to attend. I liked Marti, and right away knew she was out to help me, a newcomer, feel comfortable in a somewhat unfamiliar community.

"I had an enjoyable day," she said.

"And, what did you do today, Marti?"

"I attended a David Heyday group, in which *you* may become interested. It's a social support program for widows and widowers, and they meet once a month. It's sponsored by a really great man, from Heyday's Funeral Home. "

I sat back to listen, while she continued. "We have a nice $7.00 lunch at the Community Center in Leesburg. This groups' goal is to create an atmosphere of comfort, and support for those who have experienced the loss of a loved one, by reinvesting emotional energy through fellowship, learning and living. It's also to reinforce a sense of holiness, and to improve one's quality of life, through personal involvement and contribution. Once a month we go by motor-coach to attend a play, and have lunch. We have different activities." She mentioned there would be a Christmas luau, a trip to Sea World, and a movie. It sounded like an interesting and active group.

"One thing, Bootsy, we must make reservations through David at 787-5421. It's a local call. Dress is casual, culottes or pant suits. We had the most fun today. A registration nurse, Carol Clendinen, an excellent speaker, spoke on the subject of *Rejuvenating your Wit, Wisdom, and Wellness*. She had us all laughing. It was a fun afternoon. You would have enjoyed it."

"I'm certain I would have, Marti, thanks, but I must concentrate on finding a villa. Today, I found one I really like."

The following week, Barbara got back to me. "I haven't heard from the Bronx party, and whoever gets the money to me first, will become the owners."

By now, I had visited that particular village three times, circle-walked through the park, sat at the pool and talked to a group of nice ladies, and they said I would enjoy living there. Holidays, and even birthdays were cause for a party or picnic. They sounded like a jolly group, and I certainly wouldn't be lonely there. Thoughts were it would be a grand place to entertain.

As a whole, generally speaking, I think men can better foresee the future, and I felt privileged to be able to run to my landlord for sound advice. I called Ron Dungan, and happily told him, "I found my villa!"

"You did? Where's it located?"

"It's the one I've been looking at, in the De La Mesa section."

He stopped me with, "Bootsy, you're aware that's the only village with a park, pool and club house, and you'll have to pay an additional monthly forty-five dollars, to use them, along with the one hundred five dollar amenity fee to The Villages. Do you swim that often?"

"No, Ron. In thinking it over, I wouldn't use the pool that much."

"Then, Bootsy, think seriously before you jump. I'd hate to have you squander your money when there are nine free pools here in which you could swim without paying a penny. Keep looking. If you feel you want something, balance it out. See what makes you feel good. If you lose the house you bid on, get a rental. There's newness and advantages. Estimated monthly cost of living will vary, depending on the size of a home and its usage, as well as the type and size of the home site it occupies. When you again think you've found the right villa, I promise to go along with you and check it out."

"Alright, the search continues, and hopefully, I'll find an exact duplicate like this, but in a different location."

"Hold the good thought, Bootsy, and you will! I'm sure of it."

# Chapter 14
# Mac and Meeting New People

Wednesday, I decided to attend Singles Night at McCall's Tavern. Perhaps someone there may have heard of a villa for sale in the area in which I chose to locate. I would call a cab, go down, order dinner and, while eating, enjoy the evening watching others dance. My arthroscoped left knee still didn't feel quite up to dancing.

Perhaps I might even run into handsome Nick, the tug-boat captain from Staten Island? I met him there last year. He had been sitting at the bar. When the DJ announced it was Lady's Choice, and I courageously got out of my chair and asked if he cared to accompany me on the dance floor, he proved to be a jivey one. The rest of my village stay, we dated, and spent many enjoyable evenings, dancing at different country clubs.

The cab driver dropped me off in front of McCalls. When I threw open the somewhat heavy door, I walked inside to a burst of music, grooving people on the dance floor, and all seats occupied at dining tables. My eyes skimmed over tops of heads at the bar, to find no seats available there. What should I do now? Stand here in front of a row of all of these men, while I wait to be seated? Never had I been in such a quandary. Never had I walked into a bar, alone. Last year, friend Janie accompanied me, saw that I was seated, and left for the square.

Now, I would flag down the waiter coming toward me. "When you know of a seat which will soon be available, please think of me?" I begged.

A smile and an, "I sure will, but we must keep this section open, so it's best to go over there and stand at the door."

I did, and soon another lady entered. We chatted and I learned her name was Debbie. A charming miss, a single mother of a teenage daughter, she was the youngest and prettiest present. Besides me, of course. Giggle!

Finally we put our heads together, and she said, "If you're able to get a table, we can sit together and keep each other company." Though she loved to dance, she was mainly there to dine and *people watch*.

Once we were seated, following the dinner hour, we were able to keep our comfortable chairs. I was having an enjoyable evening, on the sly, getting dances for Debbie. While she looked elsewhere, when a gentleman was leaving the dance floor, working his way through the crowd, I would catch his eye, smile and point to her. She danced through most of the evening. It was nearly over.

I suggested, "Let's hang it up here, and run over to Katie Belles. A new and peppy band is playing there."

"I'm content here, but it you want a change, I'll go along with you."

In a little while, we headed for the door, and as we walked the full length of the bar, we were about to pass a tall, thin gentleman with white hair and matching mustache. He sat with his back against the bar, presumably, watching people on the dance floor. All evening long , I had noticed he hadn't danced, just sat there, and looked straight ahead, in line with our table. At, the time, I couldn't tell if he was studying me, as I hadn't worn my contacts.

Now, he smiled, and reciprocated when I said, "Good evening," and continued on.

Three stools away, I said, "Whoa, Debbie, wait a minute. I'm backing up."

I stood before him. "You wouldn't happen to be a man called Mac McCauly, who, last year rented the villa I wanted to buy, and when he moved in, I left a bag of oranges at his door?"

"I sure am." He grinned a cocky mustachioed grin, whiskers twitching.

"Then why didn't you say 'Hello,' to me?"

"Because I forgot your name."

Debbie and I decided to stay, and I ended dancing two slow Fox Trots, 'cheek to cheek' with Mac. Though I didn't snuggle closely, as I undoubtedly would, had I found myself in Nick's arms. By now, Nick should have received my letter. I would phone him, later.

Debbie insisted on taking me home. After three quarters of the way, we came to the Del Mar Gate and couldn't go further. She didn't live in The Villages, so had no pass, and mine was home in another purse. I thanked her, climbed out of her car, expecting to walk four blocks to my villa, when a car pulled alongside. A lady with silver hair, rolled down her window.

"Are you having trouble? Could I help in anyway?"

"I'll tell you what. Because I'm babying my knee, if you would kindly take me one more block, I'll turn right, and have only three more to go."

"Come, climb in, and I'll take you all the way home."

In a few minutes we pulled into my driveway. "My name is Eve," she said. I told her mine and she said it was a pretty name.

"I certainly do appreciate this. Thanks for helping me."

"You're welcome. People are all friendly and nice here. I wouldn't want to be any other place. I, too, am a widow. If you ever see me, don't forget to say, 'hello'."

"You, also. You're an angel."

"You are, too", she said.

I laughed. "It takes one to know one." She quietly chuckled and drove away. And so ended quite an interesting and thought-provoking day. Will I see Mac again? Eve Greenspeller? Perhaps Nick? Hopefully, and on this happy note, since it's 11:45, and I have only a pen to hang up, I'll do that, and say, "Goodnight, World."

# Chapter 15
## Barbecued Biscuits for Mac

Thanksgiving soon would be here. Where would I spend that special day? Last year, friend Del, whom I spend January with in Oahu, had flown here to visit with me, and we ate at the Chula Vista Club where we were seated at long tables, and served 'family style'. It proved to be fun. Like home, when you ask each other to pass along a dish. I'd like to do that again this year, but with whom? It certainly wouldn't be fun eating alone.

Yes, I longed for my family and became a trifle homesick. I had phoned my oldest, my daughter, Dianne, and left a message to say I had arrived safely, but didn't hear from her, nor any of my other three children.

Sunday, I returned home from church to find a blinking answering machine. My children?

I flicked the switch to hear, " This is Mac. Would you please call?"

I did, and invited him to come for lunch. It would be delightful to have such a distinguished gentleman as Mac for company.

Later, I felt proud, like Martha Stewart, while he leaned against the nearby counter, arms folded, smiling as he watched me cook. No one, not even my husband, had ever done this before. A few minutes after I slid the biscuits in the oven, my eyes began to smart. Mac said nothing, and I went about my business unaware of what was taking place. When I saw billows of black smoke seeping from beneath the bottom of the microwave door and fast filling my kitchen, I ran across the room and threw open the oven door. A blast of searing heat, along with thick black smoke, hit me in the face. I backed up and cried out, "Ah! Mac! I burned our biscuits. What shall I do?"

I went into a coughing fit, while Mac, still silent, stood there, arms folded, smiling. Hot pad in hand, I quickly grabbed the smoldering black dish, with the charcoal burned biscuits and, leaving a smoke trail behind me, rushed out into the garage.

There stood two nervous and very concerned barefoot neighbor ladies who began firing questions at me. "Is your villa on fire? What's wrong? Are you okay? What happened? Black smoke was pouring from your villa, and we thought it was on fire."

"No, everything is alright," I told them with a sheepish look on my face. "Thanks for checking. I hadn't realized I was baking biscuits in the micro-wave oven, and set the timer for twenty minutes, the amount of time they should bake in a conventional."

I brushed perspiration from my forehead. "Don't ever do this unless you want charcoal biscuits like those." I motioned to the still smoldering black dish, which I had nearly thrown on top of the washing machine.

Later, despite running around to open windows and doors, to clear the villa of smoke, our lunch proved to be quite pleasant. More so, when smiling Mac, wiped his lips with napkin, looked across the table at me and said, "We didn't need the biscuits, Bootsy. Everything was really quite tasty without them."

True gentleman that he is, he helped clean off the table, then waited in the living-room while I tidied the kitchen. While busy doing this, I pictured a daily maid on duty in his four story Cape Cod home.

When I finished my work, he said, "Come! Let's hop on your golf cart. I'll take you to see my villa. I purchased it last August. Though it's not the one I rented, it's still in the Hacienda Village where I wished to be, and on a corner lot."

As we pulled up and parked in his driveway, I could see his grounds were considerably larger than mine, and he also had a lot of grass to mow. The inside was decorated nicely, cool, refreshing and uncluttered.

"What do you think?"

"It's beautiful, Mac. Truly lovely with Floridian pastel colors. Who's your decorator?"

"A girl named Heather, from a store called Southern Life Style in the Villages. It didn't cost that much, either. Just around $8.000. She did an excellent job. I'm satisfied."

"I would be, too. I can hardly wait until I find a villa to my liking. An affordable one, without too much upkeep."

"You will find one, Bootsy. I'm sure. Keep looking. Maybe one's waiting for you just around the corner."

To this, I said nothing. I just smiled to myself, remembering how, since my husband passed on thirteen years ago, everyone had tried to assure me another prince was waiting for me...just around the corner.

# Chapter 16
# Nick

When the phone rang the next morning, a man's voice asked, "Is this Eileen McFarland?"

"No, I'm sorry. She's in a nursing home. I'm just renting here."

"My caller I D shows I received a phone call from an Eileen McFarland."

"She's not here."

Silence. Then a chuckle.

"Nick! You tease! How are you?"

"Fine. How's yourself.

"Holding in there."

"I received your letter saying you would be flying down, but I, myself, have been out of town."

"I figured as much. Say Nick! Remember last year you escorted me to the Singles Christmas Dinner and Dance? Would you like to be my escort again, this year?"

"Yes, if there would be no commitments. I have a girl whom I met last summer, during my four-month stay in North Carolina."

"No commitment, Nick. I'll wear my blue velvet dress I wanted to wear last year. I brought it along, this time."

"I know you'll look nice. You always do."

I came back with, "Thanks. Likewise, too, my dear."

"If you're free tomorrow night, Bootsy, would you like to come to my villa for dinner?"

"That would be lovely."

"I'm a good cook. We'll have fresh salmon. I'll pick you up at five o'clock."

It proved to be a delicious dinner. He smiled, when he opened a bottle of wine he had bought from Israel, eight years ago. "My dear," he said, "I've been saving this for a special occasion."

During the evening, at the dinner table and later in his living room, he tilted the bottle now and then, and I never knew how many glasses of wine I drank. Usually, two is my limit. I do know, later, when he climbed out of his lounge chair, and came over to the love-seat to view TV with me, I felt a warm coziness in his manly arms. Now and then, he kissed the top of my hair. Eventually his soft, warm lips found mine, and in time he became quite amorous. Yet, he took me home, unscathed, and when he kissed me at the door, I asked, "So tell me, are you serious about the lady in North Carolina."

I appreciated his slow easy grin and, *I don't know, now,* response.

He disappeared for ten days, and I imagined they were somewhere together, probably on a cruise.

In his absence, during the days my search for a villa continued. Nights were filled addressing Christmas cards, and writing letters.

Then on Monday, I called the Hacienda Community Center. The Singles' Club would be meeting there at seven o'clock. I would attend, and learn the date of their Christmas dance, when, I would be waltzing in on the arms of handsome Nick.

While I dressed, anxiety swept through me, as I slipped into a pair of mint green checkered shorts. Wouldn't the soft peach camisole look lovely beneath the matching jacket, with the patches of green and white checks, and embroidered blue birds and peach flowers, scattered here and there? Confident my mirror couldn't lie, I felt at my best, when a horn sounded and I ran out to climb into the cab.

The driver dropped me off at seven o'clock on the nose. However, I waltzed in alone, not to a Single's meeting, but their Christmas party, where members chatted at tables, or were gliding across the dance floor in semi-formal attire. Baffled, as to what to do, I stood inside the door near a table full of women, took a deep breath, and was about to escape, when three ladies turned, tossed me a welcoming smile, and said, "Come sit with us!" One jumped up, pulled in a chair, and when I was seated, we introduced ourselves. Amidst this marvelous group of ladies, I didn't feel alone. Quite the contrary, especially when one handed me a glass of wine, and a smiling waitress placed a plate of cherry cobbler before me.

"I didn't order dinner, " I told her.

She said, "That's okay, enjoy!" and vanished. I couldn't believe this! Here I was…a stranger, yet I felt comfortably at home.

When the weekend breezed in, I scanned the *Daily Sun News*, which I now subscribed to, and scribbled down addresses of three villas. Again, I took off in my golf cart with hope in my heart. One villa was nice, but too expensive; another, too close to the street; the last, too far away from the square. The following day, one realtor's ads looked promising.

I called. He said, "It's in a perfect location, Bootsy. Even closer to the square, than where you are now. I'll pick you up, in…say…two minutes? And yes, it's okay if your landlord tags along."

We, three, pulled up in front of a villa on Mac's street, a short walk to the square, definitely a plus. Once inside, I glanced around and was pleasantly surprised to see both the kitchen and baths were tastefully wallpapered. I snapped photos, with thoughts of duplicating the same patterns in a villa of my own.

"It needs new carpeting," Ron stated. In looking over the outside, he said, "There's a lot of yard work needed here."

"I see that, Ron. I couldn't handle it myself. Now, if my husband were alive, I would take on the challenge. Monthly cost for Mike's Lawn Care is $35. I wouldn't care to go that route, and neither do I care for the outside color of this building. Like mustard. What do you think?"

"Like baby shit," he whispered.

I elbow-nudged him. "That's awful. Would I dare to change the color?"

"No. The outside must remain the same, to blend in with the others.

It proved to be a sleepless night of tossing and turning. Would I be content to spend the rest of my life in a villa with such a color? Come morning, I called the realtor and told him I couldn't. He said he would still keep his eyes and ears open and would find a villa *just right for me*.

In the meantime, my golf cart and I swept through still many more villages. I chatted with owners, passed out fliers, and asked if anyone wanted to sell, to kindly contact me, and listed my phone number.

# Chapter 17
# My Villa

I sensed my time in The Villages and my search for the best villa for me was becoming screechingly short. Why not end this madness, give in, and buy the lawyer's cute home which was completely furnished? No need to buy furniture, no need to worry about anything. Should I go one more time and walk through? So what if I had to pay forty-five dollars more a month to use the pool? During September, in Pennsylvania, five hundred dollars was spent for lawn care, and removal of a tree. During the summer months, sometimes it costs $60, weekly, just to have my lawn mowed. Here, with neighborhood watch, there would be no cost for a security alarm, no oil bills, no lawn work.

So, again I hopped into my golf cart and drove over to take one last look. This would be my final decision. I disliked bothering the man with the key and stood at his door a tad apprehensive, and told myself, "Here goes," as I gently rang his bell.

He stood there, stared at me, and said, "I don't have time to show it," and practically shut the door in my face.

I left a note in his mailbox. "I'm sorry to have troubled you. I should have called, but didn't have your last name. Will you please contact me when you have a free moment?"

A week slipped by, and I didn't hear from him, nor did I have success in finding a villa during my continued search throughout more neighborhoods.

Still another week, and I decided to put an end to all of this uncertainty, and make sure I wasn't giving up a good thing. In the evening, after searching all day, I pulled my golf cart into the garage, and headed for the phone. I would call Barbara, the lawyer, and the owner in New York.

"I'm sorry, Bootsy," she said. "My villa has been sold. The people from the Bronx went down to The Villages, early, and they liked it. That's the reason my neighbor wouldn't show it to you."

I felt empty, emotionally drained with the loss of that lovely villa, bit hard on trembling lips to keep from crying, as I slowly reached out, quietly returned the phone to its cradle, and how long, I have no idea, I just sat there in a stupor. Suddenly, the ringing of the phone jarred me to my senses, and I wondered, *Now what?*

I heard the cheery voice of Tom, my last realtor, say, "Bootsy, I have two villas you might like to see. One has ceramic tile throughout."

"No, not that one, it sounds cold."

"The other hasn't yet been posted. The man died last night."

I didn't like to think a man had died in a villa which I might own, but I'd go see it. "I'm bringing along Ron again. For his opinion."

"That's okay. I'll pick you up in two minutes."

It seemed like a long drive to the villa, but Tom assured me, via of the golf cart trail, it was only two minutes further, than where I was renting.

From the outside, the villa was neat, clean and cream in color, and I preferred the double wide streets of grey, as opposed to Hacienda's black.

During our tour, Ron commented on every facet. "The stove and refrigerator are old. The kitchen cabinets have been upgraded. The extra two feet added to the lanai is a plus, it's glass enclosed, air-conditioned, making an extra room. The carpeting is in excellent shape". And, pointing, "There's the walk-in-closet you wanted." Then he took off to check the garage, while Tom and I went outside to look over the grounds.

I was surprised to find the gate to my villa, located between the front of my neighbor's villa, and my garage. "They're all like this,"

Tom said as he unlatched and shoved it open. "They're called 'Courtyard Villas' and are very private with the neighbor's garage on one side, a high wall on the other, and a wall in back which overlooks The Village Preservation Section."

I followed him down a long walkway embraced with white Rose Vinca in bloom on the left, and three hip-high Gardenia bushes to our right. "Gardenias were always Mother's favorite flower," I said. Directly ahead, stood a tall stately palm tree. "I've always admired such trees; their magnificence." We passed another palm of different origin, a group of red Azalea bushes, and a cute little tangerine tree with two fruit proudly hanging from its boughs. And there we stood, on a large kidney-shaped patio, surrounded by a high cream colored block wall.

I inhaled the fresh air, and sighed. "You are right. With the high wall, I'll have a lot of privacy."

"Yes, Bootsy, and with the Village Preservation fields in back, it prevents other villas from being built, so it will be nice and quiet back here."

"I would like to take a peek over the wall, Tom. Could you please do me a favor? Help me up on that chair, over there?" I pointed.

With his assistance, I looked over the wall, and drank in the beauty of lush fields of green, as far as my eyes could rove. Off in the distance, green trees scalloped blue skies. "Oh, my!" I sighed. "This is my Pennsylvania." I climbed down, and swung arms from my side. "And this is my Florida! Look up at those fluffs of white clouds. They make me feel as though I can reach up and pull one down, and they remind me of my husband's comments during our last flight to Daytona, where we would be vacationing. We were flying over piles and piles of billowing white clouds, when he looked out the window, and excitedly said, 'Darling! Look! They're beautiful! They remind you of fluffs of white cotton, and make you want to walk barefooted through them.'" I briefly closed my eyes, breathed a whiff of contentment, and silently said, "I feel close to you, my darling."

Then I told my realtor, "I want this villa."

Ron returned from the garage. "Everything looked okay out there. The water tank is insulated. And since there's not much outside maintenance work here to contend with, Bootsy, I'd say, of all the villas you looked at, this is more like what you want."

Asking price for the villa was $136.500. Later, in talking it over, I agreed to pay the full price if the furniture from the living room, dining room table and chairs and one bedroom were included. Until my furniture could be transported, I wanted a place to eat and sleep. However, I learned sentiments prevented the previous owner's children from parting with any of their parent's furniture. So I counter-offered $135.000 if this included the one bedspread which matched the valence in the guest room, and also the electric golf cart. This proved acceptable.

With no more burning of golf cart tires, now free from the task of searching for a place to live, I could relax and take it easy. I would call and talk to Mac. He thought it a grand idea to spend Thanksgiving day together. We would dine at the Chula Vista Club.

We arrived in time to occupy the last table.

"It was reserved just for us," I teased and, of course, he knew better. Dinner proved the best, with succulent and tender turkey, the trimmings, and a nice, amiable chap, called Mac, seated across from me. He ordered cocktails, and we drank a toast to good health, and happiness, especially in my soon-to-be home.

We left the club house with a doggie box loaded with turkey and all the trimmings . "You're invited to my villa for lunch, tomorrow, Mac. I insist. There's too much food here for one person."

"I'll gladly come," he chuckled. "I won't mind a bit."

# Book 2

# Chapter 18
# When Strange Things Happen

I returned to my home in Pennsylvania on December 10, this time the proud owner of a lovely villa. Then I became caught up in the hub-bub of finishing my Christmas shopping. I love Christmas, and enjoy marching along to the jubilant holiday music as it echoes throughout the malls. My favorite song, 'Silver Bells' brings a smile in my heart, and more pep to my step.

Along with shopping, I spend a great amount of my time running up and down stairs, carting items to decorate and make my home spiffy for the holidays. Not only for realtors to show, but for my own satisfaction and enjoyment. Though I'm aware one day I'll no longer be living here, at day's end, when I climb into my very own bed, I still have a feeling of belonging.

Four days after my return, a hopeful call came in. Someone wished to see my home between 10 and 11 am. They never arrived. Since my home is multi-listed, when I called the receptionist she was surprised the appointment hadn't been kept. She would have my Realtor, Bill, call. Instead, when the phone rang, it was a different and apologetic realtor on the line. She couldn't get to the phone to call and tell me the supposed buyer believed my home wasn't big enough for her four children and a

300 pound husband. This was pleasing to hear, as I wouldn't want to see my rancher abused by too many rambunctious little ones.

December 29, with Christmas behind us, and my home still on the market, I decided to get away from it all. I am flying off to Hawaii, to visit my good friend, Delene Crisorio. Del…for short. She spends half the year in Connecticut; the other half in Oahu. So, here I am, again jotting down notes.

Despite my knee bumming me once in awhile, Del and I have glorious times shopping at the International Market Place, hopping a bus and traveling 45 minutes to spend a day at the Flea Market and dining with good friends, Ginny, and Virginia from Pa, and our mutual friend, Chuck, from Ohio.

Virginia's condo is located just around the corner from Del's, and one evening she invited us over to share a delicious pie she baked from scratch, using cherries she had brought from Pa. During the evening she spoke of disappointment in not receiving her Christmas photos she had sent to the York Lab, in Pa. "They included wedding pictures of my niece, and they can't be replaced."

"Perhaps they were misplaced," I told her. "Don't worry. They'll show up. I'll say a little prayer."

She said "That would be nice", and the subject was dropped.

The following evening the phone rang. Del was out for the evening, and I hurried to answer. Friend Ginny was on the line. "Chuck and I are going to have dinner at Jack-in-the Box. Come join us. Meet us down at the corner."

Later, when I returned to the condo with arms full, including a bottle of coke, my purse, and a doggie-box containing left-overs, Mother Nature made an impromptu call, and I hurriedly placed my purse and soda on the floor in order to turn the key in the lock. Two hours later, Del returned and found the keys on the carpet outside her door. She held them up. "LOOK! Someone jimmied off the gate pass. Only a man would do that, and I thought everyone on this floor was honest."

"They probably are. Perhaps it was a visitor."

Up until now, I had been extremely careful not to lose my key, as a replacement would cost $26. I would find it. When Del retired early, I jotted off a note, saying: 'I carelessly lost my gate pass. If found, please return to room 1602.' Then I quietly tip-toed out the door, down the hall, and taped my note beside the elevator.

The following morning, early riser Del, returned from her 4 mile jaunt, and said, "Phyllis, The Palm's manager replaced your note with hers."

"What did hers say?"

"Whoever took the gate pass from the key ring in front of room 1602, please return it. Mid March, all keys are going to be re-censored, decoded and since all are numbered, I'll know who you are."

"That gal has spunk, Del. Now I'll pray someone listens." That night before retiring, I prayed, "Dear Lord, and Heavenly Father, with You ,all things are possible. I know I asked for help in finding Virginia's pictures, but since she's away, cruising the islands, could we put the pictures on a back burner and concentrate on finding the gate pass? In Jesus name, I humbly pray, and give grateful thanks and praise, amen."

The next morning Del greeted me when I walked out into the kitchen. "Sit down. I want to make your day for you."

"Ok, as long as nothing is planned that will take too much walking."

"No, it's not anything like that. When I was out walking, I saw Phyllis coming down the sidewalk with her morning coffee, and she hailed me down, and said your key has been found."

"Really? Who had it?"

"She doesn't know. She found it on her desk."

"Thank the dear Lord."

Virginia breezed in, and we excitedly shared our little key adventure. She in turn, spoke of the choppy waters on her cruise, then smiled as she pulled out a packet of her long awaited Christmas photos.

We oohed and ahhed, over them. "See!" I said. "God listens. Now that I have my key pass, I'd like to thank the person who returned it."

"I wouldn't bother," Del said.

"Still, I'm grateful." I grabbed a piece of paper, and jotted off, *Thank you for returning my key. Honesty, will set you free.*

Virginia and Del both got a kick out of this. Then I added, 'May God Bless You', and I added a smiley.

Later that afternoon, upon hearing all of this, our beach gang, regulars from New York, New Jersey, Canada, and California, shared their thoughts: "God certainly is looking after our Bootsy."

More than ever, I sense indeed He is. Especially, the following day when the phone jangled, and I found my Realtor, Bill Zody, on the line. "I just sold your home," he said.

"You sold my home? Who bought it?"

Del gasped, "Thank the dear Lord," and was bouncing up and down. I hung up, to see her with mouth hung wide open as she stood looking out the window. She pointed. "Look! I've never seen anything like it! It reaches all the way from one end of Waikiki to the other."

I followed her glance, and drank in the beauty of the most perfect rainbow ever. "Oh, My! It's even lovelier than the banner of color which stretched across the sky on the day of my husband's funeral."

Her brows raised. "A rainbow appeared in the sky, during his burial?"

"No, directly after. During a picnic in our back yard, sixty-seven of our friends and family members raised glasses to the heavens and I drank a toast to…a most wonderful husband, father, grandfather, and my best friend.' Uncle Charlie was about to leave, just then, and I rushed after him to say 'goodbye' when someone grabbed my dress and pulled me back, saying, 'you have to see this!' I turned to see sixty seven upturned faces, and only then recalled Bill's and my conversation a few months earlier, when he mentioned even the astronauts had never seen the edge of Heaven, and no one had ever come back and said they had been there." I rattled on, "Oh, Del, that day, the day of his funeral, I had been choking back sobs and smiling through tears while serving our guest, until then, when I pictured him up there, with a sweet silly grin on his pleasant face, as he stretched tall, and with paint brush in his big hand, swept the sky in prismatic colors telling me, "Darling, here it is! I've found Heaven."

"Oh, my!"

"My thoughts exactly. A doctor commented, 'Isn't that startling?' Another remarked, 'And there's not a cloud or rain drop in the sky.' A pastor said, 'Bootsy, you should find comfort in this.' There was daughter Debbie's laughter, and 'Dad paved highways and always hated paving the curves.' An agnostic and his thoughts were, 'This about blows my mind'."

I wiped a happy tear away, and said, "Look Dell, this Hawaiian rainbow is lower, with one end placed in front of trees, as if to make certain it won't be missed. See shadows of leaves directly behind? I've never seen any like it." I hurriedly removed my camera from my purse and snapped a picture.

"It's beautiful, Bootsy. I really believe this is your husband's way of telling you he's pleased with all you've done. And he's happy for you."

I agreed. How could I believe otherwise?

# Chapter 19
# The Village Helpers

The following day, Del tapped on my bedroom door. "You're wanted on the phone. A lady, named Bernie, in The Villages is on the line. She's calling about your newly purchased villa, there in Florida."

I spoke with Bernie and learned she and a group, called The Village Helpers, not affiliated with The Villages, had, over the years, been cleaning the villa for the previous owner, and now cleaned for the last time.

She was telling me, "With all the washing of the walls, there are still smudges, probably from a pet, and the walls need patched because of holes."

"Does it look badly?" I asked, thinking I had patched holes, before, and could do it again.

"I think so. My group of workers and I can be contracted and clean, patch, paint and paper for $1,000, and make it look nice." This seemed a fair price, as I remembered back in Pennyslvania it cost $500 to paint my livingroom and dining room, and she would be doing much more.

"Yes, I can supply references from different couples and also realtors."

I called Tom. "Yes, the Village Helpers are a reputable group. They're trustworthy. Quite a few of us realtors hire them for their clients."

When she sent a signed contract, I mailed photos of wall paper, and included the order number of a Japanese Garden mural which I wanted hung in my lanai. I also mailed a $400 retainer fee to cover supplies, then sat back and looked forward with anticipation, to the long road ahead.

Bernie called a few days later. "I received your check and pictures of the wallpaper. Paint has been ordered."

"That's great. Regarding wallpaper, if you can't find exactly what I want, copy it as near as possible, but keep the colors the same. Also, Will you do something else for me, please?"

"Sure!"

I'll be flying out of Oahu on January 27, and arriving there in The Villages on the 28th. Call Kanes in Ocala, and ask Anne to send out an electric twin bed? After a thirteen hour flight, I'll need a place to lay my head."

"Here, in central Florida, we have a secondhand store, called 'Bargains and Treasures.' They clear out estates and some items look like new and actually are. Want me to look there, first?"

"That's an idea. Thanks!"

Five minutes later, Del's phone rang, again, and Bernie was on the line. "Bargains and Treasures have just the bed for you. You're to call Terry."

I did. We introduced ourselves, and after she described the bed, I asked, "Truthfully, Terry, would you buy it, sight unseen, if you were me?"

"Truthfully, Bootsy, it's a steal at $209. It's clean, spotless; I don't think it's ever been used, and it has all the features an electric bed has. I'd grab it before someone else does."

"Okay, tag it and have Bernie's men pick it up. It sounds too good to be true, Terry. I paid a thousand for the electric bed I have back in PA."

January 27, on this bright sunny afternoon, Chuck, our dear Waikiki friend, arrived at Del's condo, assisted me with my luggage, and together we climbed into the cab, and soon were heading for the airport. Mixed emotions rode high. I wanted to stay in lovely Hawaii, where I usually shed a happy tear each time I fly in and see natures' colorful beauty below: Sparkling blue waters, palm trees, flowers.

They say where-ever a seed falls, a flower blooms. I especially love to walk in Waikiki and inhale the fragrance of a Palmera tree, where I usually pause to pick a handful of blossoms off the ground, to place in a dish of water on Del's kitchen counter. Yet, as we ride along now, again, here I'm wondering about the unknown path ahead. Undoubtedly, it's because the time is closing in, and soon I must travel on, entirely alone?

# Chapter 20
## Settlement on My Villa

On board the plane at the Oahu Airport, I rented ear phones, watched the movie, topped it off with six hours of rejuvenated sleep. Seemingly, time passed swiftly, and we were landing at the Orlando Airport. There, I climbed aboard The Villages Shuttle Bus, and adjusted my watch to gain the five hours lost on my way to Hawaii.

An hour and fifteen minutes later, I reached my final destination, the Spanish Springs Station, where I stepped out into Florida's bright sunshine, and there stood, a smiling Bernie. A tiny mite, with long, dark hair, she reminded me of an Indian maiden in jeans, and she had waited for me. We greeted with a hug, and I breathed a sigh of relief. I had wondered about her. What she was like? Was she dependable? Was my villa in such a sad shape as she had indicated, via phone? We gabbed excitedly, a mile a minute as we headed for her truck, and there, though a tiny mite, she hoisted my extra heavy luggage into the back.

"Are you hungry?" she asked, as I climbed into the front seat.

"Famished. All they served on the plane today was water, OJ and party mix. The last hostess gave me two packs of the mix, and one I kept in case I become hungry later on while in the hotel. Shall we go to Wendy's for dinner? On me?"

There, I relished a marvelous American cheeseburger, downed a chocolate frosty, ate a few French fries, and left carrying half of my salad.

On our way out of Wendy's, she asked, "Do you want to see your villa?"

"Would you mind?"

"No, and while there, I'll show you the wallpaper I selected, and see if you like it, since what you wanted is no longer available."

When we first stepped over the doorsill of my now to be home, I could readily see Bernie proved 100% correct. Minus furniture, ugly holes stood at attention, chipped plaster caught my eye, and carpeting needed cleaning.

"I can fix all of this. My helpers will begin painting early tomorrow morning. It's a shame we weren't allowed to do it sooner, and have it all finished by now."

"I agree. Though I had made a nice size deposit, my realtor claimed even I wasn't permitted to spend a night here, not until settlement day. The previous owner's children were concerned about accidents and a law suit."

"That's what I was also told," Bernie stated, as we paraded through the empty rooms. The one bedspread and curtain I requested were still there. After inspection, Bernie and I sat on the living-room floor, with wallpaper samples before us and I stared in amazement. "I chose ones to my liking," she said.

"I'm pleased. They're lovelier than those I had selected."

Later, we reached the Villages Holiday Express, where I had reserved a room. By now jet-lag must have overtaken me, as I somewhat wearily tagged behind Bernie, who, again insisted on handling my luggage for me.

She left, and as I checked in at the desk, Tom arrived. "Here's your keys to the golf cart. It's parked outside."

"Thanks! I hope I'll be able to operate it."

"You will. It's a little different than the policeman's cart you drove last year, but you'll catch on fast."

Five thirty, still in the afternoon . He, and Bernie were gone and I sat on the edge of my hotel bed. I lay down, stretched out, and wished to sleep the night away when, again, doubts began to cloud my mind. Had I erred in my decision? To move on…here…alone? I hadn't seen my stockbroker who recommended such a move, not since my stock took a nosedive. I neglected to have my mail forwarded here during the four months of my villa search, and my Intel nearly went defunct. Yet, my broker tried pacifying me with, "Don't worry about it, Bootsy. It's only paper." Oh, yes? I'd greedily reel in the two hundred twenty five thousand loss, stand on my head and yodel, do anything to get it back. Just paper? He said?

I dozed, awakening two hours later, hungry. I would eat the bag of party mix, and down it and the wilted salad with a glass of water. That will do for now, I told myself. If I lose a few pounds, that would satisfy me. Following a tepid bath, I dressed for bed, slipped between the covers and viewed *Everybody loves Raymond*, and one of my favorites...*Becker*. Ten o'clock. My eyes were becoming heavy. My feet were cold. Yesterday, in Hawaii, I had no such problems. I climbed out of bed, cozily wrapped my feet in a towel, turned out the light, and hoped, in time, I'd grow accustomed to Florida's winters. After a long, long day, I slept like a dream.

Morning dawned, and I pulled aside the curtain to look out on a lonely, quiet, empty world. A grey mist hovered over the swimming pool, now void of people. I called the front desk. "Yes, we have a Continental breakfast but you'll have to come right out. It closes in ten minutes."

I slapped on my clothes, my makeup and made it to the breakfast room on time, and with relish. I ate my corn flakes, a half banana, a lemon tart, with coffee and greedily drank my orange juice.

Peopled milled around, and some seated, visitors and buyers, alike, enthusiastically chatted, regarding The Villages and their experiences. They all applauded me, a widow, for my spunk and determination to change my lifestyle. Even the kitchen manager came out with a basket of apples, and urged me to take one to eat later.

Tom soon arrived, and with me and my luggage, we drove into town for settlement on my villa. It went rather smoothly. He jotted a note stating Bernie would power-wash the outside, at his expense, and shampoo the carpeting at mine. I signed numerous papers and wrote a check for payment, then together, we walked up the street a few doors to the building where an orientation of new owners would take place the next day. "Be there at nine o'clock," he said. Then it was back to the hotel, where he dropped me off.

I paid the hotel bill, received directions on how to reach San Pedro Court, then breathlessly walked out the double glass doors, stood, and slowly inhaled a breath of warm, fresh air. Beautiful puffs of white clouds dotted the azure blue skies as I lifted my face to the sun. Now, for the golf cart, a stranger to me. I eyed it from a distance, and soon, seated behind the wheel, noted controls were different, with none on the dashboard. Instead, they were in back of my legs, on the under part of the seat. No turn signals. No horn. Nearly nothing. I looked up, smiled and quietly muttered, "But we can do this, my Lord!" and together we cautiously eased out into Aveneida Boulevard, turned left, and I immediately knew the area. Great! We were on our way!

# Chapter 21
## Father Niznick's Hat

I parked my golf cart, made my way through the garage, and wondered, *How will I feel when alone for the first time, I step over that doorsill over there, into my kitchen? Utterly lost? Lonely? Never!* One cannot begin to fathom the joy which swept through me as I drank in all Bernie had done for me. Fresh towels of hers, hung in the kitchen. I opened cupboard doors to find enough dishes for two. Included were glasses. Silverware and utensils were neatly arranged in drawers. I opened the oven door to find a frying pan, and two kettles. Out in the lanai, stood two green chairs, along with a matching card table, covered in olive green, with white eyelet ruffles. I went from one bathroom to the next and found soap, towels and washcloths in both, all ready for my use. Then, I stood at the opened doorway leading into my bedroom, and happily smiled. My new electric bed , prettily dressed in Bernie's own linens, looked most inviting. I hugged myself, and thought, *Yes! Yes! This will be a nice home for me.*

Orientation went well the next day. I was the only single moving in. I returned home to find Bernie and her five helpers seated on my living room floor, eating lunch. A cute picture. I snapped it. They had been working since 6:00 AM, and my villa looked nearly spanking new, with only two more days to finish. I left to go grocery shopping at Winn Dixie where I purchased the following items:

2 tea towels
30 clothes hangers
1 pastel plate, (in case I don't feel like washing dishes)
2 bags of garden salad,
a loaf of bread
orange juice
Cascade
6 eggs
skim milk
chocolate milk
Scott toilet paper
liquid dish detergent
sliced turkey luncheon breast
carrots
cherry tomatoes
pimento cheese
tiny salt and pepper shakers
crackers
2 sponges
food wrap
tea
Lite fiber
1 box of Kleenex
salad dressing
box of salt
mayonnaise
2 cans of Campbell's tomato soup
1 broccoli
Dove soap
oat squares
onions
8 ounces of American cheese

This all came to a total of $98.86 . Now, I certainly would not go hungry.

On my way home I drove down Rio Grand, in the golf cart lane, stopped a moment, looked around, and wondered if I had missed the turn. Cars passed ahead and behind me. A man in the golf cart in back, climbed out, approached mine and asked, "Are you lost?"

"I'm not certain. Do you know where Amaya Avenue is?"

"Never heard of it." Another cart pulled behind his, and the lady driver had never heard of Amaya Avenue.

"I'll help you," the man said. "Follow me."

I did, and only a block away, I pointed, and called out, "There it is! I know where I'm at. See that gate ahead? I go through there."

He insisted on leading the way, and when we reached my villa, even carried the twenty-one bags of groceries to my front door. Before we parted, he smiled and said, "I asked God to find someone for me to help today. I'll be checking in on you."

The painting and papering was going smoothly. I told Bernie it wasn't necessary to rush. So the next day she and I spent shopping for furniture. At Bargains and Treasures I found a cream colored, Royal Lexington dining-room set: an oval white-washed oak table with two extensions and five chairs. Total cost? Nine hundred seventy-five dollars. Two table lamps for seventy dollars, and a lovely picture for the living-room, two hundred ten dollars. From there, we crossed the highway to Wal-Mart's tent sale. Andy, the salesman, had men loading a hide-a-bed and matching loveseat into a truck. I liked the colors and ordered a set. We also ordered metal glass-topped tables for the living room, and a white-washed bedroom set. In seven days, the furniture would arrive from their South Carolina warehouse.

Today, Saturday, I drove into town for the arts and craft show and the chili tasting contest. A fun-spent day. You pay five dollars, get a wristband, and go from table to table, sampling and rating. Somewhat tired, I ended up sitting on a bench next to a pleasant, plump man with a grand head of white hair and equally white beard. His eyes were blue and he liked mine. "They're a pretty green. And I feel like kissing them."

I chuckled deep. "I'm afraid my contacts would cut." My friend, Dorree, back home, came to mind. She's crazy about beards and men with 'beef on their bones'. I momentarily drifted away, remembering a doctor friend who had kissed me again and again, and I had to pull away because of my contacts. In the end, he married a nurse. Once he had asked, if I married and it didn't work out, would I consider a divorce, and I said, "No! Once in love, always in love." Yes, I'm a romantic, and deep in my heart, I will always love the goodness in that dear man.

The following day, a phone call from Pennsylvania created a stormy situation. All didn't go well with the sale of my home. The FHA, Federal Home Association was giving my Realtor, Bill, a rough time. They insisted there was Radon in my basement, and pipes needed installed to pump it out. Cost—seven hundred fifty dollars, and there supposedly was a sign, at one time, someone had a little termite test. Cost—an additional six hundred fifty dollars. Also, they wanted me to put in two new light switches, one in the kitchen, one in the guest bathroom.

My son, Keith, called. "Mom, you have a great deal here. Listen to Bill. I know the rough time FHA gave me, with little nitty gritty stuff. Pay for both tests. Sell your home now. If you hang onto it, you'll have taxes, interest on your loan and lawyer's fees, etcetera to pay."

*Tonight, I shall hang up the pen and sleep on it.* Sunday dawned and I awakened to blaring music. Where was it coming from? Oh, yes, Bernie had left her clock radio out on my living-room window sill. I lay still a moment. No repair people, painters, etcetera, would be arriving to oust me out of bed. I could relax and do my own thing. I decided to climb out of bed and shut off the noise. Only, when I returned to slither beneath the sheets, I was now wide awake. I would get up, exercise, eat breakfast and dress for church.

All ready to leave, with purse and golf cart keys in hand, I started out the door, only to glance at the clock and find I was an hour early. I would call friend, Janie, in Ocala and let her know I had arrived. We chatted, catching up to date, with my one eye on the clock, until I finally said, "I must hang up and leave. I'm off to the Church in the Square."

"Better run. Thanks for calling, Hon. I was wondering if you had returned."

The church appeared totally filled. I stood inside the double, wide open oak doors, blinked in dismay, and wondered what to do, when an usher with a pleasant face and twinkling eyes, a Ms. Lucy Palmer, came down the aisle, greeted me with a smile and said, "Come with me. I'll help you find a seat." She seated me next to a man in a wheelchair, in the handicap section. "Don't you be concerned," she told me. "It's late, and no one else will be coming in."

The invalid's wife and I exchanged greetings, and she quietly confided, saying, "He had a stroke. It's been rough. I can't go anywhere without him. I get lonely." I scribbled down my telephone number, along with a message to call sometime. She smiled graciously, and thanked me.

The organ stopped playing, a greeter at the podium welcomed us, and I shifted comfortably, and sat back to listen to uplifting and meaningful songs being sung by five singers provided through the courtesy of Central Florida Lyric Opera company. Some were old-time Baptist hymns I learned as a child. Then the congregation sang a favorite of mine, "I love to Tell the Story." Next, my dad's favorite I used to hear him sing when he thought he walked alone in the upper orchard: "I Come to the Garden Alone" and, of course, I thought of him. According to the bulletin, the pastor for this Sunday was a Mark Niznick, from St. Pauls' Polish National Catholic Church in Bellevue. A well-rounded, middle-aged jovial gent, he oozed with enthusiasm, and his sermon message read: "Don't tell me who I can and can't eat with." Scripture reading was from Mark 2:13-17, and it pertained to Christ asking Levi, the tax collector, to follow him. Later when Jesus and his disciples ate at Levi's home, tax collectors and sinners, teachers of the law, complained. Jesus said, 'It's not the healthy who need a doctor, but the sick.' He came to call the sinners.

During his sermon, Father Mark spoke about a small town in which he once lived, and there were sinners, a little group called the Mafia. Once a year his church people fed them dinner. He felt certain they looked forward to this. He stated, "We as followers of Jesus, should not be afraid to love one another. In my church, I hug everyone. There's no side doors and no one can get away. Who, in this audience needs a hug?" I thought, I could use one.

Both men and women raised their hand. I counted five. He continued, "That's alright. Men and women both need hugs." He came down into the congregation and passed out hugs. I thought this sweet. Would I have the nerve to raise my hand? I did! I raised it high and wiggled fingers, and he rushed back in the mid-section of the church and stood before me.

"I'll hug you, if you let me wear your pretty hat."

I couldn't retain a giggle. "Alright, but you must give it back to me. I bought it last week, in Hawaii." Already his strong arms had me clenched in a hug. "Thanks! I needed that," I said, and plopped my hat on his balding head.

He spoke to the people behind me, "She said I can wear it but she bought it in Hawaii, and I must give it back." With that, he turned and hurriedly walked down the aisle to the alter. There, he turned this way and that, and let the choir admire him. Now facing the congregation, he stated, "We shouldn't be afraid to reach out to people as Jesus did. There's enough Jesus for everyone." A chuckle. "But not enough hats." He ended saying, "Stay strong, committed, go forward with Christ, and we pray for this, amen."

Upon departure, I shook his hand, received a smile, and as he plopped my hat upon my head, I told him, "I enjoyed your sermon. You were terrific."

"Thanks. So were you," he said.

Upon my return to my villa, I decided to pull in neighbor Dauphine's driveway, ring her bell, and check in on her. As usual she greeted me with one of her soft smiles. "Come out back and pick some oranges to send to your family," she ordered. Together we picked forty, and I told her to keep some for her children. "I'm fixin' to pick some tomorrow, but we won't eat that many." It's a joy, visiting this dear angel with white hair and twinkling blue eyes. So, when she mentioned she wanted to teach me a new card game called Hand and Foot, I stayed and we played three games. She won one and I, the other two. She claimed I was a good player, while I insisted she was a good instructor. I discovered the game requires a mite more concentration than when one simply writes a newspaper article and has to mentally search for a special word.

I returned home to a jangling phone, pleasantly surprised to have the opportunity to talk to all of my children, except Kevin, who was out of the country. The rest were in my Camp Hill home, gathering up furniture and items I wouldn't need here in Florida. My oldest, and sometimes wisest daughter, Dianne, was saying, "Mom, we're having such fun, we're sorry you can't be here."

"Honey," I said, "If ya' all would have been there more often, I wouldn't be here." I thought they would get a kick out of the 'ya' all'.

"Mom! Don't lay the guilt trip on us. Once you make up your

mind, nothing under the sun will change it. You just barge ahead, regardless of what anyone tells you."

What could I say but the truth. "Honey, you're so right. That's a bad habit of mine."

Early tomorrow morning Bargains and Treasures would be delivering my dining-room furniture. So on this happy note, I said, "Goodnight, world."

# Chapter 22
## Unexpected Helpers

This morning the doorbell rang at ten o'clock. No, it wasn't the furniture delivery man. Instead, a senior gent, silver hair capped with a basketball hat, stood there, smiling in at me.

Puzzled, I stared.

"I'm Harry. The man who helped with your groceries."

"Oh! Hi!"

"I just dropped in to see how you're coming along."

"Fine. Come in." He stepped over the doorsill. "My place is all painted and papered. But my furniture hasn't arrived yet. If you remove your shoes you may walk through."

"No, I'm in a hurry. I'll come back another time."

"So far, Harry, everything is fine, though I'm having a little trouble with my one sliding screen out in the lanai."

"What kind of trouble."

"I tried to lock it, but it slid off the track."

"I'll take a look at it."

"Do you know anything about sliding screen doors?"

"No, but I can take a look at it."

We reached the door to the lanai. "Wait! I want your opinion on the

Japanese Garden mural the workers hung for me. The paper shrunk and I wanted to see if you noticed it. I'll have to touch it up, a bit. " I slid open the door.

"That's sharp!" He stood there, and viewed the mountain of lush green trees, intermingled with pink and white laurel, yellow Japanese trees and touches of red blossoms, and on the right, a water fall cascading down the mountain side, and bouncing off huge grey rocks below. "I do see the white separation. I'm an artist and can touch that up for you. You'll never know the difference."

"You're kidding? You really are an artist?"

"In my own way."

"Where are you originally from?"

"York, PA."

"Really? My one twin son, Keith, lives fifteen minutes away, in York Haven." The doorbell jangled. "That has to be the furniture people. Wait! I'll be right back." Anxious to have some furniture, to make my villa appear a bit homier, I took off, but heard Harry call after me ."I'll look at that screen door while you're gone."

I threw open the front door to be greeted with, "Hello! I'm Fred, and came to look at the garage floor you want me to paint and design." I led him to the garage where he got down on haunches, moved his hand back and forth over the ugly grey and black floor, then stood up. "A stain won't adhere. Someone painted it. I know someone who may be able to help," and he scribbled down some names.

Just then, I noticed Harry had come in the back of the garage, and was standing there, fooling with the seat of my golf cart. I called over, "What are you doing, Harry?"

"Can you help me?" he asked Fred.

"Why do you want to remove the seat," I asked.

"To see if there's water in the battery. If there isn't, you could burn up the motor and it will cost you three hundred dollars."

"Really? No one ever told me it needs water."

"It does, and you need to check it periodically."

Fred found the lever to release the seat. It was beneath the panel where there was an outlet in which I must plug in the cord to recharge the battery. Harry removed the sixteen caps on the water containers, stood tall, and smiled up at me. There's enough water. Check it every two weeks. Okay?"

Without awaiting a reply, he asked Fred, "Do you know anything about sliding screen doors? Hers went off the track. Come, take a look at it. Maybe together we can help her." At that precise moment I smiled and remember the Waikiki's beach crowd's thoughts, *God certainly is looking after Bootsy.*

We three were out in the lanai. I stood by and watched as they worked. Fred lifted the screen, it came off in his hands. "See?" He pointed. "This wheel belongs in that track up there. Together, let's try to get it back in the groove. I'll lift this end and you lift yours, Harry. Oh, no! It doesn't want to go up inside." He pushed harder. "There! It's in. How is it over there?"

"Mine's in, too."

"That should do it," said Fred. He turned to me. "You might want to put some oil here to make it slide more easily."

Before they left, Harry said "One day I'll be in to touch-up the mural."

No sooner did the door close, when my doorbell rang again. Bargains and Treasures' truck sat in my drive. My dining-room furniture had arrived. Justin and Rick, the owners, finished setting it up and soon departed. Yes, since I was living in a new area, I strove to get names of everyone. People take note of this, and I find it's good for business, theirs and mine.

Once again, alone, I rushed out to check on the sliding screen. Would it work for me, or slide off the track again? No problem! It worked and as I turned away, a feeling of utmost joy swept over me, with the knowledge here, I wasn't really alone. God, and many of His helpers, walked with me.

# Chapter 23
# Men at the Singles' Club

Both apprehension and anxiety still lingered in my mind as the cab driver pulled in front of the Hacienda Center this Monday evening. In five minutes the Singles Club would have one of their regular meetings, and I had no concept as to what to expect.

I was greeted at the door, given a name tag like the two hundred ten others attending, and was handed a small yellow slip of paper on which was printed the number one. On stage, club officers were already assembled, including President Laura Joiner, who called out, "Hang onto your papers. You'll need them later." I seated myself at a long table, looked around, briefly chatted with those nearest, and it appeared to be a happy and an amiable group.

We newcomers were first introduced. During the meeting Laura announced, "Ladies, we're at the age when it's permissible to ask the gentlemen to dance. So at the dances when you see one sitting, don't hesitate to approach him and get him up on the dance floor."

I liked that idea. A few minutes later, I also liked what I saw entering the meeting place. My immediate thoughts were, *Now, that's the type of man I want to marry.* Tall with a crop of white hair, and dressed in a business suit, he carried himself handsomely. Following the meeting, those with the same color and number grouped together at tables of five. I noted his name was Delbert, and sad to say, his number was different than mine, and he ended up at the table next to me, beside a beautiful lady, with shoulder-length, jet black hair. There were three men and only two women at my table, including me. We were supposed to be having a discussion and come up with something we all enjoyed, then, in the future, pick up on it and do it together as a group. At first, we reached a stalemate. Frank, rather quiet, was into golfing, as was Carl, a big husky farm boy, with a comical grin, who was now asking "What do you think? Bootsy?"

"Well, I must confess I'm not a golfer, though one day I would like to take lessons. I'm not an excellent swimmer, but I do enjoy ballroom dancing, and fine dining." They all agreed on dining, so plans were made to go out to dinner.

During refreshment time, I watched as Delbert left his group for the second time, and alone, headed for the refreshment table which held all sorts of yummy pieces of cake. I, rather boldly, made my way there, too, and turned side-ways to coyly slip a note into his hand. It read, "During our next dance, will you please save one for me?"

A delightful smile beamed in his gentle, near look-alike, Carey Grant face, and in a soft, Jimmy Stewart voice, he said, "I surely will." I returned to my table, and felt a little guilty, as I sat beside Carl.

After the meeting, Frank invited me to see his lovely villa. The outside was peach in color, and the interior decorated so beautifully, it nearly made my mouth water with envy.

That Sunday, Frank picked me up, and we met the rest in Albertson's parking lot, where we formed a cavalcade and traveled to a quaint restaurant that resembled a little farmhouse with a rambling porch. There, we enjoyed a remarkably delicious meal, and chatted the afternoon away. When we parted, Frank told me, "We'll have to get together again."

"Yes," I said. "I think the group would like that." He never called again.

Instead, Carl, whom I call my 'Kentucky farm boy' checked in on me, now and then, and loaned me one of his sweepers, plus a green sweatshirt, and a warm jacket to wear during cool evenings. During the next four weeks we were quite busy, shopping for items needed to get my palace more homey, and during our trips, now and then we stopped along the way for lunch.

One day, an unfamiliar car pulled into my driveway, and the doorbell noisily rang. I sauntered out to find a nice looking, mustachioed chap smiling at me.

I asked, "Do I know you?"

"Nope!"

"Am I supposed to?"

"Nope!"

Just then, Carl bounced out of the side bushes. "You!" I gasped in surprise.

"Yes! I want you to meet my kid brother." I thought that was nice, and imagined he was there to check me out. In the short time Carl and I have known each other, through our interesting chats we have reached a camaraderie plateau of understanding, and I could tell he was looking for someone special, and made no bones about it. I laughingly told his brother he should hear some of the outlandish things his big brother talked about.

To this, Carl, my farm boy friend, sheepishly blushed. "Well!" He grinned, and paused a moment, as if wondering what to say. "How do you expect to get any, unless you ask?" This threw me into a fit of laughter. To me, it was as much as if to ask, *If hens don't get busy soon, how do you expect to have eggs for breakfast?*

Another week passed. Wednesday, my phone jangled, and Delbert, the man I admired at the Singles, was on the line, inviting me to dine with him that evening. Over dinner at Sunnys, I learned he frequently golfed, picniced and, with the pretty lady named Julie, attended cocktail parties with her neighborhood friends.

During the next two weeks, tired of golfing, he shared time with me, and on two occasions we went shopping and out to lunch. Twice we dined together, here in my villa. He appeared to be everything I had been searching for in a man. Yet, from our conversations, he appeared to be growing quite close to Julie, who was outstanding, lovely, a charming lady, and was keeping herself for their wedding night. I accepted this. Yet, one quiet, peaceful evening, eating a simple sandwich, and downing it with pink lemonade with him out in my courtyard was worth a million to me. Like a moonlit night on a ship's upper deck.

The next time we were together here in my villa, while the kitchen radio played soft music, I suggested we dance. He grinned down at me. "I dance very little." I told him that was okay. I had Nick Felix's tape. He had taught the movie stars how to dance, and we would use it. Delbert's next statement had me more than a little puzzled. "I've been taking dance lessons, with Julie."

"That's nice."

"I'm not doing so good."

I tried to teach him how to smoothly do the 'ballroom break', rather unsuccessfully, as it was far from smooth.

The kissing session which followed, when we stumbled into each other, made up for that. Shockingly, we were both turned on, and we ended laughing, as I shoved him and his manly body out the door. Oh, my, yes! I bowed my head and blushed with the knowledge I was still very much alive.

Now as I wrote, Carl was gone. Off to his last residency, Indiana, for the sale and settlement of his property. I missed him. Truly. His silly grin, when he saw me, and "Hi, there, Toootsy", instead of *Bootsy*. The last I saw him was on Sunday, over at the Paradise Swimming Pool. On my way from shopping that day, I again, became lost and a rather tipsy younger lady stopped to show me the way home, and coaxed me to go swimming with her. Yes, that's where I last saw Carl. Oh well, life does go on. Delbert, a Snow Bird, though certainly not cool in any sense of the word, also left for his home, leaving me wondering if we would ever see each other again. And yes, I, too, would soon be departing for my home in Camp Hill.

**Jane Stem entertaining me and my West Indies friend,
Carol Joseph, from Trinidad**

# Chapter 24
# Saying Goodbye to My PA Home

March 7, because my travels had me away for two months, when I returned to my home in Camp Hill, I expected to walk in and find it empty, looking sadly bleak. Not so! My children had carted up furniture from the family room. The rattan sofa, patterned in an island motif of tan, cream and greens, along with a champagne cushioned rocker, and a wicker table, were all attractively positioned in the living-room. It appeared cozily uncluttered. Thoughts were, *Good going, kids!*

The dining room looked rather empty, with boxes piled along the one wall. Only the kitchen remained the same, with the exception of an ant, which slowly moseyed across the counter. Ants? With winter not totally over? I gathered him up in a tissue and flushed him on his merry way down the Susquehanna. I would miss that smooth flowing river. Two days later another ant came visiting in the same area. I watched him turn left, cross the counter, up the wall, down again, then up half way and stop. Had he made a pit stop, or stopped to take a bath? Ants build rooms and add chambers underground, and keep their rooms, as well as themselves, spotlessly clean. Recently I learned Florida's red ants build their homes above the ground in mounds. Already I have been warned their bite is excruciatingly painful.

Nope! This ant was neither making a pit-stop nor polishing his body. He simply lingered to ponder which route to take. Then he moved slowly up the wall toward the window and vanished beneath the opening lever.

That afternoon, Bill Zody, my realtor, stopped in and told me, "Bootsy, nearly everyone has ants in their home this time of the year." Later, when Jim Clisham, the exterminator, came to make certain there were no termites or other critters creeping around, he told me he was using Premise 75. It's not for ants, but he would make a clean sweep across the window base and it should help. It won't cause coughing or any discomfort. It's made by Bayer, a division for pesticide and just last week he had attended a National Pest Association Seminar with Bayer Corporation Division in York.

There were no ants in my office, just my computer with AOL's e-mail box loaded with messages and forwarding notes. Pressed for time because of packing, I would read only a few messages each day. My first, surprised me. It was about me, and had been sent by an unknown to Virginia, a friend of mine in Oxford, and also Hawaii. She's the one who, when I was visiting her neighbor Del, invited the two of us over for cherry pie baked from PA cherries. The message read:

> Subj.: Fw: The Villages
> Date: 2/18/02
> From Virginia Rebate
> To: Arbutus E @aol.com
>
> SUBJ. Fw: The Villages
>
> ALOHA!
>   I WAS READING AN ARTICLE IN THE SENIOR CITIZEN NEWS I PICKED UP AT THE POST OFFICE ABOUT AN ARTICLE BY A ARBUTUS FOCHT. SHE WAS DESCRIBING HER VISIT TO THE PALMS CONDOMINIUM, OWNED BY HER FRIEND SHE

122

CALLED DEL. SHE TALKED OF THE VIEW OF THE GOLF COURSE. THE CANAL, ETC. SHE LOVED SHOPPING AT THE INTERNATIONAL MARKET-PLACE AND DUKE'S. SHE IS BUYING A PLACE IN THE VILLAGES WHERE HER NEW VILLA IS LOCATED. [A RETIRED SENIORS]. HER SETTLE-MENT DATE WAS JAN 29TH.

THOUGHT YOU MIGHT LIKE TO LOOK UP A FELLOW PENNSYLVANIAN WHO IS STAYING RIGHT THERE IN THE PALMS WITH SOMEONE SHE CALLED FRIEND, DEL

GOD LOVES US.
HOWARD

Another read:

Howard to Virginia
Date Mon. 18 Feb.2002 11:08 44-0500 2

ALOHA!

I THOUGHT YOU WOULD KNOW WHO I MEANT BY DEL'S CONDO. LET ME GET THIS STRAIGHT, IS BOOTSY THE ONE THAT WROTE THE ARTICLE? I THOUGHT IT WAS FUNNY THAT THEY HAD A RETIREMENT PLACE IN FLORIDA CALLED THE VILLAGES. WE KNOW THAT PLACE VERY WELL. WE WERE THINKING OF BUYING THERE BEFORE WE CAME TO CROSS KEYS. I HAVE A CD ON THE VILLAGES. THEY HAD A DEAL FOR $150. YOU WERE A GUEST FOR 3 DAYS IN ONE OF THE CONDOS. AND WITH THE $150 THEY PAID YOU IN THE VILLAGES DOLLARS, WE HAD LOBSTER AT THE CLUB HOUSE, KEPT THE GAS TANK FILLED WITH THEIR GAS AND EVEN HAD FRANK AND JANICE, OUR FRIENDS FROM SCOTTISH HIGHLANDS COME UP AND VISIT WHILE WE WERE THERE.

WE LOVED THE VILLAS THAT YOUR FRIEND IS INTERESTED IN. ESPECIALLY ONE THAT WAS FACING THE GOLF COURSE. ALL THE OTHER HOUSES WERE REAL NICE, TOO. A FELLOW I USED TO WORK WITH, A GEORGE GIBSON AND HIS WIFE MOVED DOWN THERE SHORTLY AFTER OUR VISIT. I THINK HE LOST HIS WIFE AND I LOST TOUCH WITH HIM. I THINK IT IS MOSTLY A GOLFING COMMUNITY AND I KNOW YOUR FRIEND WILL LOVE IT THERE. SHE MAY HAVE TO DO LIKE WE DID. KEEP BOTH PLACES UNTIL WE COULD GET A BUYER. WE STAYED IN THE OLD PLACE BECAUSE THE NEW PLACE WAS SAFER TO LEAVE EMPTY.

DOWN AT THE VILLAGES WE HAD TROUBLE SPENDING ALL THE MONEY SO I BOUGHT A NICE GOLF JACKET. (I'M STILL WEARING). FILLED UP THE TANK WITH SUPREME GAS AND BOUGHT SNACKS FOR THE TRIP HOME. WE HAD ONE CENT LEFT OVER SO I THINK WE DID VERY WELL. WE WILL HOLD THE ARTICLE FOR YOU AND SHOW YOU THE TAPE WE HAVE ON THE VILLAGES WHEN YOU GET HOME TO PA.

GOD LOVES US...
MARY ALICE AND HOWARD

Admittedly, I can truthfully vouch for everything good this man shared about The Villages. After rereading his and Virginia's forwarded e-mails , I still shake my head in disbelief, and find myself laughing, and, yes, singing that ever popular song I first heard while visiting Disney World with my husband eons of ages ago, so it seems. Remember? "It's a small world, after all."

During the nitty-gritty job of sorting, packing, and clearing out my home of fourteen years, I couldn't believe how much one can accumulate in that amount of time. I was extremely grateful to have friends come in to help because I had to be out in six days. The new owners expected to move in the day of settlement, March 13. I had hoped to stay on and rent from them, but they, too, had to vacate and make room for new renters.

Saturday morning, when the phone jangled, and sorority sister, Eileen Young said, "I'm on my way to see if there's anything more I can help you with," I breathed a big happy sigh, and told her I was extremely grateful. The previous day we spent eight hours gathering junk together and placing it in one corner of the room, for the junk collector…Not really. My junk may be another man's treasures.

Next, in the late morning, came my youngest daughter, Debbie. She would go through the give-away pile down in the basement. It pleased me to hear her say, "I want this, this, and this. I give my students who achieve, little presents. This green soap dish with a little frog on the side, will look cute with a pretty cake of soap wrapped and topped with a colorful bow. These gold bows and canes on this little tree you're throwing away, will be nice to trim a tree for in my class room."

Soon, all confusion broke loose. The auctioneer, his wife, mother, son and his wife were scooting up and down stairs, emptying rooms, carrying lamps, marked boxes of books, china and crystal out the back door. Then, the packers, Jill and Jay, arrived, and together with Eileen and me, a total of nine, we were like a swarm of busy bees, flitting from room to room. Bernice, yes, a younger Bernie, in charge, called down the hallway, "We have to clear your office." Eileen and I followed her in, and shelves and bookcases were cleared of albums, and boxes of my writings, in what seemed no time at all.

Next, came the refuse collector with his son, and in a few hours, the downstairs' paint closet and the main basement shelves were emptied. And, too, in a short while their truck was filled with garden tools and all sorts of imaginable paraphernalia.

Then came my son, Keith. "Mom, I can give you an hour and a half, and no more."

Surprisingly, his brother Kevin's wife, Lynna, arrived a few minutes later, having traveled three hours from the Poconos. I had to laugh as she and Keith worked together, emptying the guest room at the end of the hall. Lynna picked up a colonial lamp, and I asked, "Keith, remember that lamp?" No, he hadn't, so I told him there was a story about it. I began, "One rainy week when your dad worked out of town, I was alone with you four children. You and Kevin were 12 at the time, and I bought…"

"Mom! I don't have time to listen..."

"I just wanted to tell you, I purchased that lamp as a 'happy day' gift for myself, when I felt blue. And don't you remember what happened to it?"

"Mom, I told you, I don't have time to listen."

Lynna, now with lamp in hand, hurried down the hall; I followed with an armload of items. "You'll get a kick out of this, Lynna," I told her. "One day, your Kevin was upset when I gave him a job of dusting in the living room, and he angrily shoved in the leaf to the gate-leg table, and the lamp came crashing down on the hardwood floor. I couldn't find a duplicate shade to match the blue and yellow flowers on the base, so bought a white glass shade and painted it myself."

"Gee, Mom! You did a terrific job."

"Thanks. It looks nice in the daytime, but when it's lit at night one can readily see I used the wrong kind of paint."

"That doesn't matter. It's still pretty." Mid-way down the corridor, I could hear the shade grating on the metal rim. Lynna was having difficulty holding it together. In her attempt, it toppled loose and came crashing down, and lay broken at her feet. She groaned, "Oh, Mom! I'm so sorry!"

"That's okay, honey. No one wanted the lamp. Though, it's odd. Your husband broke the first shade, and you, the second." I chuckled to myself. Whether Keith wanted to hear or not, he did, and even helped to sweep up the broken glass.

Daily, we progressed, with most of the furniture removed by my children, and what had been my cozy home, soon appeared obliquely bare. As I stood in the living room and drank in the solemnity of it, thoughts were it looked like a comfortable hat with the finery missing. The day before settlement, my neighbor's cleaning lady, Pat, called. "My daughter and I will be over at your home early tomorrow morning. We'll have your house 'spanking clean' by three o'clock."

When I returned for inspection, it looked, and smelled *spanking clean*. I breathed deeply and brought a smile to their faces when I said, "You've done a fantastic job. If I needed a place, and saw this, I would say, 'I want it!' Yet, now, I must move on."

Then I called friend, Peggy DeStephano. Before, on several occasions, instead of flying in and traveling out to Keith's and Marsha's home in the country, Peggy had graciously opened her doors to me. Now, here I was, again asking, "Would you like to take a lady in off the street?"

"Who?"

"Me."

"I'd be delighted." Original plans were to stay with another friend, yet, Peggy's home had an open third floor level and we both laughingly call it *Bootsy's room*. It consisted of twin beds covered in fringed white spreads, a TV, a dresser and a white fur-covered chaise lounge. At Peggy's house, I felt like a pampered princess. This time she greeted me with a hug and concern in her voice. "Oh, my! I've never seen you look so tired."

"Yes," I told her. "This move has been rough on me. Though I devour food like a hungry horse, I've lost eleven pounds." I would have enjoyed being spoiled a bit longer at Peggy's. Yet, there were still sixteen days before my flight to my new and permanent home in The Villages. So I jimmied my time, dining with friends who wished to say a last 'farewell', camped at Peggy's for two more days, Keith's for seven, two at youngest daughter Debbie's, off to Kevin and Keith's Godparent's Wally and Wiebe Jelsma's 50th anniversary party...then on to daughter Dianne's for four days. Then back one more night at Keith's and Marsha's, closer to the airport.

During all of this time, via phone, sporadically, I kept in touch with Bernie from The Village Helpers. Regarding the movers and car carrier, she assured me I had nothing to worry about. "I'll make a point to be at your villa and intercept the moving van, and check off the numbers of each box as they're unloaded. And yes, I'll be there when the car carrier arrives with your New Yorker."

I could breathe more easily, now, knowing everything would be handled satisfactorily at the other end of the spectrum. She would go one step further. She could have my ugly, black garage floor painted in speckled shades of tan and brown, with a darker brown border, for the same fee which had originally been quoted by two teenagers. Yes, things were looking up, and now appeared to be running smoothly.

# Chapter 25
## Unprepared for the Unexpected

True to Bernie's word, as she had been before, she did everything she promised, and then some. Only now, my new home was stocked with my items and not hers. When I walked into my tidy kitchen, I choked on happy tears. She and her helpers had unpacked dishes and pans, and neatly put everything away in cupboards. Boxes of bed-linens and towels, had also been emptied, and neatly stacked in the linen closet. My bed had been freshly made. Bathrooms were the epitome of neatness. Boxes of cosmetics, lotions, shampoo, etcetera, had been emptied, and items placed beneath sinks and in medicine cabinets. Those three rooms gave a semblance of *home*.

However, I couldn't say that about the rest of the villa. I stood in horror, and recalled an award winning article I once had written, titled, "The Muddled Mess of Moving", THIS WAS IT! Seven wardrobes stacked full of my clothing, boxes and more boxes, totaling eighty-one, huge, tall, low and long, though placed in their proper rooms, covered floors, and stared me in the face, announcing the tasks ahead in days to come. They were long. For four weeks, I attempted to empty one room of boxes at a time. Then, in need of a breather, I shoved a big amount of them, mostly boxes of my writings, out into the lanai. Eventually, it would become my office, when I could finally get around to buying furniture.

During all of this, troubling me most, were the many hours wasted on the telephone, ironing out important issues caused when one moves into another state.

I hadn't given *health insurance coverage*, and obtaining *a state license plate* enough thought. Regarding health coverage, though I had been a member of Blue Cross and Blue Shield in Pennsylvania for sixty-one years, I discovered my company, and Florida's Blue Cross and Blue Shield in Jacksonville, were not affiliated. More upsetting, I learned here in Florida, our premiums are judged by our age, which means cost is considerably higher. However, one can receive a two and a half percent discount with automatic payment withdrawal from one's bank account.

I also learned car inspection isn't compulsory here in the state of Florida, and I wouldn't have had to take the time to run out and have my car inspected, the day before I moved here. Another shocking surprise was to discover, though I had already received my Florida driver's license, in order to drive, I needed a Florida license plate, and to apply for one, my car title was necessary, and it became lost during my move. In an attempt to request a duplicate from Penn Dot, (PA Department of Transportation) in Harrisburg, with automated telephone communication in vogue today, I spent many exasperating hours on the phone. On several occasions, I was put on hold, and after a ten minute wait, was disconnected, only to have to start all over again...if this is this...push this button...If this is that...push that button, and on and on and on, until I wanted to pull hair. Not my own!

When I finally did get through, I waited two weeks, without hearing a word. Finally, Ron, my former landlord, suggested contacting the local sheriff's office in Sumter County. They came to my rescue, faxed a message asking for a form for me to fill out, it was notarized, and returned to Penn Dot, along with another check for twenty-two dollars and fifty cents. In the end, the original title was found amongst boxes of items the movers had removed from my filing cabinet, I never received a remuneration from Penn Dot for the one check, and I now have three titles. It took four weeks until my license plate arrived. Until then, I used my golf cart for shopping outside The Villages, I relied on friends, and couldn't have managed without my Kentucky farm boy, Carl. And, too, my PA church friend, Carol Furlong, who, with her husband, Tom, had lived here for three years. Bless them!

# Chapter 26
# Alone on Mother's Day

Then came a day to remember. Attending nondenominational services in The Church in the Square had become a highlight of my week. Yes, as I have down through the ages, during church services, I still wear hats. Some of the eighty-one boxes brought from Camp Hill contained many of my favorites. I enjoy doctoring them to match outfits. I switch flowers, ribbons, feathers, and even brown and gold flower pods to go with leopard. Today, Mother's Day, as I stood in my closet, I chose a see-through, brimmed, green mesh hat, trimmed in rose and purple flowers to wear with a lime green linen sheath. The latter fools everyone into thinking I'm quite slim. Later, as I sat behind the wheel of my golf cart and zoomed my way down the golf cart path, into town, I felt slim, prim and proper, in that pretty fifty cent hat which I had found on a sales table in the Camp Hill Boscov's department store.

Before church services began, I would take advantage of Katie Belles special Mother's Day buffet, honoring mothers. Luckily, there, directly across the street I spied an available golf cart parking space, and as I pulled in, I smiled to myself, lifted my face heavenward and quietly whispered, "Thanks, God!" Then, with heels rhythmically clicking against the concrete sidewalk, I hurriedly made my way up to

Katie Belle's front door, there to be greeted by a man named, Jim, who was checking ID's. This has become necessary, as too many outsiders have been coming in, crowding the restaurant, as well as the dance floor during Katie Belle's nightly dances, leaving little room for Village residents. While I stood there, and rooted in my purse, I told Jim, "I'm sorry, it's taking so long, but I know it's in here."

He smiled sweetly. "Take your time, and Happy Mother's Day. How are you this lovely day?"

Tears spurted from my eyes and I sobbed, "I miss my kids!" Up until then I had no idea about this. I had been doing well on my own. Lips quivering, I looked up at him. "This is the first I've been away from them."

"You'll be alright." He gently patted me on the back.

By the time he opened the door for me, I was dry-eyed. However, the maitre de and three waitresses behind the counter, all chorused in a bubbly voice, "Happy Mother's Day, and how are you?"

Again, tears rolled down my cheeks. I sniffed, "Okay, but I miss my kids. I've never been so far away from them. I m going to attend The Church in The Square service, and just came in for a scrambled egg, toast and coffee."

They consoled me with, "You'll be alright. We know it's hard the first time."

I received a hug, and the manager said, "We have a special Mother's Day buffet over there. You can help yourself." Nodding to a waitress, she added, "Misty, show her the first table." Breakfast proved quite tasty, though eaten on the run, and when Misty slipped the bill on my table and walked away, I read: *Happy Mother's Day. It's been a pleasure to serve you. This is on me. Come back to see us again. Misty.* As I exited out the door and headed for church, my eyes misted not due to sadness, but to her sweet thoughtfulness. When I entered and went to sit down in the church pew, I turned to the ladies behind me and smiled, greeting them with "Happy Mother's Day." Again, came the tears and, "I miss my children, terribly."

The lady in a green and pink floral dress, said, "I know. I went through the same thing last year. You'll be happy when you leave here." I thanked her, and the lady to my right, held up her hand, and ordered me to please not cry or she would, too, and I couldn't help smiling Later, I sat spellbound, and listened to the vocalist — beautiful, 20-year-old Annie — as she stood up front amidst five singers, and filled the air with her lilting rendition of "Ave Maria."

Now, with no longer frayed nerves, I turned to the lady in pink and green, smiled, and whispered, "You're right! I'm happy."

So life goes. My feelings on Mother's Day had surprised and shocked me, yet I recovered. Maybe even a little bit stronger. I did get to converse with all of my four children, that evening, including Kevin, in Spain, and under the circumstances, my first Mother's day in The Villages ended quite nicely. The following week, I received a gift from my oldest daughter, Dianne, commemorating that day. When I opened the little box, it contained a hand twisted silver wire necklace of a swan, with my birthstone as its eye, and across its back was written "Mom." The bottom of the swan contained tiny silver beads, and dangling in between, were my four children's colorful birthstones, and their names spelled in silver wire: Keith, Kevin, Debra, Dianne. Yes, I stood there as I sniffed and read Dianne's sentiments. "Mom, this is to remind you that you are never alone, we are there, always hanging around your neck." Love, and Bunchies of Hugs, Dianne."

# Chapter 27
# Nice Gentlemen,
# Jake, Roy and Don

June 8, and one never knows what to expect here. I'd been a resident only two months and seven days, and they do whiz by so fast. Today, I decided to goof off, rest a bit, then scoot out and meet some people at the Singles Club.

It proved to be a pleasant evening, like the last one, and before leaving, I signed up to help escort the men to their tables at the Father's Day Dinner two weeks away. I also said I would attend the Singles picnic at the Chula Vista Club on Saturday.

That was to be my first extraordinarily happy afternoon.

Joan, recently widowed, called and suggested we attend together, and I was rarin' to go. No sooner did we arrive when we were whisked in with a peppy group of shuffleboard players. There, on the first set, I was paired off to play with a man called Jake. When it came time to change partners, he said, "I want to play again with Bootsy. I'd like to get to know her better." A fatherly type, older with gray hair, and blue eyes which peered from a solemn face, he asked, "Where have you been? I've never seen you before." After our second game, I decided to go indoors, out of the sun, and into a glass-enclosed room where tables were scattered about, and card playing was in progress. One table had only three players. Another was needed to play Hand and Foot, a popular card game here, one I had played months ago, with Daphine. I was coaxed to join in. It was quite fun. Next to me sat a nice-looking gentleman with a twinkle in his brown eyes, then there was Laura, a retired school principal, our Singles' Club president, and her friend, Pat, a skilled player.

Later, I met up with Joan and together we went through the food line and ended seated at Laura and Pat's table. We were finished eating when Pat shared her Listerine Mouth Fresheners, slips of mint flavored squares of translucent paper.

"They're wonderful!" I said. "My tongue tingles, and they do make one's' mouth feel fresh." Joan spoke up, telling us she could catch a whiff of my Listerine over where she sat. Just then Jake moseyed over, asking where I had disappeared to. He had been looking all around for me. I told him, "I played cards, and now I'm here." He leaned over, and with his cheek so close, I pointed to mine and said, "Kiss me." When he attempted to kiss my cheek, as a naughty lady, I swiftly turned my head and brushed my lips on his. This brought an uproar of laughter from everyone. Quiet man that he was, he didn't quite know what to make of this. Nor I.

"I wanted you to sample my Listerine Mouth Freshener," I told him. "Kiss me again." For a fraction of a moment he stared at my mouth, and I wondered if my lips were colorless, minus lipstick from eating, but he lowered his to mine, kissed them and told me I tasted fresh, and just as quickly…nearly bounced away.

Monday, June 10, the phone jangled, and the unfamiliar voice said, "This is Laura, from the Singles. You're a jolly, gregarious lady, and I'm making you my welcoming chairman." She was serious. "Will you do a big favor for me?"

"Surely! If I can."

"A Mr. Holmes, from Chicago called, and needs someone to show him around town. Maybe you could meet someplace for coffee? He's supposed to be here in The Villages for a month."

"I can do that," I told her.

I called him on the phone. "No, I don't want to get together. I'm sorry. I rented for a month, have been here only nine days, and I'm leaving for home on Wednesday. I'm dissatisfied. I talk to people and they walk away." My thoughts were, they couldn't be Villagers. He continued, "I never see anyone on my street."

"You undoubtedly are on a street where mostly snowbirds live. They go home for the summer months. Did you have your dinner yet?"

"No."

"Let's meet at Katie Belles. The food is good. You pay your way, I'll pay mine."

"No, I don't want to."

"Maybe we can meet in The Square, and sit and chat."

"No. It's been rough since my wife died. I never cried so much in all my life."

"How long ago did she leave."

"A year."

"I know what you're going through. It will take a while for you. Each day will get a little better. My husband passed away fourteen years ago, and at times I still get weepy-eyed. Especially when I hear Bette Midler sing "My Hero." My Herb truly was my hero and I told him I was dedicating the song to him. After he died, a year later, when it was sung at the Harrisburg Singles Dance, I was in the arms of a man named Frank, and when the dance ended his tan jacket was soaked with tears. Mine! I had sniffed all through that dance. I'll tell you what. Since you don't want to dine out, I can whip together a turkey and cheese sandwich and we can eat down by the lake and listen to the music coming from the band playing in the square."

"No. That's very kind of you, but I don't want to."

"That's okay," I told him. "Well, you have a good night." He wished the same for me, and I hung up.

Then I told myself it wasn't okay. I thought about him all alone on an empty street, and crying. He had said he was on Medira. Wasn't that the street where my friend, Suzanne, lived? I would call and have her go over and check on him. Just to let him know someone cared. Suzanne wasn't aware of any newcomers in her area, I should call Denny, across the street. He worked for VHA and may know. Denny wasn't in, and his wife also wasn't aware of any newcomers. I looked at my watch and realized I'd have to leave soon, as my golf cart had no lights. First, I would call Laura, and get the number of Leroy's rental. I was right! It was close to Suzanne's. I would stop by, and coax her to accompany me.

As I rang her bell, I hoped with all my heart her answer would be in the affirmative. "No, Bootsy, I'm sorry, I don't wish to go, but you go. You're better at this than I am. You can do it."

"Alright!" I smiled at the underhanded compliment, turned and marched down her sidewalk as I sang "Onward Christian Soldiers," and envisioned her own smile. In a few minutes I stood outside his door. I took in a deep breath, gave three hurried presses to the bell, and waited. No sound from within. Could he be sleeping? Crying? I wrote the following note to put between the door and screen.

"Hey, there! Was here. Where were you? Call me."

I changed my mind and decided to go next door to the neighbor's and have them check in on him. Only to discover indeed, I was now standing in front of his door at 923 Medira. He wasn't answering. Now, what? Leave the note? No, he may be out. I returned to my car, sat, and pondered a bit. The screen on the garage door had been pushed half way shut. To get out his golf cart? Certainly, and if that were the case, The Village rule insists all golf carts must be off the street at sundown. I'd simply sit in my car and wait until I saw him in person, and make certain he was alright. I would even sleep there awhile, if need be. 8:15, I rested my head against the car door and closed my eyes, and breathed a sigh of contentment. The night before, I hadn't slept well because an ant had taken a walk near my pillow, escaped, and thoughts of it were never far behind. Now, in a comfortable state of mind, almost asleep, the sound of tires grating on gravel spoke of someone nearing. The noise stopped beside my car. I didn't raise my head, but lay ever so still, and heard a gentle chuckle and, "My, you are a persistent young lady, aren't you?" When I looked up and grinned, he said, "I wondered who that woman was, sleeping in her car in my driveway."

"That's me," I chuckled.

"Would you like to come in for a drink?"

"Such as what? I only drink at parties if accompanied by a date."

"Pepsi?" We stepped into his villa, and when he took me on a tour, I discovered it was an exact duplicate of the one I wanted to buy last year, in the same neighborhood. At that time it proved too costly.

Ironically, only five months ago, January 29th, I paid an extra eight thousand more for my villa, but my courtyard is more regally landscaped. I stood in his kitchen and watched as he poured the soda. He had a steady hand. He looked over at me, and a smile showed white, even teeth, even for a man 79 years of age. Tall, slim, a tad thick in the tummy region. "I'm happy you stopped in," he said. " I've been very lonely."

"That's because of the area you're staying in. On my street, people stop by in golf carts and chat once in awhile, or at least yell, 'Hi!' or 'Good morning.' Want me to take you there to see where I live?"

"That would be nice. I'd appreciate it."

"I'll finish my soda later. Come, we'll go, now."

He liked the wider streets of my neighborhood, and my villa. Together we slid open the lanai's large sliding glass doors, and stepped into my courtyard. "My! This is lovely out here. It's much nicer than mine. You were wise to buy this villa." He looked skyward. "It's so open and wide out here, and look at those beautiful billows of white clouds."

"Yes, Roy, when I first saw them, I thought of my husband, and the comment he made during our last flight to Daytona. He said they reminded him of white cotton and made one want to walk barefoot through them. I think of him every time I'm out here."

We returned to Roy's villa and he asked, "Have you had your dinner?"

"Are you kidding? I didn't have time to eat. I was too busy tracking you down." He got a kick out of this. His laughter told me. "Have you eaten?" I asked.

"Yes, at Katie Belles." He walked to his refrigerator, opened the door, and asked, "Would you like a sandwich? How does spiced ham and cheese on rye sound?"

"Wonderful!" So while I fixed a sandwich, he prepared my dessert, a bowl of chopped watermelon, and together we sat on his sofa and watched television, until 11:00. It was an enjoyable evening for both, and when we hugged goodbye, I told him, "1 will call you in the morning and check on you."

"Thanks, that would be nice."

I kept my promise, and called him. "What are you doing?" he asked.

"My friend, the decorator, is coming to hang pictures in the lanai."

"Tell her you must leave at four o'clock. I'd like to take you to the theater and to McCall's for a steak dinner."

"That would be lovely, I'll be ready." We saw *Insomnia*. A man's movie, with a lot of the *F* word. Not to my liking. Soon, after the show began, Roy reached over and took my hand in his. That was nice, but his fingers kept running up and down mine, distracting me, until finally I removed my hand, and whispered, "I can't concentrate when you do that." He whispered he wasn't aware of what he had been doing, and apologized.

During an enjoyable dinner, he said "I wished we could have met sooner. I would have stayed. We could have fun together. But my son made flight arrangements, and I do miss my little grandson. I often take him fishing down at the lake, so I'm going to leave tomorrow."

Back at his villa, we scribbled off each other's address and phone number, thinking we may want to keep in touch. We set my alarm clock which I was loaning, and set the one owned by The Villages, so both would sound off early in the morning at 5:00 AM, and he wouldn't miss his shuttle bus ride to the airport. Then he cleaned out his refrigerator, and insisted I take all the food from it and also off the closet shelf. It consisted of milk, watermelon, cereal, sugar, a grapefruit, a banana and two apples. We viewed a little TV and when I was about to leave, he kissed me goodbye, and said, "I'll walk you to your car." Seated behind the steering wheel, I looked up at him, standing there, so tall. Six feet, one hundred eighty-five pounds. A nice figure, a nice man. "I'm going to kiss you once more," he told me, and leaned over into my opened window and lightly captured my lips "This is my first time," he said, now standing even taller. "And your kisses are overwhelming. Thanks for everything. We'll keep in touch."

"Yes, and Roy, thanks for dinner, for everything."

"You're welcome. It was a fun night, and my thoughts regarding The Villages have changed. It can be a nice place." He was truly a nice man, and I told myself if he should return next year, I'll keep my promise and assist in finding him a nice villa, help show him the ropes, and introduce him to others so he won't feel lonely. He said it's harder for a widower to pick up and move out into the world after their wife dies. When he said this, I swallowed hard, thinking of my friend DJ, back in PA. I shouldn't have given up on him. Oh, well, today, he is married, and undoubtedly that's how it should be. Who is to say? Though once in a while I think of him. Perhaps as all my friends have told me down through the fourteen years, someone is really waiting just around the corner for me. As I write the phone is ringing.

"It's me, Laura, again, from the Singles. Would you mind if I shared with the Club how you helped Mr. Holmes?"

"No. Just don't tell them he thought my kisses were overwhelming." I giggled.

"No, I won't. I'm calling to ask another favor. I received a phone call from the Sales office. A friend told me there's a man named Ron Long in town, and he's here for only four days, and needs someone to accompany him to the Auto Show and go to dinner. Would you be interested?"

"Well, I've been at the computer all afternoon. When did he want to go to the show?"

"I have his number, you can call. Maybe he will end up being your prince."

"I'm too busy to look for one. I'm hoping he'll find me. Laura, why don't you accompany Mr. Holmes?"

"I recently met my prince, and wouldn't feel comfortable going out with another man."

"How did you meet this prince of yours?"

She laughed. "One girl said she knew this man and he was right for me, then a man I knew said he had a friend who was just right for me. We finally met. They were one and the same, and we liked each other instantly."

"That's great! Tell me about Don. Is he nice? Single? A Christian?"

"I don't know anything about him. All I know is his name, and phone number. A lady realtor gave them to me."

When I dialed Don's number his line was busy. The next time I called, I left word on his answering machine, explained who I was, and left my number. I was taking a nap, my body jerked, and I was about to slip into dreamland when the phone on my nightstand jangled. Don was on the line. He sounded nice. Grammar perfect. "I'm a bit confused, now. A lady realtor set me up with another girl, named Sheila. She called, and said she could go to the auto show. Then I received your call."

"That's nice, you can have a girl escort on each arm tonight."

"There's a thought," he chuckled.

"Go out with Sheila, since she's undoubtedly expecting you to call. And if you want, we can go out tomorrow night."

"You won't mind?"

"No. In fact, I'm happy. Now I can continue my nap and catch up on sleep."

He laughed. "You're a good sport."

The following evening when he called, I agreed to meet him at Katie Belles for dinner. "Sit on the bench," I told him. "And, I'll be there at six o'clock."

"How will I know you?"

"I'll wear a pink flower in my hair."

When the time came to leave, I ran outside and snipped off a pink Mandera blossom, and pinned it to my hair. Yes, I was anxious to meet this man. His voice was peppy, free with laughter, and not hurting like Roy. I parked behind the restaurant. When I went to enter the main entrance, three men were seated on the outside bench. One, in the middle was tall, wore glasses and had gray hair. I walked up to this man, smiled and asked, "Is your name Don?" It wasn't. Neither was the man next to him, who said when I found Don, if he smoked, I was to ask if he'd share his cigarettes. I told this man he looked like my Uncle Charlie, who always said smoking wasn't good for us, and he should know better. The man to his right piped up, and said, he, himself didn't smoke. I chuckled and told him, "You're the smart one,"and marched indoors. There, next to a white pillar, and alone, stood a dream of a man, impeccably dressed in gray suit, blue shirt, and white, white hair. He could have walked out of Esquire. Our eyes caught and held, bringing a smile to my lips. "Is your name Don?"

"No," he soberly said.

I wanted to say, *Ah, shucks*. Instead I said, "Oh, I'm sorry."

A tall, thin man then approached me, and a cheerful smile beamed on his pleasant face. "I'm Don, Bootsy." I liked him immediately. His English and manners were perfect. We climbed Katie Belles stairs to the upper level, and he, like Roy, also seated me at the table, and over dinner, conversation, too, proved pleasant. I learned he became a widower after fifty years of marriage, Also, this past Christmas, his home was struck by a plane, and burned to the ground. He, himself, was forcefully whirled out of the house, but not too seriously burned.

He said, "The only thing which remained from my past, was a box of love letters which I found out in the yard. Love letters, my wife and I had written each other before we married."

I felt a tug at my heart, as I recalled the box of love letters found amongst my belongings during this move: Letters my husband and I had written to each other during his college years.

Don, I learned had been extremely ill, recovering from a new artery replacement, and was working at gaining weight. With dinner finished, we sauntered out onto Katie Belle's balcony. There, I sighed, as I drank in the perfect postcard panoramic view. A full moon glistened on tree tops, and below, in the town square's gazebo, a band played, while dancers swayed to the melodious music, which drifted skyward on the fresh night air, for even us to enjoy.

"They're playing The Tennessee Waltz, my favorite, Roy. Do you want to dance?"

"I haven't danced since my wife died. But I'm game if you lead." We stumbled through. I complimented him, mostly for being a good sport. When we parted at Katie Belles, he thanked me for a lovely evening, and said he would like to stay a bit longer, if the insurance company would agree to a settlement worth the value of his destroyed home. He definitely wanted to settle here.

So ended a great evening, with truly a nice gentleman.

# Chapter 28
# A Good Hair Day

Monday evening following our Singles Father's Day dinner, president Laura, before everybody, asked me to stand. Yes, I'm somewhat shy, and my heart thumped wildly as she now introduced me as the club's Goodwill Ambassador. Then she added, "If anyone needs help, call on Bootsy."

Two men, from opposite directions zeroed in. Charlie, from New York, a little jovial fellow whom I enjoyed dancing with last Friday at the Swamptime Jamboree, leaned over my table. "Will you go to dinner with me tomorrow night?"

"Thank you, Charlie. Not tomorrow. I'm all tied up for the next four days."

Next, to my right, came Jake, my shuffleboard partner. "I've been looking all over for you." Evidently, while I had been busy escorting men to their tables, he had missed me. We now made plans for a Saturday night date.

Two days later, we cancelled due to the death of a friend. A week passed, and he called again. We decided to meet for breakfast at ten o'clock the next day in front of Bachara's Bakery. We would enjoy one of their yummy pastries, along with a cup of cappuccino.

I awakened to the sun shining gloriously, and birds singing sweetly outside my sliding glass door here in the lanai. A grand day in which I would work Jake into my morning schedule. My appointment with Natalie's hair dresser wasn't until one o'clock. Yesterday, she had driven over there with me. Would I find my way, today? I recalled when I first met the beauticians, both appeared saddened. Why? I wondered. Perhaps they could use a moral boost today. Should I take an apple for each? No. What, then? My favorite fudge which Dr. Joyer and his crew back in PA enjoyed, came to mind. It would take only five minutes to whip up a batch. Yes, I would do this! So, into a large mixing bowl...though the recipe called for two...I scooped off one and three quarter sticks of Blue Bonnet margarine, and watch it melt in the micro-wave oven. Next, I added one cup of peanut butter, a teaspoon of vanilla, and stood on tip toes to search in the cupboard for a box of 10X sugar. None there! Quickly, I called neighbor, Dauphine, and bless her soul, yes, she had an extra box. As I ran next door to her villa, an exterminator, working across the street, came around the corner of neighbor, Elaine's villa. I called over, "When you're through, may I talk to you?"

"Wait a sec, and I'll come right now."

While he screwed a top on a long metal tank, I met Dauphine at her door, grabbed her box of 10X, and scooted back to my home just as the bug-man moseyed over. Yes, he could spray through my home...this morning. Cost, forty-five dollars for one session. I had checked with neighbors, compared prices of numerous exterminators and found prices differed, but all were much higher. "We set our price and hold firm," Jeb, this exterminator assured me. "And we come whenever you want us."

Later, in the kitchen, he told me he and his friend live in the country, and they had no children but a pet pig, named Gehron. I laughed about this, and told him, when I was 20, in my tender years, I dated a nice fellow by that name. He was no pig, but a dear who allowed me to get behind the wheel of his red convertible. And...the first time out, I brushed the side of a culvert, and caused four hundred dollars worth of damage to his car. That was a lot of money back in those days. Thoughts now, skipping through my mind were, if ever before I die, I win the lottery and he's still alive, I'd surprise him and pay back every cent. Jeb finished in the garage, returned to the kitchen and told me he didn't find any termites. Only two baby spiders, and gave them a double dose. No, he didn't spray for wasps. Only seasonal, and they would be hiking out of there, soon. I paid him, and no, he didn't want a sample of my finished fudge. He had just eaten his lunch a little bit ago. He handed me a business card, a large form which I signed, and told me, "Call, whenever you need us."

My watch showed I would have to hurry to meet Jake on time. I quickly slipped in my contacts, grabbed my purse, and hurried out the door. Only to pull up before Katie Belles' entrance, and caddy-corner across the street, see Jake prancing past occupied tables. I slammed my car door, locked it, and called out, "Hello, Jake!" I finally caught up to him. After we exited from the bakery carrying our ordered goodies, we found a nice corner spot in the rocking-chair section. At the same time I reached for my chair, I attempted to sip my cappuccino topped with whipped cream, but what I thought was a straw, ended as a spoon stuck in my nose. I laughed about this. So did Jake. He proved to be a nice, amiable chap.

When I told him about my morning, he said, "There used to be a lady with red hair on TV, and you remind me of her. Her name was Lucy. And she got in all kinds of predicaments."

"Yes, I feel like her, sometimes. There's always some sort of excitement that pulls me back" We sat rocking, and talked the morning away, about our pasts, our spouses. What we wanted in life. He was hoping we could connect. Already we had two dates made, and he booked me for a shuffle board partner at his Fourth of July neighborhood picnic. I was thrilled I wouldn't be alone. This would be the first time I wouldn't be tubing down the Shawnee on the Delaware with my children. Undoubtedly, like on Mother's Day, I wouldl miss them. But I wouldn't be alone and crying.

I looked at my watch.

"You have to leave, don't you?"

"No, I have fifteen minutes." We talked about sex, naturally.

"I'm quite a bit older than you," said Jake.

"Age is just mind over matter. If you don't mind, it doesn't matter. If you're worried about sex, don't be, Jake. A lot of men our age, can't perform." I purposely make a point to say 'our' and not 'your' age. "In fact , Jake, when my former doctor told me he was never going to marry again, I told him he should masturbate . You know what they say, if you don't use it…"

144

"You lose it," he gave a little smile. "My doctor told me the same thing. I don't have any problem, yet. But I'm old enough to be your dad."

"Do you want to be my dad? Shall I call you 'Poppa'"?

"No, I want to be your friend. And maybe more. You said you were a one man woman. What does that mean? That you try one man at a time?"

"No! I want to fall in love again. I want one man of my own, one who does not sleep around with other women. I will not frolic in the bedroom with any man. Not unless I'm in love, there's a ring on my finger and there's a future in it."

"Do I have to get you a ring?"

"No. We'll take it slowly. You say I'm your first date in ten years. Well, now that your ex is gone, you'll find the ladies will be chasing after you. We'll be good friends and see where it goes." We stood to say goodbye, and we kissed. I don't know who kissed whom, but it was nice. His lips were sweet and gentle. Again, we kissed, and again. Ladies in the corner, surreptitiously glanced over at us, and I broke away, once again a lady.

"You're turning me on," Jake softly murmured.

"I don't mean to," I said, and wished he were the big strapping fellow like my man, yet, though older, and a cigar smoker like my dad had been, I genuinely enjoyed being with him. He would call regarding Sunday's date. I plopped myself behind the wheel of my car, eased away from the curb, threw him a kiss, he reciprocated, and I was on my way to the beauty salon.

Yesterday, it seemed so far out in the country, yet today I pulled into their parking area fifteen minutes early. Following my permanent, while Crystal cut my hair, she told me not to cross my legs, or the cut would throw my body off and the hair cut wouldn't be even. When she was through working with me, and I looked into the mirror, I was pleased. "My hair looks thicker since you layered it. I like the cut, perm and curl."

Yes, I returned home, content, and lay down on my bed, and drifted away to the musical swishing of rain upon my window. I awakened when the phone rang twice, and stopped. The clock on the night-stand read 5:20. Three hours earlier than when I rose in the morning. Yet, I felt so refreshed. I would get up and work at my computer. Then it dawned! It was evening, not morning. It had been a pleasant day, far exceeding my expectations. The girls at the beauty shop had loved my fudge, and I couldn't truly say which was most pleasing to me: my hair, or having a nice man in my life, even for one day.

# Chapter 29
## Decorating My New Home

More and more, things are looking up. I have met Natalie's husband, Glenn, a likeable chap, and very much like his peppy and spunky wife. Nearly every other day, for five to eight hours, they assisted in helping me to not only settle in, but comfortably and beautifully. Bless them! First, Glenn hooked up my computer. Then, we three went shopping for a virus scanner and an electric surge protector, and I was back in business.

Both, also refused to allow business people, especially handymen, to monetarily take advantage of me. When the air-conditioner in my car no longer worked, Natalie suggested Glenn drive it to the garage, so the mechanic wouldn't know it was owned by a helpless little lady...me. Freon and dye were added and it was working. Thanks to my friends, Natalie and Glenn! Now, I also had a new lock on my door, and Glenn even installed a 'peek-hole' for me to look out and see who was on the other side. He told me, "I've been planning on doing this for you. Some workers you had, may still have one of the keys. You never know."

Most importantly, he rewired and hung my two crystal chandeliers. A handyman hadn't grounded the one in the kitchen, and the other, purchased in Paris, hung in a lopsided manner, and blinked off and on when I cleaned it. Glenn purchased a brass chain, to match the original, extended it, and that chandelier now gracefully hangs over my dining room table. When he handed me a scorched cap which had held the live wires, I shuddered."Bootsy, see this? You could have had a fire here, if I hadn't discovered it."

Recently, I came across a picture in a magazine, and Natalie agreed, saying, "That's a clever idea. Yes, we can do that." So, today, we three drove to Ocala, and there flitted from mall to mall, and found twelve picture frames in the Dollar Stores. After four hours of tedious and time-consuming work, they are filled with favorite pictures of my family, and now hang from red ribbons, on brass curtain rods in the guest room. Natalie chose red to tie in with Susanne Pleshette's Strawberry Patch twin spreads, favorites of mine, purchased thirty years ago.

Another day, a stay at home, goof off, day. While clothes whirled in the drier, I enjoyed catching up with *The Young and The Restless* on TV, after missing three sessions. My soap opera excuse? My lunch hour. Back home in PA, everyone knows this, and refrains from calling, yet, here, my phone was now ringing.

Natalie on the line. I tell her, "I'll buzz you back in five minutes."

In five minutes, I made a quick stop in the bathroom, ate a piece of chocolate, and dallied a bit longer, viewing TV. Thoughts were, she too, was simply taking it easy in her villa, and wouldn't mind waiting a bit. The phone rang again. Natalie, to say, "I'm going into Dockside to pick up the metal umbrella for in your bathroom." Dial tone! Stunned, I blinked in dismay. Why hadn't she told me this beforehand? I would have liked to tag along and pick out my own umbrella. Yet, come to think of it, while out in the laundry room, I had missed a call from her, and unsuccessfully tried to get back to her three times. I was steaming with hurt, as I dialed her number. No answer.

My phone is ringing. Sis Kathy, from New York. "You shouldn't have kept her waiting. That's not nice."

When son Keith phoned, he believed as Kathy. "Keep your word." I caught him up to date, then conveyed concern about how Natalie fusses. Particularly when she arrives and finds the coffee table cluttered with newspapers. "Mom, don't let her change your individuality. You're perfect the way you are."

"Really, Keith?" No one had ever told me this, except his father. Silence on the line, then, "Well, nearly."

"Natalie is one uncanny lady, Keith. Never having children, she's the epitome of perfection when it comes to neatness, and she's attempting to teach me how to live quite regally. Me, who had you and three other whooping children jump off the school bus at the same time, and run wildly indoors, arms loaded with books, jackets, hats, and all that clutter. Then me, with my office clutter."

"Just don't change, Mom. I love you the way you are." That one sentence was a nice *pick me up* for the day.

The next call coming in was Natalie. "Remember all the metal umbrellas Dockside had when we were last there? About 15? Today, there were only three left. I bought one of the small, and it will look nice in your bathroom. I bought more silk flowers, and matching hand towels. Also, a lot of little things you needed. You'll be pleased."

"That's nice, I'm sure I will be, but you were so curt on the phone, and I was upset because I couldn't go with you. So I ate two dishes of ice-cream, and, in the mixed nuts I bought yesterday, I ate all the hazel nuts I had saved for you."

"Good!" A slight hint of laugher. "Before I left, I told Glenn I was going to call you, and he said we'd hang on the phone. I said it would only take a minute. You told me you would call in five, and he was timing it. When it reached ten, he insisted we leave."

"Oh, I'm sorry I held you up. Glenn went with you?"

"He wanted to go to Dockside to get certain bolts to hang the heavy plaque outside your front door. The pretty plaque you and I bought yesterday. The one with pastel flowers and blue butterflies. Oh, and wait until you see the 'Welcome' sign I bought! You'll love it. It will go nicely with the plaque. On our way home, we were so tired Glenn took pity on me, and insisted we stop for dinner."

"That's nice. Then you didn't have to cook."

"We'll be over tomorrow morning at eleven and hang everything."

We wished each other a goodnight, and I said, "I still love you."

She reciprocated with, "I love you, too. Goodnight."

The following day, Natalie and I were out shopping again, and upon our return when we pulled into my driveway, I was utterly shocked to see her husband in the unmercifully hot sun, with electric clippers in hand, cutting back my hedges. No one had told me he would be there. Yet, there he was, with blue and white plaid shirt, perspiration soaked, and clinging to his back, while driblets of sweat dripped from salt and pepper hair onto brows. I couldn't believe he was doing this for me, and on such a beastly hot day. Hedge clippings lay at his feet, and to the left of the driveway, lay four long, dead cuttings from my five trunk palm tree.

Natalie bounced out of the car, ran into my garage, grabbed a broom and called to me "Go into the kitchen and get some large garbage bags." I did, and together, we gathered enough shrub cuttings to fill eleven.

Then Glenn said, "Bootsy, I'm anxious to know your thoughts regarding the way I trimmed the palm tree out back in your courtyard." I couldn't wait even a moment, and hurried over to the gate on the left, and sauntered down the long pathway, and there, straight ahead stood my tree. Beneath its graceful spreading fronds, it had been artfully trimmed to resemble a pineapple. For a moment I stood in awe, admiring its beauty, while wiping away tears of joy. Then I stooped and began to gather cuttings, and jammed them into the garbage bag in my hand.

Natalie, perspiration dripping from her face, came back and said, "We're through out front. Go rest. I'll take over. You've done too much today." I heeded her advice and went inside to telephone chat with sis, Kathy. Finally, I cut the conversation short, and returned to find my helpers in their van, all ready to leave. Natalie gave a short hand-wave, and pictured on her flushed face, as she rolled down the window, was a look of sheer exhaustion. "I'm not coming back. If there is anything you want me to do tomorrow, you call me."

As they drove away, I stood there and drank in the beauty of my neatly trimmed front yard, with the thoughts, *It's truly phenomenal, in today's world, for anyone to do so much for anyone, simply out of the kindness of their hearts. Yet, these two wonderful Christians insist God would want them to help me.*

I turned, opened my front door and walked inside, to find my villa bathed in sunlight. Everywhere I turned, I saw beauty. The Camp Hill table cloth I had sewn, years ago, Petunias with green leaves on white, blue and yellow plaid, was now a pretty valance and hung at my kitchen window. Another work of art, by Natalie. We had hung it together, and when we stood back and looked at her handiwork, I was amazed and pleased when she smiled and said,"See? How it picks up colors of your border and brightens the room.?"

Mostly, I'm happy with the guest room, its strawberry border, the wall grouping of pictures, and particularly Natalie's latest seam work: I ran my hand across the red and white striped cushion on the white wicker chair with its matching ribbon climbing the back and tying in a tidy bow at the top. Magnificent!

How can I not be happy, in viewing all she has accomplished? Never did I think everything would come together so beautifully. I turned, and from off the white wicker dresser, I picked up the red covered address book I had given to Natalie when we first began working together. She had handed it back to me, and said, "Write in a little something, so I know it's from you."

Today, I did. "To Natalie Martin, my wonderful decorator and friend, who walks in the beauty of God's love and so freely gives of her own. My sincere thanks, and deepest appreciation."

# Chapter 30
# Cutting Costs

I have now come to the conclusion I should have listened to my children, and hired my own lawyer and inspector when I purchased this villa. Instead, I believed my realtor when he said, "Bootsy, it would be a waste of your money, in view of the fact we have our own good men."

I believed him until settlement day, when I read all I had paid for, and felt I did not get a fair deal. The termite inspector's report stated: "Did not check the eves. Did not check water traps. Reason: Too high. Too low." Also, when I had called from my villa and asked Tom if we were going to have a walk through I was informed, "You're there, and you walked through, didn't you?" When I discovered the dishwasher didn't work, I called again, and he came, got down on the floor and showed me the fan which needed to be turned, as the machine hadn't been used for six months. At the time he said, "From now on, get someone else to come in and help." I did. I called Carl, from the Single's Club, when I found the hose to the clothes drier on the top shelf in the garage.

Then, I found water on the carpeting outside of the master closet, and felt Tom should know. I called his office and spoke to his associate, but no one came. It dried the next day and was sloughed off. Two months later, in June, two smaller spots appeared, now in the living room, near the coffee table, and no one returned my call. (In all fairness, at that time Realtors weren't handling many resales, and I hadn't known their policy was when you bought a resale, the problems were yours. Now, I understood the inspection policy was identical for both resales and newly built homes.)

Secondly, had I to do it over again, I wouldn't uproot and move from one state into another during the months of March or April. For me, it involved flitting back and forth, waiting for settlement dates, switching insurance from state to state: car, home and hospitalization, bills for there and here to pay, setting up moving dates with movers, car carrier, auctioneer, refuse collectors, and Merrimaids. Then there were change of address cards to fill, disposing of nearly a library of books, emptying six double closets of clothing, etcetera, etcetera. Though I downsized, and previously breezed through my Camp Hill home, with tablet and pen in hand, noting what I wished to take, what should go to my children, which to leave for the auctioneer, the job was tiring and seemed unending. Also, time had to be weaseled in, to comply with my PA tax accountant's demands.

Thirdly, I've learned not to shorten time in choosing an auctioneer, and to choose wisely. If unable to be present during the auction, have someone there to represent you. Never entrust items you value the most to an auctioneer. I've lost a hefty sum of money, along with lovely items I've cherished over the years. Then it took three months for my auctioneer to contact me, and only after I phoned his wife. I looked forward to receiving a check, in the vicinity of at least twenty-five hundred dollars, to help fray the cost in purchasing new furniture. Instead, I received a check for four hundred sixty-eight dollars. In the two long, folded, yellow sheets of listed items sold, I found no mention of the appraised four hundred dollar, antique, white leather baby carriage, nor my white glass top wrought iron kitchen set. Near tears, I wrote voicing my grave disappointment, but never heard from him again.

Number four, I should have had a relative or friend oversee the packing. I was surprised to find several items had vanished along the way, and I obtained a few which weren't mine. The most import loss, consisted of a dark brown leather backing of a one thousand twenty-one page book on the Revolutionary War. Inscribed on the inside page it states, "1889, read 20 times by Isaac Barton, Williamsport, PA." It had been passed down to my husband, Herbert Oliver Focht, from his father Herbert Spencer, who received it from his father, Herbert Mason Focht. I'm still discovering trivial, yet meaningful items which have fallen somewhere along the wayside. I'm minus my favorite pan in which I cooked potatoes and macaroni. Items which showed up amidst my belongings, and I'm now heir to, included an electric iron, a bed pillow and two cake tins. All in all, this move proved to be quite pleasant, with the help of Bernie, from The Village Helpers.

What significant importance have I noticed the most, while living here? The Management looks after its people. We are warned not to pay in advance, and to be extra cautious when hiring outside workers. In conversing with other villagers, I've been told there are a lot of unscrupulous rednecks who come in and swoop down like vultures, on widows. I've since, sensed they have mentally corralled us into a category as older, richer, forgetful and not too wise. Yes, this is a completely new ballgame with different rules. To score, one must be canny, on their toes, with a mathematical mind and have patience.

Regarding car insurance, I expected rates would be decidedly cheaper in this golf cart community. Yet, when the agent and I discussed my policy over the phone, nothing was said until I finally blurted, "Listen to me! I'll be driving my golf cart in The Villages, and my car out of town for shopping, approximately three times a month." We went down the list and I said, "Cut this! Cut that!" We did, and cut the cost in two. At the time I wondered about those who might sit back, go with the flow, and pay the higher premium, and end finding themselves hurting financially.

Yes, I'm still keeping my eyes open. Last month, when I received my $99.01 monthly electric bill, the highest ever in my entire life in Pa, even when burning Christmas lights all during the month of December, a lady representative from the company arrived, and we went through my villa to check for a possible problem. I shared the fact that, after a six months vacancy, I had replaced a dust-filled filter.

"That's good," she told me. "Check the filter once a month, and be certain it's changed every three. Also, remember, during the hot months, for every degree your thermostat is set below 75 degrees, your bill will run six to eight percent higher. To cut cost even more, use cold water for the laundry, turn off ceiling fans if the rooms won't be occupied for four hours, and when you go away on vacation, set your thermostat at eighty nine. It's good to save wherever possible. We're seeing more and more people moving away. They lost a great deal of their retirement money when the stock market tumbled, and now with our economy slump, some chose to work part-time, but wages are low here." Before she left, I mentioned in order to keep an eye on my incoming and outgoing money flow, I wished to discontinue bank draft payments, and instead, receive a monthly bill. Through all of this, I'm happy to say, my bill this month was twenty dollars less.

Next, came a $43.48 monthly water and sewage bill, too high to suit me, and I called the water company and talked to Tony, the office manager. "There must be a leak somewhere, and this should have been noticed last month. I'm sending out Joe to see if he can find the problem. You'll be receiving a rebate. Probably enough to pay a plumber." Joe found the water meter running, even with the water turned off, and a new male adapter was needed for the automatic sprinkling system. Joe also felt a month's rebate would at least pay for half of the repair bill. The next day, the plumber came, and ended presenting me with one for $176. Twenty four dollars for parts, and the rest labor. Only now, no water came from the sprinkler. Another trip, and a bill this time for thirty cents for a part, and $124 for labor.

I called and asked the office manager, "Which bill am I to pay?"

"Both, which comes to three hundred dollars."

"That's ludicrous!" I explained to him that my friend, Glenn, had seen the plumber drop a screw, and spend quite a bit of time to find it amidst a pile of rocks in my garden. Next, the plumber sprayed a pipe and said he had to sit there until it dried. He had also noted on each bill, "1 trip. Job complete." I would pay $124.

The man, on the end of the line, backed down somewhat, and said, "I'll talk to the plumber, see what he says and then get back to you." I had heard, here in Florida, there are two speeds...slow...and stop. Sometimes I feel they have added Hawaii's slogan..."Hang Loose." People, including those in doctor's offices say they will call at a certain time during the day, you wait, and no call comes in. This happened to be the case with this particular office manager. However, instead of his call, he sent a new bill for $124.

Then the telephone company representative called, and suggested I get their monthly $46 package, and proudly rambled on, noting all the goodies I would receive. I asked "How did you derive at that price?"

She replied, "Because that's what everyone there is getting, and can afford."

"I don't think so. I live on a budget. So please remove call-waiting for me." Later, I also discontinued caller ID, then added it, for $8.50 a month. Everyone here thinks I'm a spunky lady, keeping adrift, and doing quite well by myself. I like to think I am, and I shall hold the good thought.

# Chapter 31
## Keeping Cool

Today, I'm excited. Dear man that he is, Jake, volunteered to take me to Ocala. We'll be picking up my friend, Janie. She is now settled there in a delightful, more moderately priced, rental, in a retirement community called On Top of the World, and it's close to relatives. On the way, we stopped at Piccadilly's in the Paddock Mall. Over a delightful lunch, I was surprised when Jake said, "Had I known Janie was coming back with us, and the two of you weren't just spending a day shopping together, she could have joined us here." I had been under the impression he knew of our plans.

"I'll make up for it later," I told him. So, before we left Piccadilly's, I stopped at the dessert counter and purchased some yummy looking apple dumplings, swimming in cinnamon syrup, for Janie's and my dinner tonight. That would surely please her. Indeed it did, and it topped off a thrown-together meal.

The following day, we phoned our former next-door neighbor, Suzanne Lee on Medira, down in the Hacienda Village. Perhaps, we former jolly three, could get together again. Two years ago, when Janie and I were minus a car, she had graciously taken us to all the wonderful and exciting spots this area has to offer. Yes, now she agreed, we would meet at Katie Belles, for lunch and the fashion show.

There, we had an enjoyable gabfest, rattled on a mile a minute, and caught each other up to date. In between, we admired the lovely fashions, as models wove in and out between tables, and answered questions pertaining to materials and price. Suzanne looked grand. Ah, yes, I reiterate: It's always fair weather when good friends get together.

Especially, later, when we left Katie Belles and motored here, to my villa. I, quite anxiously, flung open the door and awaited Suzanne's response. With eyes sparkling and astonishment mirrored on her face, she glanced around, smiled, and simply said, "Your villa is lovely," and that meant a lot to me.

"Better than our last year's rental, near you?"

"Positively! This is much roomier."

To me, it seemed unusually warm. Perhaps I was simply flushed, due to excitement of the three of us being together. Like old times. Then I heard Janie say, "I just switched on the ceiling fan."

According to the TV weather report, the temperature outside was 96. I checked the thermostat and discovered the air-conditioner wasn't working. Perhaps it needed a fuse? I excused myself, rushed out into the garage and checked the circuit breaker. Number 17-19 read, *Air conditioner*. I flipped on the switch, and flipped it back and forth. Nothing happened. In a panic, I ran next door, to neighbors, Jo and Lu, who returned with me. Lu discovered, while the condenser motor ran inside, no sound from the outside compressor could be heard. "Place an emergency call for help to Suters Air Conditioning," he advised. I did, and soon our neighbors and Suzanne departed.

Outside the sky darkened. While we waited for a return call, Janie and I scurried around in an attempt to cool off the place, and make it comfortable for the night. A fan from the garage was brought in for Janie's room. All windows were opened as well as three sliding glass doors. However, despite having screens on all doors and windows, as I now write, tiny gnats are breezing in and taking turns dancing upon my computer keys. The phone is ringing. Emery, a man from Suters.

"What temperature do you have the air-conditioner turned to?"

"Seventy five."

"What degree does it read now?"

"Eighty two."

"I couldn't come until much later. It's already ten-thirty and none of us like to work outside at night, because of mosquitoes and the West Nile disease."

"I don't blame you for that." I said.

"Would it be alright if we put you down for tomorrow morning?"

"That would be fine."

"Turn off your lights and the bugs won't disturb you."

I hung up and Janie said, "If we open the queen-size hide-a-bed, you can sleep there, directly beneath the living-room ceiling fan, and keep somewhat cool. I'll help open it."

We struggled; however, the mattress wouldn't budge and the front end of the couch kept lifting off the floor. "Janie, I think this band of ribbon at the bottom is holding it fast. Do you think we should remove it?"

"We can try."

I hurried to the kitchen and returned with a serrated paring knife, and while my stomach nervously churned, I began to saw away. "There's staples holding it. In fact, not just on the bottom, but on the edges of the inside. There! Two came loose."

"I hope we're doing the right thing," Janie fretted. "And not ruining your new hide-a-bed."

"Me, too. I hope it won't be. . .there, the underside is unfastened. See if you can pull it up over there on the inside of the metal frame."

"Got it," she said. "Whew! That was some job!"

"Tell me about it." I took a deep breath. "NOW! Let's see what happens." We both pulled up and out, and presto! "Oh, my! It's beautiful! The mattress is pretty, and look, Janie. What's this metal bar up here?"

"You can actually elevate the head."

"Great! I won't need my electric bed. I don't know if I want to keep the sliding doors open, tonight. The one screen won't lock. Supposing someone comes in and...?"

"Try him out, and if he's good, send him to me!"

We giggle. "Can I quote you on this, Janie?"

"Sure," she laughs. "I'm going to bed."

"Me, too, in a little bit."

Now, a soft breeze caresses my back, and it's coming in the

unlocked screen. Shall I leave it open? Or just the one in the dining room, and feel perfectly safe? Perhaps the overhead fan will grant enough coolness? Let's hope so. On this happy note, I close with, "Goodnight, world."

True to Emery's word, come morning, I flung open the door and found a repairman, named Mike, standing there. "I have been here before," he said.

"No, you haven't."

"Yes, I have. I remember the fence around the air conditioner."

"I've never seen you before. I moved in here, permanently, four and a half months ago, on April the first."

"Well, I remember being here and telling the man the air-conditioner wasn't in good shape. He would probably need a new one within a year." I wondered if my realtor had been aware of this.

After Mike volunteered, and succeeded in helping Janie and I fold up the heavy hide-a-bed, getting that out of our way, he left for the garage to check the air conditioning panel. There, he worked in the sweltering hot 110 degrees. Two hours later, dripping with perspiration, he appeared in the kitchen and wiped his forehead with a grey rag. The expression on his face worried me, and rightly so.

"I have bad news. I can't get a response from the compressor."

"Can it be fixed?"

"Possibly, for five hundred dollars. Then maybe not, and you'll end having to call me back here again." He told me a new unit would cost $1,529. This is the route he would go, if it were up to him. While he talked to Janie, on the sly, I went into another room, and called a competitor.

"Yes, Suters is an excellent company, run by honest people. The Lennox unit is one of the best, and the price quoted is quite reasonable." The lady continued, "We would have loved to have been able to help you, but all of our men are tied up until next week, and with this heat, you can't wait that long. You did right by calling Suters." Somewhat relieved, I still wasn't sure which way to turn. The Villages recommends comparison shopping with three estimates, but in this case, neither the heat, nor time would allow. In the end, I chose to get the new canister, and was informed the men would come later in the afternoon. Two, did, but because of rain, which progressed into crashing thunder and swirling lightning, the job had to be postponed still another day. I was unaware Florida was considered the lightning capital of the world. It can strike from nine miles away.

Janie suggested, "Let's go to town, take in 'Signs' at the local theater, and afterwards, dine at Katie Belles, then stop at the Square and see what's going on there." A wonderful idea! A wonderful night. In the Square, I found Charlie from The Singles' Club, and as we danced, I laid the burdens upon his shoulders. He, too, suggested three estimates, especially when it came to air-conditioners. I was satisfied I had the time to check out the Lenox and learned it was a fine air-conditioning unit, and Suters who sold them was an excellent firm.

Our second morning, Janie's door was still closed when I awakened, dressed, and unsuccessfully attempted to close my cumbersome hide-a-bed. She suddenly appeared, stretched, and said,"I slept well. Did you?"

"So, so, but my hair is damp, again. But just think! Tonight will be much better."

All morning long, we were beside ourselves, anxiously keeping out of the way, and watching men, a total of five, breeze in and out of my sliding-glass dining room door. It led to my courtyard, where the old compressor was being removed, and the new would be installed. All morning long, I noticed my pretty sea-mist green carpeting becoming dirtier. By mid-afternoon, installation was complete. The men left, and Janie and I plopped ourselves down on couches in the living room, and breathed a sigh of relief. Janie said, "Regardless of how lovely it is here in sunny Florida, with this tropical climate, one absolutely and positively cannot live without air-conditioning." Of course, I agreed.

When she retired for the night, I decided, since her brother and wife would be arriving the next day to take her home, that sad, messy looking carpet had to be cleaned. Surprisingly, in a matter of minutes, I was finished. Sleepy-eyed, I went out into the garage to put the can of Resolve Rug Cleaner away. Only then, I discovered ...I had cleaned my carpeting with ...Hornet Spray. Come dawn, anxious to find the outcome of my midnight toil, I hurried out to discover the rug had never appeared so fresh.

Through all of this, I've come to a firm conclusion, when purchasing a home, at least a year's warranty should cover all appliances, especially air-conditioners. I had included a clause to that effect in the sale of my Pennsylvania property.

# Chapter 32
## Carl's Ideas

Alone again, and now, this morning while at the computer, my phone has jangled eight times. Most irksome! Because there's yet to be a phone line installed in my lanai where my desk is located, each time I must run out into the living-room to check Caller ID. If the screen shows 'Unavailable' since I am here in a new area, I am now back to avoiding answering calls, as I'm aware they're tele-marketers attempting to sell something. Seven of the calls proved to be just that.

I chose to ignore the eighth, until curiosity struck. The name didn't mentally register. However, the voice did, when I picked up the phone and heard "How're ya' doin', girl? I just called to see how you was."

Carl, the Kentucky farm boy who loaned me a warm jacket and sweatshirt last January was on the line. He returned from Indiana where he had gone three months ago to sell his garage business, and now here he was again, bringing me, not more oranges for myself and my four children, as he brought last year, but a lift to my day which had me smiling. We chatted briefly, and I growled about all of the telemarketing calls which disrupted my writer's chain of thought while at the computer.

"Yes, they're annoying. I'll tell you what I do. When such calls come in and a woman says, 'Good morning, and how are you today, sir?', I tell her, 'I'm sitting here, horny, without someone to service.'"

I gasped. "You don't!"

"Yes, I do, and she hurriedly hangs up."

"Now, I know you are indeed a rascal. So tell me what do you do when a man's on the line?"

"I just say, 'I'm not altogether here', and hang up."

While living in The Villages, I now believe I have seen, heard, and shared it all. Except I haven't mentioned our new, sixty bed hospital. Nice! I even tried it and came out smiling when enzyme reports showed my fluttering and skipping heart was fine, that my problem was an acid reflux attack. In all probability due to all of the shortcomings and unexpected worries. I couldn't rightfully tell.

Despite all the ups and downs, the pros and cons, I'm happy to be alive, and where I've longed to be since first discovering this retirement community and all it has to offer. Everywhere I look, I'm still amazed at its beauty: From the grass which remains richly green all year long, the beautifully landscaped grounds, with their lovely flowers, water falls, lakes and palms, all well-cared for. Others feel as I do. Especially a lovely, petite, senior lady, whom I met when I happened to be shopping in Publics the other day and found her outside on the weighing scales.

"My guess? One hundred twelve," I said.

Eyes sparkled and she smiled. "You're right. That's amazing."

What struck me as truly amazing? We chatted a bit, until her husband, Bill, motioned for her from the parking lot. The lovely lady was none other than the mother of Susan Lucci, the TV star of All My Children. She agreed, this is the closest place to Heaven without being there.

Then she told me, "We live in West Palm Beach, but spend two weeks out of the year here in The Villages. It's a beautiful place and we love it."

What more could I say, except, "I do, too!"

# Chapter 33
# The Famous Poets' Society Convention

This lazy, August morning, as I wiped off the chairs in my courtyard, I listened to a happy bird sing quite noisily in Daphine's tall orange tree, on the other-side of my stucco wall. Though invisible, I attempted to duplicate his sweet melody, in hopes he would respond like the birds in my back yard in Pennsylvania. I ended giggling, as his notes were too high. Then it dawned. This little bird and I were alike. We both were delighted to be alive and live in such a beautiful place.

Later that evening, still in a frivolous mood, though now indoors and perusing *The Daily Sun*, I was amazed to see there was something going on, something to do, somewhere to go, and one needn't be bored in a retirement community, not unless they choose to be. Listed among the upcoming Labor Day weekend activities was The 2002 Famous Poets Society convention in Orlando, Florida. Orlando? Nearly in my back yard.

Poetry? Not my forte. My greatest joy is writing. Yet, I remembered fourteen years ago, in Professor Wallace's English Comp 102 class, at Harrisburg Area Community College, he insisted we spend a half semester writing poetry, and I did. Purposely, most of mine were humorous, and kept the class in stitches. Students claimed this grandmother wasn't boring, but fun, and begged me to tag along with them, and take other courses.

Now I wondered, *could this kid over fifty become a member of the famous poet society, attend their 2002 Poets Convention, and possibly win some of their $50,000 in prizes?* I hungrily yearned for some of that green stuff, and I don't mean broccoli, lettuce, and spinach. I mean honest-to-goodness money. Even a little would be nice, to refurbish my bank account after dishing out two thousand dollars in one week for that air-conditioning unit and a male-adapter for the automatic sprinkling system.

Yes, I told myself, added money at this time of the month would certainly come in handy. I would check into the convention.

Since we, as seniors, have been warned of frauds which usurp us of our retirement money, I dialed the hotel's listed 800 number to check and see if the newspaper write-up was what it claimed to be. A gentleman answered. He would transfer me to their Orlando number.

"Yes, the poet's convention will be held here on Labor day weekend. And, yes, the Mears Shuttle Bus runs daily from the airport to the hotel."

I hung up, and with pen in hand, I tried to recall a free style poem which, years ago, won an honorary award in a international contest. It had been inspired during a cross-country trip with my Parisian schoolteacher friend, Christine Barreau. She, quite excitedly, had called from Paris, and said, "I just purchased a book of Greyhound Bus tickets, and will be flying from Paris, into Phoenix, Arizona, to attend an Astrological Seminar. Please come with me and be my traveling companion." That little minx continued, with, "You can fly to Phoenix, attend the Seminar's cocktail party. They already know you're coming, and told me you're invited." Breathlessly, she continued. "We will fly from Phoenix to Reno, and begin our bus tour from there. Once we reach Long Beach California, we will rest a few days, then ferry over to Catalina Island, a popular place where celebrities are known to frequent, and there, we will spend a splendid day on the beach. Think of the fun we will be having." At the time, we hadn't seen each other for three years. Not since my husband's death, when I flew away to Paris and she turned her apartment over to me for five weeks.

Now, with pen in hand, I recalled that last trip with her, and the long, tedious twenty-one hours on our way home to Harrisburg, as the bus lumbered across desert, down highways, through small towns, down country roads, and the words of "Travelogue" flowed on paper:

> The Greyhound bus caterpillar crawled to the stop light.
> Seen below, from its window-pane eyes were pedestrians.
> Dressed in blue jeans, long skirts, ponchos and such,
> Only one stood out amidst that cross-walk din.
> She wore a SMILE, and granted joy to the weary traveler.

I typed the poem, mailed it, then sat back and patiently awaited a response. It came on a Monday. The executive board of The Famous Poet Society enjoyed my poem, and entered it in their contest.

Imaginary dollar signs nearly blurred my vision as I dialed the hotel's number and made reservations for a three day stay. Still, mentally, I fidgeted. I dislike traveling alone in unfamiliar places, as I have an uncanny knack for becoming lost. Even here, it took nearly three weeks to learn my way out of my village. Yet, in a sense, I'm improving. No longer do I panic. Now, I'll simply take a deep breath, tell myself 'I can do this', and surprisingly, I work my way out of difficult situations.

So, I picked up the phone, and without too much fuss, reservations were made at the Spanish Springs Shuttle Bus Station, for both trips to the Orlando Airport and back home here in The Villages.

When the final day arrived to leave, my friend, "Kentucky farm-boy", Carl, would be here to escort me to the bus station in twenty minutes. Only terrible stomach cramps had me doubling over. Nerves? Three trips to the bathroom. I was scheduled to check in a day early, to prevent confusion of any sort. Now, I would call and cancel one night's lodging.

"No, Ma'am!" I was told. "In order to cancel, a seventy-eight hour notice is necessary."

So, now what? Two Tums might settle my stomach? I called Carl, no answer. I chewed a Gaviston, downed a glass of water, and felt somewhat better. My door bell rang. In came Carl, all smiles.

"Ready?" he asked. His thoughts? "Maybe you'll feel better once you're on the road." So, now, I scribble this, as our bus smoothly laps up the highway, heading for Orlando's airport.

Bless the driver's heart. He just said, "If any of you find it necessary to stop along the way, let me know. Time will allow two stops."

I settled back into my seat, and became acquainted with the two other ladies. One, directly across from me, a directress at Savannah, has grandparents who live in my development. The bus driver jokes, "Do you know what they call a senior citizen's retirement village?"

"Nooo," we chorus.

A chuckle, then, "It's a place where the woman can't get pregnant, and the men look like they are."

Still another from Charlie. "Two ladies in a nursing home were talking, and one asked, "Hey, Doris, what are you going to do today?"

"I'm going to take my clothes off, strip naked, and run through the recreation room."

At her word, she does, and as she flashes by, two men stand there and one asks, "Did you see that?" The other said, "No, I didn't have my glasses on. But whatever it was, it sure needed a lot of ironing." Yes, our trip to the airport was pleasant. Likewise, to the Wyndham Palace Resort Hotel in the Mears Shuttle bus.

Originally, I requested a room close to the pool. However, I discovered it was located out in the open, and due to a lightning scare, changed my mind and opted for room 1528. Also, I hadn't been thorough when reading all the convention information, and was gravely disappointed to learn food would be provided only for our Sunday night banquet. After settling in my room, I studied the hotel's map, and took off for the Watercress Café. There, I purchased a thick sandwich of turkey, ham and lettuce for $6.95, and a small strawberry smoothie for $2.50.

The café appeared sparsely occupied. Yet, as I carried my tray and was about to pass a gentleman seated alone, he looked up, and smiled. "You may sit with me, if you like." How nice. It broke the ice, and I sighed, not feeling so utterly alone in a strange place. It proved a delightful evening. His last name was Valentine, a Mormon with eleven children, 34 grandchildren and four great-grandchildren. They lived on a one hundred acre farm and he raised cattle, and in cross breeding, bred his own chain. I found him interesting and ran into him on our first day, Saturday, August 31, on my way to our champagne reception held in Hampton Court.

Early afternoon, we all gathered again, and were introduced to our teachers: Larry Maraviglia, Annette Ackerman, Chris Kusznir and Joyce Meadows. At 2:30, Peter Massey presented the fantastic Verses of Ogdon Nash. A marvelous actor with a well enunciated voice, he held us all spellbound.

Day two, September 1, our scheduled workshops began.

My first was conducted by lovely Joyce Meadows, an actress with a self-assured air. She welcomed us, laughed, and shared thoughts regarding conventions. "It seems nobody ever takes into consideration that we are people who must eat, sleep and…visit bathrooms."

Never had I been totally smitten when it came to Shakespeare, yet I found her rendition of his English Sonnet amazingly and profoundly interesting, as I sat on the edge of my seat for forty minutes, totally engrossed. She was magnificent, to say the least.

All workshop teachers were helpful in the art of acting poetry naturally, polishing poems and fulfilling one's dreams in winning big. Would I win?

While in classes and on my way there, I was fortunate to meet some spectacular and noteworthy poets. One was publisher and editor, Joyce Hailicka, from Oregon, nearly young enough to be my daughter, but we had a lot in common and fancied ourselves as sisters. She kept telling me,"You look like a movie star." Now if that doesn't build confidence. We formed our own mutual admiration society, because in my eyes she was a near copy of Grace Kelly, when it came to serene beauty, composure, and grace.

In her book ,*Voice of The Rogue*, which she had so graciously given to me, she touches one's soul with pure passionate beauty of the wild and majestic Rogue River, in her little logging town of Butte Falls, Oregon. With a flip of a each page, and a colorful, scenic view of her beloved river, one can hear its stirring and powerful voice speak to us, as though from another place in time.

She also introduced me to a friend named Nancy and I, in turn, introduced them to Sid, a nice gentleman who attended several of my classes, and ended saving a place for us in the crowded banquet room. He had waited inside the door and said I looked fantastic when I entered in my black, slinky Oleg Cassini evening gown, bought on sale in a little PA shop. Yes, later we four enjoyed snapping pictures, and laughing. The young claimed it was like being in high school again. Not for me. Years ago, Dad warned me, "Get on the honor roll or I'll take you out of school and put you to work."

The next day, after the completion of classes, came the anticipated Mary Rudge's presentation of Poetry and Peace in the World. All eight hundred of us had eagerly strived to write a poem on peace, and as we lined up outside the Convention Room, we were handed a balloon, red, white or blue, on which to tie our poems. I chose red, and told our little group, "So I can keep an eye on it." From the Great Hall, in an unorganized fashion, we eased ourselves through the mob heading for the outdoors. Here, beneath sunny Florida skies, we lined up four abreast, began our Famous Poets Parade and Poets for Peace Balloonathon, and marched to the music of our Famous Dixieland Band, led by Mickey Mouse, our Grand Marshal. It proved great fun.

When we released our balloons, a moment of revered silence seemed to overtake the crowd. Then a noisy cheer was ushered up, as we stood in awe and watched the sky become sprinkled in red white and blue. I believe I was a tad noisy, as I pointed and yelled, "Look! That red one at the top is mine." My poem was titled 'Up, Up, and Away' and away it went until it disappeared from view.

Then, on my left, out of the corner of my eye, I noticed a white balloon slowly bobbing up and down, between cars in the parking lot. Saying nothing, I took off on a merry run. A poem had been written on a sheet of paper, too heavy to allow it to fly into the air. I hurriedly tore off the sides, the bottom, not touching the printed prayer, and was about to release it when beside me, a mother stood, with her little daughter's hand clenched in hers.

We spoke briefly. I learned the little girl was five years old, and when I asked, "Is this balloon yours?" she solemnly gave her head a positive shake.

"Now, that it's lighter, let's see what happens, shall we?" Again, she nodded, lips turned upward in a faint smile. I held the balloon in front of me, and the string slowly slipped through my fingers. We watched the balloon ascend, catch up and mingle with those remaining. A spectacular sight, but not as thrilling as the joy which danced in the youngster's eyes.

Following the parade, we returned inside to the Great Hall, the convention room, where we listened to two celebrity actors present *Poems That Touch Home.*

Then came the presentation of winning poems. It reminded me of Academy Awards Night on TV with all the fanfare, and screen stars seen coming up out of the audience and appearing in front of a large movie screen.

No, I was not one of the twenty to receive a whopping big cash prize during this Eighth Annual $50,000 Poetry Contest. I had been slightly nervous during my rendition in class, and could tell it showed. Yet, I had tried.

Later, when all was said and done, with the convention over, I pulled my luggage outside, and headed for the parked Mears shuttle bus straight ahead; possibly the one to take me to the airport? A slightly built man, wearing a smile, hurried to catch up to me. I had noticed him in the one class of about sixty-five, as he stood out with his white cotton hat perched upon his silver hair. In a flurry he told me, "Oh! I'm happy I found you. I wrote a poem about you."

Puzzled, with brows raised I asked, "You did? Can you recite it?"

"Yes. 'There goes the lovely lady in the lime green hat. I wonder where she got that.'"

"That's nice." I couldn't help grinning. "Now I think that could be my bus over there." I pointed and took off.

The driver of that bus said mine would be arriving in five minutes. I turned in surprise to see a solemn-faced Sid with suitcase in hand, hurrying towards me. I had left him in the convention room when he had been cornered by four younger ladies.

"Hello, I was so afraid I wouldn't see you to say goodbye." A handsome, single man, recently divorced, 56, he was too young for me. Yet, had I been Elizabeth Taylor, I would have taken the chance. Unlike her construction man, who needed polishing, Sid was the epitome of perfection. His head of dark brown hair was still beautiful, wavy in back and just a distinguished touch of gray at the temples. We discovered we would be traveling to the airport on the same bus, and decided to sit on the concrete curb, off from the others, where we chatted while waiting.

I asked him, "Did you see the man with the white hat talking to me?"

He had and was about to ask what that was all about when the bus arrived, and so did the poet. Now, with tablet in hand.

"I remembered the poem. I'll read it to you. 'There goes the lovely lady in a lime green hat, I wonder where she got that, and would she like to stop and chat? About this or that?'"

I couldn't hold back a grin. A professor from Philadelphia, Pennsylvania, he hurriedly scribbled his e-mail address and told me to write. All in all, I arrived home safely and soundly, not with a cash prize in my purse, but with a *Shakespeare Trophy of Excellence* as a famous poet of 2002, and also an engraved medallion with my name inscribed as 2002 *Poet of the Year, from the Famous Poets Society.*

In looking back, I enjoyed the convention, and found it quite titillating to have been among the eight hundred with a head start in sending prayers for peace skyward. Not only that, meaningful friendships had been established with kind, sensitive people. People who can, so freely, bare their souls in poetry.

Now as I write in a pensive mood, it gets me to wondering. Do birds quote their own poetry when they fill the Heavens with their sweet songs?

# Chapter 34
# I Will Not Cry

Admittedly, it's strange how once in awhile, life seems so beautiful one moment, then takes a sudden twist in the road, and you're left puzzled, floundering near tears.

At our last sorority meeting, during our social hour, I felt it unusual and surprising to see one member, and the hostess depart from the group and leave for the lanai. They were gone for at least fifteen minutes. Something was going on. What? I had no idea.

I returned home, called and asked the hostess, "What was that all about?"

"She wants to break away and start a chapter which meets during the day."

"That would be great. Count me in. I get lost when driving at night." I chuckled, and added, "Sometimes, even in the daylight."

"Me, too. She thinks we should hold membership to around eight, and no more than ten, because some of the villas won't accommodate many more. Marti Rowland wants to join, and with her, you, me, and a few others she had mentioned, we'll need only three more."

"What does the present chapter's president and the others think about this?"

"She hasn't told them yet. By the way, I'm a Snowbird, and will soon be leaving for my home up North. Call and tell her you'll join, and while I'm gone, look around and see if you can help drum up more members."

Three times, I called the supposed president of this new group. Three times I left a message saying I wished to be included. I also sent an e-mail telling her this.

Then I flew home to visit my children for fifteen days. While there, I became all wrapped up visiting my offspring and theirs, along with wonderful friends whom I had left behind when I moved so far away.

Upon my return to The Villages, I finally got through. Quite excited about not having to drive at night, I told her, "I'm back in town. Is there a place for me in the new daytime sorority you're forming?"

"We have our quota, and there's no room for you."

A cold chill swept through me. Asked if friends Joanne and Marti were included as members, she said, "Yes, they both signed up before going home."

Thoughts were, here I am, after five months in a relatively new environment, with no one to pal around with. No one to go shopping with or out for lunch. I thought of friend, Joanne, still in her home up North, and called her and bemoaned this situation.

"I won't become a member if you're not welcomed. And I don't think Marti will, either."

"I was told you and Marti are members, as you both signed up before leaving."

"I didn't sign anything." Joanne stated.

Had Marti, a special and dear lady, who all summer long, kept me posted via postcards regarding her exciting travels? I would call to welcome her home.

"Yes, we had a marvelous time motoring across country."

I spoke of the new chapter, and she said, "Since I'm home, I've already been invited to a picnic at our new president's home."

This hurt, but I told her "That's nice. Joanne told me she wouldn't join unless you and I did. It's too late for me. I hadn't signed my name before leaving."

"I didn't either, but I was asked to join. What are you doing now?"

"Nothing, I've been staying close to home because the doctor's nurse gave me medicine to help curb inflammation in my knee and I've been fighting the diarrhea for ten days. I think I'm winning."

"My dance class is having a get-together in Leesburg and I'm meeting two of my friends in front of the Catholic church at five-forty-five. Why don't you come along? It will be fun. What time is it, now?"

"Five-twenty. I'll try to make it. If not there by six, leave without me."

I scurried around like a mad-hatter. Picked out a long turquoise jumper dress with a white short sleeve top, purchased last year in Hawaii. Simple, with dancing figures on the bottom, just looking at them, lifted my spirit. Next, wiped off edges of fingernails to repaint, finished, fluffed hair with a tease-lift, grabbed a purse, and was out the door at ten of six. Twelve minutes later, I pulled into the parking lot. The lined up cars were minus drivers and passengers. My watch showed I was two minutes late. Had Marti and the girls been there and left? Or hadn't they arrived? I would wait fifteen minutes.

The rains spit tears on my windshield, and for a fleeting moment I felt desolately lost; lonely without a soul to care, yet, I told myself, "I will not cry!"

A car with an elderly couple pulled in front of the church, and now, there they were, carrying a cooler. No doubt a picnic was going on inside? I wished I could go in, anywhere, just to be with someone.

At twenty after six, I slowly ebbed my car out onto the highway. My thoughts were, *I'm all dressed-up to go out on the town, so why not breeze down and see what's going on at Katie Belles?* Yes, I would do that.

There, a cute mustachioed gent with the bluest eyes, an attendant at the door, checked ID's. "I left mine home, when I changed purses. I have my voting card, and drivers license. Will either do?"

"Your driver's license will be fine." So I was free to march inside. Lighting was subdued. A band on stage struck up a jivey tune for the Country Western Line Dancers, approximately sixty, with faces depicting concentration while performing what appeared to me, intricate and confusing steps. I stood at the railing and watched awhile. At the far end of the floor, on the other-side of a roped-off section, a lone couple glided across the dance floor. Not wishing to appear conspicuous, I turned and looked to the left, contemplating what to do next.

Two ladies were seated at a high table. "Good evening," I said.

"Good evening," both chorused. "You may come join us at our table, if you wish."

My sober-side smiled, and thoughts were this was bound to happen in a nice place like this. We enjoyed becoming acquainted.

Sheryl lived in The Villages. She and sister, Ann, were both from Alabama, and Ann was here visiting for two weeks. They ordered margaritas and I, a Piña Colada. Mine was yummiest, topped with mounds of that diet stuff, called whipped cream, a red stirrer, a fan-shaped sliver of orange and a cherry.

We were all caught up to date, family-wise, when I voiced wishes of dancing, just once, and I would be happy.

"At our age, it's a woman's world, and permissible to ask a gentleman," Sheryl said. Ann, agreed.

"Yes, I've been told that before." I glanced to the left. Three tables in a row. At the first, a man with a gray mustache sat alone. Two men at the next, and a couple at the third.

"Ask the man with the white hair and mustache," both chorused.

"Alright! I can do that." So off I went! As I approached his table, my heart thumped a bit, telling me I wasn't as confidant as I appeared. No, that man didn't know how to dance. The other two didn't feel like dancing. "That's okay." I smiled, and flitted on up to the bar.

"No," said a gentleman seated there. "I'm married. My wife is out there line dancing and she would kill me if she caught me with you."

One lone man, younger, at the end of the bar, with his head bowed over a drink, refused. But with a little coaxing, agreed, saying, "I'm not a good dancer."

"That's okay. I'll teach you to jitter-bug." Yet, it wasn't until the last dance, when I decided to follow his steps. He was doing the Western swing, and I, the Eastern. Still it proved fun, getting these bones agroovin'. The dance finished, and the gent whose wife would have killed him had he danced with me returned to his drink and gently touched my shoulder. He introduced me to his lovely wife just as Sheryl came up to me and said she and Ann were about to leave.

I, too, decided to walk across the street to the Square and see what went on at the dance over there. The band in the gazebo played a peppy tune and I noted some of the Snowbirds had returned early. Quite a few were gliding across the concrete dancing area. I looked over the people seated in chairs on the outside perimeter. There were no single men, none that I could see. I walked by, on out to the sidewalk, and was about to pass the waterfall, ahead, when I spied a middle-aged gent, in sneakers, shorts and a white and blue printed shirt. Alone and nice-looking. I slowed, pretending to admire the flowing waters. "A lovely night." I said, surprising myself.

"That it is." he smiled.

"I'm about to leave for home, but hoped to find someone to dance with."

"I'm available."

"You are?" His finger was minus a ring. "Are you married?"

"Yes. But my wife won't mind. We just returned home from vacation and she shooed me out the door, telling me to come down to the square and have fun while she finishes unpacking."

"I don't date married man, and never intend to."

"That's okay. We'll just dance." It was truly a delightful night. Paul proved not only light on his feet, but several times, a classic clown with his silly and hilarious feet, knee and hip movements, and I, in front of him, laughed and moved my feet back and forth. All the while, those seated watched and clapped their hands in time to the music and his dance steps.

The night ended. He escorted me to my car, parked in front of Katie Belles. There, we shook hands, kissed cheeks and parted. That was that! and I came home, not the lonely soul, but content; feeling complete. And as I always do, before closing my eyes and escaping into sweet slumber, I thanked God for yet another day, which turned out to be lovely.

# Chapter 35
## Safe From the Storms

Monday, another daytime sorority group of sisters invited me to their luncheon at the StoneCrest Country Club. A super meal, and the ladies were pleasant and nice. Three attend the Lutheran Church group which meets at the Savannah Center. I, too, am Lutheran, but feel their meeting place is too far away for me to attempt to arrive on time. One married sister, Judy, said, "We have a nice group of people. When our new church is completed, attend. You're bound to meet a nice man there." Yet, I wonder.

Surprise! Surprise! Tonight, the president of the newly formed sorority, whose door on membership was closed, called and told me she voted to include me as a member. Nice! The next meeting is next Wednesday. I told her, "I'll be present."

I hung up and, due to a bruised ego, a shadow of sadness still lingered, but I told myself I could climb over that. I did! Before the evening ended, my phone jangled on two more occasions. Marti Rowland, and another member, Karen Schultz, both called to tell me the good news. I was now their sorority sister.

**A Happy Group of Zi Zi Mu Beta Sigma Phi Sorority Sisters**

Tuesday proved somewhat stormy. I shot eight hours shopping and helping Joan, a rather new widow, pick out a TV for her kitchen. I noticed hereafter, I'll have to speak up around her. When I helped hook up the TV, I kept pleading, "Will you please move your car, so I can get my golf cart out? It's lightning. A storm is brewing. I must leave." She kept fiddling with the remote control, trying to insert batteries. I became more antsy as I looked out her back door. Only a fringe of gray daylight appeared beneath ominous black clouds which spanned the entire sky. "It's going to rain, SOON," I exclaimed, a bit louder this time.

"What's a little water?" she asked, still fussing with the remote. I reminded her I had placed bags of my purchases, including packages of printer paper in my golf cart and they would become wet. Finally, she backed her car out of the drive and I was on my way.

The winds whipped up in a fury. My golf cart swayed at times. Steering became difficult. The sky was totally black. Three blocks from my home it began to rain.

I prayed, "Please, God? Hold off the storm just a bit longer?" I pulled into my garage, and on the other side of the now closed door, all Heaven broke loose with heavy winds and pelting rain. I leaned my head on the steering wheel, gleefully laughed, and said, "Thanks, God! We made it."

# Chapter 36
# Gordon, the Cute, Lovable Rascal

Thursday, I took off in my golf cart for the mail station five blocks away. There, I scanned the mail received, threw the majority of magazines in the junk bin, and stepped off the curb. As I backed out, I noticed a man turn around in his nearby cart. "Nice afternoon," he said.

"Yes, it is."

He studied me a bit. "Do you live here?"

"Yes. Do you and your wife like it here in The Villages?"

"Cancer took her away from me, nine years ago."

"I'm sorry. I lost my man fourteen."

"I'm sorry."

"Thank you. My husband and I did spend thirty-eight beautiful years together."

"That's great. My wife and I had forty-eight."

He asked where I lived and I told him. We exchanged names, and I learned he lived only three blocks from me, on the corner. "You'll pass my home on the way to yours. Stop by on your way home."

My brows furrowed. Truly, he had a nice shock of white

hair...blue, blue eyes, and a rather come-hither smile. I wanted to meet more men, but had never seen nor met him before. "Oh? I don't know," I finally said.

"I'll show you my villa." The way he looked at me, blue eyes dancing, got me to wondering. I can't say he drank in my every curve. They're more difficult to find at this age. Nevertheless, I could nearly read his mind.

His villa was simply furnished. A bachelor's pad. One came directly into his kitchen and there, before us stood an oval table dressed in green plaid. Evidence of a hurried departure was in full view. Papers scattered hither and yon, and directly to the right, were two framed pictures. "Yes, one is my wife." He picked it up, handed it to me, then replaced it. I agreed, she was a pretty woman.

I picked up the other. "Your girlfriend?"

"Yes."

"Going steady?"

"Almost. Since December."

"Oh!" I got tongue-tied, then added, "That's nice."

He passed the bedrooms, and walked straight ahead to his lanai. There, he lifted the lid to his hot tub. "I use this every day. Want to come in with me?"

Whoa! Just as suspected. I grinned, and imagined, with me by his side, his temperature would soar far above the 95 degree point.

He touched my shoulder. Lightly, not in an urgent way, and simply said in a gentler tone, "Come in with me."

I chuckled, and startled myself with "No way, José", and invited him, instead, to join me for a swim in the family pool located on the other side of the mail station. He reneged. "Well," I said. "I must leave." Then to appear more sophisticated, asked, "Would you like a tour of my villa?"

"That would be nice. I'll get out my golf cart."

"No! Come with me, on mine." Silly thoughts were he may take off with me. Why? I hadn't the vaguest.

He liked my villa. "It's nicely decorated." We reached the lanai. "It's enclosed. That's great. Was that attractive mural on the wall when you moved in?"

"No. It's called, 'The Japanese garden'. I saw it while in Waikiki, and ordered it from a Sherwin Williams paint and paper store here."

I reached beyond him, slid open the double glass sliding door, and stepped out into my courtyard.

"Enchanting. Not like mine. Here, you have privacy. One can actually walk around in their birthday suit, if they wanted. It's really nice."

"Thank you." I didn't share the fact that if I breakfast out there, at times I walk around in my nightie. Instead, I reached both arms to the sky and told him, "Here, it's mine. The sky, the clouds, the sun, the moon, the stars…everything. I sensed my husband would want me to have this villa, that's why I bought it."

"Have you seen the courtyard of the villa at the other end of my street? It's the largest and prettiest I've ever seen. Come, I'll show you!"

He sat beside me in my cart, and it felt good, taking a man for a ride for the very first time. I zoomed down the street, as if more than in full control. "Go right at the cul-de-sac. Now, go out of the neighborhood. Now, pull over there to the right and stop. You'll get to see the back of their house."

"How?"

"You've got to climb that wooden fence in front of us."

"You're kidding?"

I was well covered in culottes, down to my knees, so I climbed out of the cart, and with him beside me, walked over and anchored my foot on the first rung.

"Now, another! Another! Another one to the top," he was saying.

Over my shoulder, I asked, "To the very top? It seems so far up. Do I have to?"

"Yes. I'll hold onto you. His hands grasped hard on my ankles.

"Oh, my! Gordon!" I breathlessly gasped. "Truly it's the loveliest. Over top of all the purple flowering bushes, I can see their Olympic-sized pool. I'm coming down! Hold on! Don't let me fall!"

As I slid down, his hands slid up to my knees. I laughed. "Now, I see why you had me climb so high." To this he gave an impish grin.

Back at my place, when I pulled into the garage, I said, "I've been told I should periodically put water in my golf cart. I haven't had time to do it, yet."

"Yes. While I'm here, let me take a look."

I couldn't remember how to lift the green covered seat. My cart differed from his. Then, beneath the cap where I plug in the electricity, I found the lever.

"You are a lucky young lady," he told me. "Beneath all of these sixteen white caps I've unscrewed, there's barely any water. I can see the bottom. It's a good thing you happened to ask about it. You could have burned up your motor."

Before we left for his villa, I gathered up mail from the table in the foyer. I would drop him off and continue on to the mail station. When we reached his home, he discovered a stamp was missing on one of my envelopes. "I'll get one for you," he said, and took off on a run, and soon returned with the envelope stamped. "That was nice, I owe you," I told him. "Hop in and you can go to the station with me." He didn't renege on this and later, while there, I could feel his burning eyes, keenly watching, as I hurried around the corner to slip the mail in the slot. Thoughts were, walk tall, don't let your knees knock like some I've seen. I felt foolishly happy, actually liking this man.

I whisked him back to his villa, and returned to mine for an afternoon nap. An hour later I awakened to the jangling doorbell. Hurriedly, I slipped into a black and white floral printed, floor length pants dress, buttoning it up the front as I made it to the door. I opened it to see Gordon standing there with a silly grin on his face.

"You look nice. Is that what you sleep in?"

"No." I flicked his hand away from the top button.

"You didn't give me your phone number."

I rattled it off, he scribbled it down and thanked me.

"But since you have a girl, I'm not interested."

"Don't you like me?"

"Yes, but I don't want someone else's man. I live by the Golden Rule. You know! Do unto others as you would have them do unto you?"

"Okay. Goodbye." He turned away and the sound of his footsteps seemed to grate on the concrete as he hurried down the driveway.

That evening my phone rang. "Come, go for a moonlight walk with me."

"No. I'm busy." I peered out the window. A full moon did indeed shine beautifully, lighting the entire sky with its silvery beam A lovely night for a walk, hand in hand with a nice gentleman. But alone with one I knew so little about?

"Busy, doing what?"

"Removing fuzz balls off a favorite sweater of mine."

"Finish, then come walk with me."

"No, I'll be working at the computer."

The following day, because of a sore neck, I took time off and lay down with the heating pad as my companion. I nearly fell asleep when I heard footsteps on the pathway leading to my front door. Through the window blind, I saw Gordon.

When I opened the door to allow him in, he kissed my cheek. At a loss as to what to do next, I asked, "How does a game of Chinese Checkers sound to you?"

"Great." He followed me into the living room. I went to pick up the game from the shelf under the glass top coffee table. "I'll get it for you," he said. picking it up and placing it on the table. "Gee, it's quite heavy!"

"Yes, I know. It's made from marble. Can you believe I hid it from my husband, in my suitcase, and carried it all the way home from Mexico? It was his Christmas present that year."

"It's beautiful. I'll bet he was surprised?"

"Yes, he was."

While Gordon sat on the loveseat, I took my position on the floor, where I could better watch his uncanny moves. A fast thinker, he won. "Do you want to play another game, or Gin Rummy?"

"Gin Rummy." This time, we both sat on the floor, and rested our backs up against the entertainment unit. And while I shuffled and dealt the cards, he enjoyed rubbing and playing with my bare feet.

"Do you mind?" he asked.

"No," I surprised myself. "It feels good."

Once, when he shifted I asked if anything was wrong, and he said, "No, I don't have on any underwear and don't want you to see anything. "

I didn't let him know I had already seen the edge of one of his soft pink powder puffs. Instead I asked, "Didn't you do your laundry?"

"Yes, my clothes are all washed, but I don't wear any underwear under these grey knit shorts."

The game was over. He had won that one, too. Since he didn't wish to play another, I asked , "Would you like a bowl of soup and a toasted cheese sandwich?

"That sounds good, but no, I don't want to put you to any trouble.

Are you trying to win my heart through my stomach?"

"No, it's dinner time. I'm hungry and thought you also may be"

"No. I think I'll be leaving soon."

We talked a bit, and I told him I'm a one man woman, and will not marry until I find another prince.

"I'm not marrying again, either. Though, I might, if I find the right girl."

I sensed he wanted to try to make it with me. I studied him a moment and said, "Gordon, do you know if you break up with Dawn, you may not even like me."

"The same goes with me," he said.

He kissed me at the door. Lips were soft and nice. He kissed me again, and his thick tongue tried to probe deeper. I pushed him away, with a "No!" and shoved him out the door. I never had French kissed anyone in my whole life, except my doctor friend. Yes, I had totally, and unequivocally loved that man, and had taught him how to kiss.

The following day, arms loaded with bags of groceries, I shoved open the kitchen door to find Gordon's message on my answering machine: "Call me!"

My message on his machine simply said, "Returning your call."

Later in the afternoon, after I spent hours at my computer, I heard the sensor birds chirping in the wreath on my front door. Someone was approaching. I jumped up, and hurried to look out through the peep hole, and strangely, it made him look so far away. Yes! It was Gordon. I was attired unprofessionally in a jersey pink halter, and pale blue shorts, yet, still felt somewhat business-like in my tortoise shell reading glasses. As I flung open the door, I recalled an adage which stated *a man won't make passes with a girl who wears glasses*, yet there he was, telling me, "You look sweet, shapely, and adorably young. Are you going to invite me in?" His compliments were pleasing, but no, I would not thank him for them.

Instead, I closed the door, and told him, "I'll turn on the TV, and you may sit on the loveseat over there, while I shut down the computer." My plans were to sit on the sofa across from him. However, when I returned from the lanai, I said, "I just realized you can't see the television too well over there. If you wish, you may take the sofa." He obeyed, while I, with remote control in hand, crossed over and seated myself on the love seat.

"No, don't sit there. Come over and sit by me," he ordered. I did, and he gently placed his arm around my shoulder. "Do you mind if I muss your hair?"

A silly question. My husband used to do this. "No," I said. I enjoyed it, too much, and rested my head upon his shoulder. Thinking better of it, I jumped away, and said "Excuse me! I'm going to slip into something more practical." I took off for my bedroom.

"No. Don't change," he called after me. I was about to close the door, when he said, "I'm coming in!"

"No, you're not!" Already his foot was inside, and I shoved him through the opened doorway into the living room.

"I won't do anything. Don't change. You're perfect the way you are. Come, sit with me." We struggled a bit, when he pulled me back on the sofa.

"I know karate," I lied.

"No! Don't use it."

We were on the edge of the seat when his hot and pleasing hand slid inside my halter. I pictured my Bill, and longed to stay. But my mind reeled, and I flung myself out of his arms, twisted, and landed on the floor with a scream.

"My sore knee," I moaned, and rubbed it. "It's my left, the one I've had trouble with." I looked up at him sitting there, so nonchalant.

Instead of assisting me to my feet, he said, "You should protect it."

"Me? You're responsible. Not me." I vowed to stay away from this fresh kid. That's what he was. A kid who wanted me, and golly Moses, yes, I think I actually wanted him.

"You shouldn't have done that," he casually remarked.

"Me? You better leave, now." I shoved him on out, through the living room, and out the door."

The next day, I couldn't get him out of mind. Actually, I had handled the situation poorly. What I should have done was feed him, and not given in and sat beside him on the sofa. Now, I would end it. I would jot off a thank you note for his help in fixing the golf cart, and take down two stamps...I double what I borrow.

He smiled at me when I rang his bell. "Come on in," he said. He enjoyed the note, and said I wouldn't have had to bring the stamps. Right away, I told him I must leave, and he said, "Come into the hot tub with me."

"You gotta be kidding," I managed a chuckle. "No, I really must go."

"I'm a nice guy, I'm kind, and very gentle, and I could make you very, very happy. Stay with me awhile." I gave my head a negative shake. "You'll be sorry," he said.

Again, I told him, "No, thank you. I really must go."

His remark? "Don't go! Stay for awhile. I'm truly, a really nice guy, gentle, kind, and I could make you very happy." His blue eyes flashed, and his hand swept downward into his gray plaid shorts, and I turned away, covering my eyes.

My thoughts were, *I'm not going to let him think I'm naive, and afraid of him,* so I quickly turned around and said, "No, don't show me. But tell me, does it work?"

"With Viagra."

"Do you know , it's not kosher to act this way in front of a lady?"

He didn't apologize, but stared at me. "Why did you call me?"

"Because you asked me to. I'm leaving now."

At the door, he stood there with a twinkle in his eye, and tossed me a gentle smile. "Goodbye," I said. As I pressed my face to the screen, he leaned over, our lips touched and I kissed him. Don't ask why, even I don't know. Except I love to be kissed, and am used to men kissing me. I do know, on my way home I laughed myself silly. Now, there's a message on my answering machine, asking me to call. I won't. In fact, I disconnected the machine.

Over the next two days, he called twice. I wouldn't answer. Then, just a few minutes ago, he phoned again. I counted eight rings, and he finally gave up. For some reason, I sense a great loss. He awakened my senses. He made me feel alive. And yes, admittedly, I shall miss his kisses.

# Chapter 37
# A Fun Day with Jake

Admittedly, I like men. I want one I can call my own: A golfer so he can be away at times, while I'm busy writing at the computer for the paper, magazines, and whatever my heart desires. However, today, at precisely 10:35 AM, Jake, a non-golfer called.

I greeted him with "Good morning, you're lucky. Usually, I have a rule not to get off the throne to answer the phone."

A chuckle, and, "I'm sorry."

We made plans to head down the highway for brunch at Sunnys restaurant. "Do give me twenty-four minutes more?" I asked.

"That will be eleven. When I'm to pick you up."

"Yes, I know. I'll hurry. Goodbye."

No, I didn't wait for his "goodbye", it was *full steam ahead*, as I try not to keep a gentleman waiting. At least, not too long. Back to the bathroom and the phone jangled again. "Do you want me to pick you up at your villa, or the parking lot on the other side of the gate."

"Other side of the gate. This way you won't get lost."

In fifteen minutes, I dialed him back. "I'm ready."

"I'm leaving."

In a few minutes, when I walked out my door, he was coming from my neighbor's home. "I can't believe I was at the wrong house. I don't know what's wrong with me."

I clasped his hand in mine, as we walked down the street toward the golf cart gate. "We all make mistakes," I said. We stepped aside to allow a couple to pass, and I was proud to have others see I had a nice man by my side.

On the drive to the restaurant, Jake chatted on about the bible. Jake was the adamant one when it came to not attending church services of any kind.

"Did you know artificial insemination...and invetro fertilization was in vogue way back when Mary became impregnated by the Holy Ghost?"

"No? I never thought about it."

"Writings claim, in the beginning, there was God the Father, the Son and the Holy Ghost. How could there be the Son, when he hadn't been born yet? And do you believe in the Holy Spirit?"

"Yes, I believe in the Holy Spirit, and in, Jesus, our savior. It's all in the Apostle's Creed." It surprised me, to hear him, a Catholic, speak of religion. This conversation differed from normal. Usually, they all leaned toward sex. He would like to awaken in the morning, and find a soft warm body snuggled up to his. He liked to see a lady in shorts. Just as suspected, he was switching.

"Years ago, I was teaching a young girl to drive, windows were down, and suddenly, she veered around a corner, her skirt flew up, she took her hands off the wheel and the car headed for the river. I steered the car back on the road and told her, 'I'm taking you home to put on shorts.'" He reiterated, "I like shorts. Like to see women's legs. See them in their bras and panties. See them naked. Women don't think like men." I silently grinned, as I surreptitiously, out of the corner of my eye, looked over at the edge of his shorts, and wondered a bit about him.

Brunch was fantastic. Enough for me to take home for dinner. Previous plans were to return to my villa for strawberry shortcake, but both of us were too full, and we postponed it until tomorrow. Instead, I asked, "How far away is the Russell Stovers candy warehouse?"

"Quite a distance, in the opposite direction. Why?"

"Just wondering'. I'm hungry for chocolate. Remember the fun time you, Janie Major and I had visiting there, and sampling the yummy sweets? Speaking of chocolate, I'm glad Hershey didn't sell their company."

He eased out of the parking lot, into traffic. "You're not heading for Leesburg and home, are you?"

"No."

"Where are we going, now?"

"To the chocolate factory."

"You're a sweet man." I reached over and gave his hand a squeeze. As before, we had a delightful time tasting various chocolates, and when I went to pay my twenty-seven dollar bill, I felt guilty spending so much for candy. In fact, so guilty, when Jake's back was turned, after I handed my check to the clerk, I whispered, "Could you clear the cost from the cash register before he turns around?"

Next day, upon my return from church services, I busied myself at the computer. The flying keys worked overtime, as I tried to catch up to date, when the sudden interruption of the jangling phone made me nearly slip out of my office chair. It was Jake, asking, "What are you doing?"

"Working at the computer. What are you doing?"

"Looking forward to your strawberry shortcake."

"Oh, my goodness, Jake! I just remembered you were to come over. Okay, I'll close shop. Come over."

I checked the biscuits we brought from the restaurant and they appeared somewhat dry. I would bake fresh...For Jake. Later, they cooled on a trivet, when my doorbell rang. I looked around. Everything appeared in order. Yet, I wondered about my attire... The pink halter and blue shorts. Plans were to slip on a cover-up, once the kitchen became somewhat cooler. An idea sparked. Would Jake think me adorably sweet, dressed in this, as had adorable Gordon?

At the door, twice, Jake kissed me lightly on the lips. "Did Don call?" he asked.

"Who's Don?"

"The gentleman at The Singles. He likes you."

"Oh? He does? No one ever told me. How do you know."

"Didn't you see how he wanted to sit near you at The Single's dinner at the Cracker Barrel the other Sunday?"

"Come in," I ushered him into the dining room. "Regarding your question, 'no', all I remember is Don asked where he was to sit. By the way, I thought fresh biscuits would be nice. They're cooling in the kitchen, sit at the table, and I'll be back." On my way to the kitchen I remembered the one evening I had met Don, at The Singles Pool-side Chat. Jake wasn't present. Admittedly, I liked Don's looks; simple, clean-cut face . He sat at the far end of the semi-circle, and when it came time to introduce ourselves, I proudly laid it on about everything I enjoyed doing; ballroom dancing, particularly writing for a paper back home, and the unpublished author of eight books, now working on my ninth. Later, how I silently laughed, when, following dinner he told me, "I don't hear too well, and couldn't hear a word you were saying out there." No, Don hadn't called me. However, I did learn from one of the girls, he had made a date with her, then later left word on her answering machine canceling it, saying he met someone else. So much for Don.

The golden biscuits looked terrific. Their homey scent permeated through my cozy kitchen. A feeling of pleasure swept over me. Jake would be proud of me. I had done this for him. However, I cut one in half and discovered they hadn't baked completely and had to be returned to the oven.

"I'll eat the ones we brought home the other night," Jake was saying. "I'm hungry."

Later, I placed a hot biscuit in my dish, left it to cool in milk while I excused myself and slipped into my bedroom for a shirt to place over my halter. Upon my return, I told Jake, "The biscuit is still warm, but tastes better than the store's."

He reached over with his spoon, took a bite from my dish. "Yes, it's tastier, but I'll finish what I have. But you shouldn't have put the shirt on. I liked you the way you were." He continued with, "I don't think we'll get along. You use skim milk. I use regular. You eat peanut butter, and I don't,"

Later, we played Chinese checkers. I attempted to allow him to win and moved my marbles back and forth, and he said, "You're prolonging the game," and it ended a tie. We sat on the sofa and viewed TV for awhile. When he was about to leave, he stood, leaned over, and scraped the bottom of my bare foot with a fingernail. "I'm seeing if you're ticklish. You're not." He tried again, and my foot moved a bit. "Yes, you are, a little." I thought of how Gordon had played so tenderly with my feet.

At the door, Jake kissed my lips twice, said he would be leaving town in the morning, attending a funeral, and would return in three days.

"Take care of yourself," I said. "Drive carefully."

"What if I don't want to. It will take away all the excitement."

"Then don't."

Thoughts were, *he manages to exasperate me with his confrontations. Over the silliest things, and when least expected.*

As he walked to his car, he chuckled, and I heard his, "I can get you riled up once in awhile, can't I?" Only then, I began to wonder about this man. He's aware I love the ocean, and said when he returned he'd take me away for a day, perhaps three, and I said on one condition, we have separate rooms. To this he had said, "That's no fun. It will be like marriage." Mine had been fun.

# Chapter 38
# At Marti's Home

Today, Wednesday, October 2, and my calendar reads: "Sorority with the new, daytime chapter." I would be in the presence of our new president, who, at first, closed the door on me when her quota of selected members had become filled. Before I left home, to soften the situation, I would personally speak to her. She wasn't in, so I left a message saying "Hope to see you soon."

Yesterday, because I'm still inclined to become lost, I made a dry-run to Marti's home where the meeting would be held. Today, bless her heart, she opened the door, all smiles, when I surprisingly found I had arrived an hour early. I dislike when friends do this to me, and apologized profusely.

"That's fine," Marti said, in her soft Southern voice. "We can have a good gab session." We chatted like true sisters, tossing back and forth ideas as we went, from kitchen to parlor, setting up three tables, getting ready for the group to arrive.

Soon, car doors slammed and one could hear chatter and footsteps out in the sunporch. I greeted all sorority sisters with a hug. I liked each and every member. Yet, I also had detected a genuine warmth amidst the other daytime sorority.

Lunch was delicious, homemade soup that Marti, herself, had whipped together. Dessert was the yummiest cake ever, baked by her sweetheart, to share with us.

During our business meeting, the girls all welcomed me.

"I'm attending today," I said, "But I'll give it some thought as to which daytime group I'll eventually join."

"Too late, now, Bootsy," the Vice President told me, as she handed me a Program Book. "We already have you listed as a member."

I soon learned my hurried call to the president hadn't been necessary. She was out of town. Later, as I rifled through our program book, I read in awe, the lovely welcoming message she had written to each of us. She wasn't the ogre who slammed the door in my face. She wasn't the one who even suggested starting a daytime group. This surprised me, too, when the Vice President said, "We're going to have a fantastic year, with a fantastic group." Yes, I was chosen to be their Scrapbook Chairperson. Karen Schultz would be my photographer, and her friend, Marilyn, would also help.

A super meeting, a super parting, though I stayed and helped clean up. Marti and I chatted on, while I washed dishes and she dried. Then we sat and talked about men, her sweetie, and my hopes of finding one.

Before parting, Marti told me, "Tonight, a friend named Art will be going to the ballroom dance with me. He's a nice man. Come along with us. You'll like him. They'll be serving champagne, punch and cheese, plus crackers. We'll pick you up at the Catholic church at 5:15 to 5:30."

I called her at 4:30. "I can't find my watch. I'll be lost without it. Tonight is Fiesta Night in the square, so I'll run in and buy one. Wait for me!"

I hung up and changed my mind. Rather than chance arriving at the church late, I searched in the armoire drawers, and came up with several watches. None worked, but still I found an old-time favorite, suitable to give a secure feeling of being totally dressed, and I arrived at the church ten minutes early. Time to fret a bit, wondering if she and her two girl friends had left without me, as they had before. Male voices sounded from the side of the church, and I followed them to be certain I was in the right parking lot of the right church. "Yes, this is the Catholic church," the men assured me.

I thanked them. They smiled, and asked if there was anything else they could do for me. To this, I grinned. "No, but thanks, again." I took off for my car. Ten minutes slipped by, and a red convertible pulled beside me. I stared as Marti clamored out. "Hi, Marti," I called to her, as I climbed out of my car and walked over. "Is this your significant other?" I peeped in.

"No, he doesn't dance. This is my friend, Art, you can sit in the front, and I'll climb in the back. I guess the girls aren't going tonight."

After introductions were made we were off, sailing down the highway.

I tried to watch in which direction Art was going, and said, "You haven't lost me, yet." He seemed amiable. A nice chap, well-dressed.

Once we entered the dance hall, while Marti chatted with the dance instructor, I told Art, "I'm going to the bar and will bring back glasses of punch and cheese and crackers for the two of us." His pleasure showed in his smile. When I headed back to where he sat, I noted Marti was already waltzing across the dance floor with her instructor.

"I can't dance," Art said.

"That's why you're here, to learn."

"You're right. But if you want, we can try the next fox trot."

We couldn't jive together. I seemed to be forever, tramping on his feet, so I had mercy on him, and spent the rest of the time dancing with others. I was especially pleased when, here, like in PA, they had the *get acquainted dance.* Ladies line up on one side of the room, the men on the other, and a gentleman picks up the girl across from him, dances around and drops her off at the end of the ladies line, and returns to his.

In teacher, Randle's arms, I felt serenely happy, as though I floated on air. He proved to be such an elegant and smooth dancer, I believe he could gracefully maneuver a bull dozer up a garden path. "You've had lessons," he told me. "You're light on your feet, and follow beautifully."

"Thank you. It's because I have a good leader. And yes, I've had four years of ballroom lessons."

"You can tell."

Peter, another teacher, small, wiry, resembling a school kid, was equally good, but without any extraordinary, sophisticated movements. Then there was Charles, Monte, Bob, and others. One elderly gent, with shoulders that sagged, danced remarkably well.

Dance lessons over, Art suggested we drive back to Paneras in The Villages, for soup and sandwiches, instead of Katie Belles, as it was Cowboy Night over there. It proved to be a worthwhile day, a worthwhile evening. Marti hadn't ordered soup, but sat at our table, while Art and I waited in the soup line. While there, we reminisced about Marti, and what a wonderful lady she is. "She reminds me so, of this one TV actress. A mystery writer," I told Art.

"Yes, she does. I can see her typing away, but can't recall her name."

"Me, neither. Marti is somewhat prettier, and more stylish. Let's see who remembers first." Soup bowls in hands, neither of us could come up with the name by the time we reached our table. There, we verbalized about our stock market losses, and hopes of climbing over the present slump, then switched to doctors here, and how they differ.

"That's because the majority are from other countries," I said . "If I could find one good American doctor who would take time to report back to me when tests were taken, I would be content."

Art suggested "Call Dr. Meade. He's good. He takes time to listen and doesn't rush you through."

They dropped me off at the church, near my parked car.

Come morning, I emptied cereal in a bowl, nuked tea just as A-n-g-e-l-a- Lansbury flitted across my mind.

I dialed Art's number. He answered on the third ring. "Angela Lansbury," I said.

"I'm sorry. Who do you want?"

"Art, this is Bootsy. Her name is Angela Lansbury."

"Who? I'm sorry I couldn't hear you."

"It's Bootsy. Remember we were trying to remember who Marti looks like?"

"Oh, yes. It's funny. After I got home, it was such a nice evening, I went outside for awhile, looking at the sky and the stars, and suddenly I remembered, too. But it was 9:45 and I thought it was too late to call."

We talked, and talked some more. About our spouses, and I spoke of the dear doctor I had fallen in love with, who married his best friend's wife, and how I would have erred, had I married him. Art

194

spoke of a situation somewhat similar, and together we laughed . He seemed so somber last night. Yet, now, here he was opening up. So freely, so sensibly, about Paris, about times we each had spent in lovely Hawaii, with no mention of sex, and wishing to see me in my nightie, and undies, and it was nice. I spoke of the man who wanted me to join him in his hot tub, and after our last kiss goodbye I didn't answer his phone calls.

"I thought you said you were a romantic."

"I am, but I don't want to hop into a hot tub, nor someone's bed. My husband said I was worth a million. Men would be flocking at my door. But I don't want just any man. I want to be appreciated, courted, with flowers, candy, adored, and in time, love and be loved."

"I don't blame you. Things have changed over the years. By the way, how did you get home last night?"

"With difficulty." I laughed.

"When we saw you turn around, we wondered where you were going?"

"I was getting lost. After circling around the church parking lot, I came out in the front, and knew I was right back where I originally parked when waiting for Marti. The Episcopal church supposedly was across the highway. I crossed over, and also ended circling in their parking lot. Finally, I came to a driveway which led me out on Avenida Central Boulevard. Once on the main drag, I breezed along the wooden fence, now certain I was on the right road. I laughed to myself, thinking it was a mystery as to how I became so fouled up. Just as it was a mystery why I couldn't remember the mystery writer's name."

He would be leaving town to visit his brother, and upon his return would call me. Later, in thinking about Marti, and how they luncheon together, I would call and tell her about Art's and my friendly chat. Also, I would let her know I would never infringe on their time together.

# Chapter 39
# An E-Mail to Keep

It had been a long day, and I was near the end of three hours spent at my computer in the e-mail department. 12:45 AM, I looked forward to a nice warm bubble bath and my inviting bed. My mailbox was almost empty. One more message to go. Then, here I was, joyously reading my last message. . .from my youngest daughter, Debra Jean. No attachments requesting I send inspiring stories or prayers to five or ten friends, so I can be blessed, happy, or else no one will love me, or I'll run into a day of bad luck. This message was real, honest to-goodness from the heart. Debbie's own. It read:

"Hi, happy Monday, September 30,02. I feel like I could do another 10 hours of sleep this morning. I am still recouping from the weekend trip to Philadelphia. 'Women in Faith' was wonderful. Where else can you lift your voice unto the Lord with 20,000 women?

The two college girls who were missionaries in Afghanistan were there. They told about how they prayed for release, but yet had to minister to the 30

Afghan women who were in prison with them. They sang and worshipped God the entire time they were in jail. Heather, one of the girls, prayed for a message from God, because she was fearful and needed to know what God wanted her to do. The next day, Taliban soldiers entered the prison and handed out sanitary napkins. There were two brands. One was of the brand name, Always, and the other was Trust. Heather said, God is miraculous. He can even answer prayers using sanitary napkins.

When the U.S. bombing started, the girls were terribly frightened, and prayed for safety. One of the Afghan women came to her and said, "I saw Jesus, and he told me he was sending his angels to protect us." When Heather looked out of the prison, into the compound, she saw angels standing shoulder to shoulder around the prison. Shortly afterwards, the U.S. scared off the Taliban soldiers and freed the women. What a witness!"

Debbie continued, "Other witnessing was great, too. Lisa Beamer, wife of Todd Beamer, the man who attacked the terrorists in the plane, and died in the crash, also witnessed. It was fantastic.

I probably won't e-mail brother Keith at work. The position he has is all time-consuming, so I will only e-mail when the situation requires it.

I best be going. Today is my worst and most challenging day. I have to phone a parent right after class, because so far this year, I have kicked her son out for poor behavior. His mom says it is all my fault, and indirectly threatened me. So now I have to teach the class, and remind myself the whole time that this kid does not misbehave...Yeah, in a cold day in Hell. Bye.

Love, me, Deb."


I closed shop, breathed a sigh of relief. Since I moved so far away from my family at this tender age in life, e-mail is a great way to keep in touch with loved ones.

Following church on October 6, I decided I didn't want to hop into my golf cart and return home to eat alone. Perhaps Marion, the lady I met a month ago at Bichara's Bakery, may be there today, downing one of their yummy cappuccinos?

There wasn't a soul I knew amidst the rather large dining group. I ordered an oriental chicken salad sandwich. Stephanie, the cute, long-tressed young one, waited on me. I discovered if you work up a conversation they won't skip on the innards to sandwiches. In fact, I told her I always scoop out the inside of rolls, and she said, "I can do that for you." That was one swell sandwich. She filled the gap with raw onions and lettuce.

I chose to eat outside, in the shade under a covered roof to the right, and there, found an unoccupied rocking chair. Nice. After nearly everyone left, a young chap moseyed over. "Do you want this cushion?" He asked, lifting the green padded one off the chair on which he planned on sitting. I gave my head a negative shake, and watched him sit and begin rocking. He could be rather handsome, I mused, when he began to talk, showing prominent white teeth. His name was Gusepi.

"Greece?" I asked.

"Quebec." We talked on, about our families, about everything, except his occupation. I neglected to ask. I spoke of my joy in writing, and about my latest experiences while living here in The Villages. Yes, he, too, is enjoying life here. This is his sixth year. He moved here after his wife died. He had been in the service, had six sisters, and never was in France, though would have liked to go there.

Soft music from the nearby radio station drifted on the afternoon air. I took a big swig of my coffee, looked up at him and asked, Do you like to dance?" My feet were itching to.

"A little. Slow."

"Do you want to dance, now?"

A grin, and "Sure". People on the other side of the street smiled over at us. The Village Trolley turned the corner, and the driver waved. "I'm liable to be tapped on the shoulder by a policeman, for dancing with the lady in the pink dress. What color would you call it?"

"Raspberry."

"It's nice. When we returned to our rockers, he picked up a cushion from a foot-rest, next to him, and brought it over."

"What's this for?"

"For on your foot-rest, to put under your feet." Unconsciously I had propped up my feet.

"Thank you. That was nice. I'll have to take off my shoes. I do rest this leg whenever possible." It was the one on which three arthoscopies had been performed. After a half hour slipped away, I stretched with hands over my head, and told him, "I'm going to leave you now, to go home and hit the computer keys. Have a great evening. Will I see you here next Sunday?"

"Yes! Don't work too hard, and are you going to write about Gusepi?"

I grinned and over my shoulder tossed, "You betcha! I'll share this pleasant day, spent with you."

So there, I did, but I didn't remember to go for another Cappuccino until two weeks later and I never saw Gusepi again.

# Chapter 40
# An Ill Wind

The clock on the nightstand blinked 8:00 AM. No, I wasn't sleepy, just a tad lazy. The previous night I attended the dance at Mulberry Grove, and stayed until the end. At the moment, nothing was pressing—only a make-up and brow sculpture, my first scheduled appointment at the Merle Norman Beauty Salon at 2:00 o'clock. I wanted to look my best tonight, at our PA talent show when I was expected to recite some of my poems. The phone jangled. I listened to the answering machine click on in the kitchen, then picked up to hear the rest of my message, which is light-hearted, wishing the caller a great day.

"Hold on," I said. The machine stopped. "Not bad," I chuckled.

"No, it isn't. You're good at this."

"Who is this?"

"The lady who sat caddy-corner across from you at the table, last evening."

"Oh, hello there, Elise!"

"Let me tell you something. When you see me, don't sit by me."

"Alright." Puzzled, I wondered if she had some infectious, transferable disease. Walking pneumonia?

She continued, "Last night, Jack came over, sat beside me and said, 'Finally I got a seat. I sought you out and came over to dance with you.' What you did was uncalled for, I'd never do that."

"What did I do?"

"You took over, sat there scratching his back then danced with him all evening."

"Oh! I'm sorry. I didn't know he was with you."

"No, you're not sorry. This is the way you behave. You jump around until you get your clutches into the men, then you hang on. You danced with him all evening, and I didn't have a chance. Bud asked me to dance, but I told him I don't dance the polka. So I just sat there, then got up and went home."

"I'm so sorry."

"No, you're not. This is the way you behave. Do you know who noticed this? A lady at the table behind you. Just don't go near me. You infringe on someone's good fortune. Thank you, I can do without this. You behave the way you want."

I blinked in disbelief. Here was one of the prettiest ladies, a former model, stylish in every sense of the word, yet I refused to allow her to continue. "Look," I said. "If this is what you think of me, I don't even want to sit by you. I had no idea he sought you out. Last night when Jack went to sit down, I shifted my chair to make room, and accidentally bumped the back of his arm. I reached over, gently rubbed it, only a second, and asked if he was okay, and he grinned saying, 'You can do that all night. It feels good.' Now, because of your sharp tongue, I honestly wish he had refused to dance with me. I had never seen him before and thought he was a newcomer, like Doug, the nice chap across the table from me, who monopolized me on the dance floor. I told him we were supposed to share the men, and then I brought him over to dance with the girl seated across from you. Remember?"

"No, I didn't even see him."

She reiterated, "You picked up Jack, took over, and I didn't have a chance."

I bit hard to still my trembling lip. "Truly, I'm sorry."

"No, you're not. You think of Bootsy, and that's the way it is. Just stay away from me when I'm with a man." Her voice trembled with anger.

"Please! Please, listen to me? Over the past six months since living here, when I force myself to go out alone in the evenings, and I do force myself, I do with hopes I'll end up having a good time. I don't sit around and wait for the world to come to me. I reach out and embrace it. Wherever I may be, if I see a stranger, and feel he or she may want to chat, or sometimes dance, I attempt to help make them feel comfortable. I began doing this years ago, during the war, when I belonged to the Hostess Club in Williamsport, PA, and we welcomed and entertained our wounded soldiers when they returned home." Silence on the line and I imagined she was interested, so I continued.

"One evening our Hostess Club held a dinner dance at the 'Y', and one particular soldier stands out in my mind. We sat together at a table, and watched others on the dance floor, when he said, 'Before I went in the service, I loved to dance. Now, I'll never be able to, again. Not with this bad leg.' I studied him a moment, stood, reached out, took his hands in mine, and slowly pulled him to his feet, and though he sometimes dragged his one leg across the floor, tears misted his eyes and he said, 'I can't believe this. I'm really dancing.' So you see, because of that one little incident, I truly believe somewhere out there he still may be dancing."

She had worked up steam in me, and I had to let it escape. "Elise, people of late, don't reach out to others. Not as much as they used to. This is understandable in this fast pace we live in. I could be one of them, but choose to be different. Thirty five years ago, I joined another meaningful and worthwhile organization, and took their pledge to think of the other person before myself, and I have kept that pledge. It's amazing the wonderful things which happen because of this. Yes, I had fun dancing with Jack. It was nice. Though the-Tag-Along was extremely long, too fast, and tiring, and I kept telling the leader to slow down, but he couldn't hear me. Because of this, when I returned home I had to put an ice-sock on my sore knee. I did not dance with Jack after the Tag-Along. He danced with someone else, while I danced with a Paul, Frank, and a man I call Silent Sam. Do you know Sam?"

"No, I don't."

"He's a smoothie. Said nothing, just held me closely, our bodies molded, with my hand curled beneath his chin, exactly as my husband held me, and all the time he smiled, holding my eyes with his. When I asked, 'What are you thinking?' he told me, 'About you!' I gracefully moved away, with elbows spread out to the side, and said, 'My dance instructor, back home, said we're to dance like this.' We did for awhile, with him, still the Silent Sam, beaming that tantalizing smile down on me."

"Why are you telling me this?" she asked.

"Just to let you know, there are still some men in my life, and I'm not reaching out to grab yours or anyone else's."

"So how many others are you involved with?"

"None, really. No one special, though I do sit back and scrutinize. And when I do go out, I usually go Dutch. For instance, last week, friend, Jake, asked if I wanted to do something this Wednesday, and I told him, 'Yes, I'll take you to the movies if you pay my way.' He laughed, then I added, 'I'll buy the popcorn and soda.' Then there's Gordon, the man I met two months ago at the mail station, dates another, yet called three weeks ago, and asked me to go for a moonlight walk. I told him I was busy. Two weeks ago he showed up at my door. That conversation went: 'Did you miss me?'...'No, I hardly know you. Why should I miss you?'...'I was away on a seven day cruise.'...'That was nice. Were you with your girlfriend?'...'Yes.'...'Did you have a good time?'...'Yes'...'Do you love her?'...'No. Will you come on a cruise with me?'...'No.'...'Tomorrow, I'm flying to Wisconsin.'...'That's nice'...'I'll be attending my class reunion. Come with me?' and I said a flat...'No!'

"Have you ever gone out with him?" Elise asked.

"No! He has a steady girlfriend. Yet, he again knocked on my door last Wednesday and asked, 'Can I come in?' With a mouth full of chicken, I told him 'no', I was eating my lunch. 'Can I have a chicken kiss?' he asked, and I told him 'no', stepped out and sat beside him on the bench, and we chatted. Before he left, he hugged me, kissed my cheeks, and said, 'I want you.' I laughed, kissed his cheek and said, 'So do one hundred other men.'

"There are so many women to men," Elise murmured. "Then, there I was, looking forward to dancing with Jack when I saw him walk across the room, and I felt you didn't give me a chance."

"I'm truly sorry about this, Elise, and how things turned out. I agree, men are somewhat scarce. I also learned the ones going steady, find it so easy to find a playmate on the side. Not one. Not two, but maybe three. With so many women out there craving for a male's companionship, they become easy prey. Yet, there are still some nice men left. JoinThe Singles Club. You'll find someone. That's where I met Carl, a nice brotherly type. Whether they like to admit it or not, men still need us. Just yesterday, Carl arrived with an essay paper I had typed for him last week. He's going to become a clown. He'll make a good one. Together, we edited, added a little, and I retyped it. He smiled, and said, "Now I owe you one," and I told him, "Okay, one day you can come rewind my garden hose for me."

So you see, Elise, through all of this you have pegged me incorrectly. I'm not out to take another woman's man, I'm simply waiting for another special prince to walk into my life. I'm a one-man-woman...actually, a born-again-virgin..." I gave a little giggle. "I'm saving myself for him. All of my friends and relatives have been telling me he waits just around the corner. It doesn't matter that much. I'm happy. But, I would like to have a nice, trustworthy gentleman of my own."

"I'm looking for the same thing, and perhaps it could have been Jack."

"What will be, will be. I'm sorry I wounded your feelings, but was truly mortified, when you verbally chewed me up and spit me out for something I hadn't been doing." With her light chuckle, then silence on the other end, I took a deep breath, and continued. "I felt if you or the lady from the next table wish to talk about me, that's not a problem of mine. I have always lived by the Golden Rule, and walk in the beauty of God's love, and will not change. Life is what we make it. Mine is beautiful. Each day begins with a wiggle of my toes, while I chant: *This is the day the Lord hath made, I shall rejoice and be glad in it.* At day's end I thank God for still another one."

"I thank Him, too," Elise said. "We're all in the same boat, and at this age, one never knows what the future holds. "

"Yes, incidentally, you say you watch me and see how I act? Well, last night, I studied you, and my thoughts were, you weren't feeling up to par. Were you?"

"No, actually, I felt lousy after just getting over a headache, and, like you, I also had forced myself to go to the dance."

"Well, Elise, after all is said and done, I consider our slate wiped clean." Nothing more was said, and we were still on speaking terms, and I left it go like that.

During breakfast, I looked back on last night when I danced with Sam, returned home, showered, and refrained from washing my face. I chose to allow his manly scent of after-shave-lotion to linger close to me all night long. Momentarily, I now replaced the spoon in my cereal bowl, reached up and smoothed my hands over my cheeks, and with eyes closed, I again could see him, eyes tantalizing mine, as I inhaled his fragrance, and could once more sense his arms around me. There was no getting around it, I was smitten with this playboy, this womanizer.

I could never share this with Elise. Nor, how, last night, during certain dance movements, through my yellow silk dress, now and then I could feel Sam's manhood gently brush against my inner thigh, with young thoughts of a cottage behind a picket fence, and several little 'Sammies' running around. Nor how, the second time I pulled away from Sam, and smiled up at him and asked, "Now, what are you thinking?" and he said, "You know!" I had guessed correctly, and when I told him, "You are bad," he beamed that tantalizing smile, and like the young boys of yesteryears, and today's now older boys in long pants, he said, "When I'm bad, I'm very good." Perhaps I should have shared this with Elise. Should have warned her that Sam was out to get what he could. He was smooth, like polished silver, which goes with a fine gourmet dinner, and if a lady was hungering enough for love, as I was, she could be gobbled up, spit out, and later wonder what in the world had happened to her? I also hadn't told Elise, when the music stopped, I slipped out of Sam's arms, and escaped into John's, a staid, righteous gentleman, who had been standing on the sidelines near a group of occupied tables.

Despite the morning's upset, as the rest of the day wore on, I forgot the dance, forgot Elise, forgot Sam, and concentrated on this evening's talent show. Off and on, I would recite a poem out loud, to make certain I remembered it.

Later, I shared them with the girls at the Merle Norman Beauty Salon. Amy, who waxed my brows, laughed and said my poems tickled her funny bones and, "You'll do fine tonight. You look great!" While Penny, in charge of make-up added, "I agree. And I picked just the right color to enhance your green eyes."

That evening, I arrived at the Hacienda Center in plenty of time. Yet, while seated amidst others circled around the many tables, toward the end of the show, I mentally fidgeted. According to my watch it should soon be over. Perhaps I hadn't been registered? The last contestant walked off the stage, and now the man at the podium said, "I'm reading here, about a lady who will be reciting some of her poetry. Is she in the audience?"

I turned, looked around to see no hands, and raised my own. "I'm not certain, but I think that might be me!"

"Well, then, you just march right up here, and tell us who you are."

With microphone in hand, alone on the big stage, I introduced myself. "My name is Arbutus Focht, though as a toddler, I couldn't pronounce Arbutus, and since I liked to wear white boots, they nicknamed me, 'Bootsy'. So if you like, that's what you may call me." A chuckle came from the audience. I continued "My father raised me, and I didn't meet Mother until I was 21, when she found me through an ad placed in our local paper. Later, while visiting her in New York, we shared lunch together in a quaint little Italian restaurant, called The College of Complexes, in Greenwich Village. That's where I first became introduced to humorous poetry, far off the beaten path from Shakespeare's. There scribbled across one wall I read:

> There once was a judge in this here land,
> Who granted a divorce to my old man,
> I laughed and laughed at the judges decision.
> He gave him the kids, and they ain't his'n."

The crowds' laughter, assured me I had captured their attention. Now, confident, not the least nervous, I asked, "Has anyone ever been to Greenwich Village, and visited The College of Complex Restaurant?" One hand raised out of 211. Everything went well with my poetry recitation, and when through, I politely bowed to the crowd and walked down the stairs to return to my seat. On my way, men and women at tables I passed, looked up, some smiled, some thanked me, some said, "You did good."

Once I became seated, an English teacher came over to my table to speak to me. "If I were still teaching, I'd have you come and share your poetry with my class. You were grand. I couldn't have done better myself."

It proved to be a successful night, despite my morning start with an ill wind blowing cold. Before climbing into bed, I shared my thoughts in prayer. "Thanks, God! Together, we did it! In the end it proved to be fun." I closed asking Him, "To bless my kids, and my kid's kids, and above all, do bless Elise." Then, as usual, I breathed a sigh of contentment, and expected to sleep fitfully, but sleep wouldn't' come. As I tossed the night away, I came to the conclusion I had drunk regular and not caffeine-free coffee, at the Pennsylvania Club.

# Chapter 41
## Smoothing Ruffled Feathers

Come morning, when I awakened to see a sprinkle of sunlight dancing upon my ceiling, I realized it was going to be another lovely day. What would I do with it? Yesterday started out to be the pits, but ended quite successfully at the talent show.

Following breakfast, with a cup of tea in hand, I headed for my office, and was comfortably seated when the telephone began to ring. Surprisingly, Jack was on the line. "You must be popular, the answering machine beeped twenty-five times."

"I'm sorry. It's the machine. I believe sometimes the calls don't erase."

"What are you doing?"

"I'm at the computer. Why? Do you have something in mind?"

"No, I just wanted to know how your day was going?"

"Fine, thank you, kind sir. Question, Do you know a girl named Elise Williams?"

"No, why?"

"You sat across from her at the dance. Look up her number, call, and ask her to go out."

"Really? Why?"

"She called and scolded me."

"She did? What for?"

"She said the other night you sought her out, came to our table to chat and dance with her, and I gobbled you up, took you out on the dance floor and she didn't see you the rest of the night, so she went home."

"Yeah! Yeah! I know who you mean. I danced with her one night. She's a pretty lady."

"Yes, posh and pretty, the most beautiful of all the ladies. Except me, of course." I added a little giggle.

"Naturally."

"Tell me, Jack, did you ask me to dance, or had I asked you?"

"You grabbed me, pulled me out on the dance floor and pushed me around. You can grab me anytime you want to. During the three dances, I wasn't sure, but you led me through them. You're a good leader."

"Thank you, kind sir. Call Elise, but don't tell her I told you to."

I waited awhile, to give him enough time, then phoned. "How did it go? Did you ask her out?"

"Yes, and I'll work at settling things straight between you two."

"There's no need. I cleared the air."

"That's good. Are you free on Saturday? We could go to a movie. A late one, as I have a golf tournament."

"Wait until I run to the kitchen and check my calendar." I picked up the phone out there. "Saturday will be fine."

"What movie would you like to see?"

"*White Oleander.*"

"I'll phone you after the tournament."

Today, Friday, four days later, I was in the midst of preparing a chicken and onion sandwich for lunch when cut short again by the jangling phone.

Our Singles Club president, Laura Joiner, was on the line. "Don't forget! Tomorrow evening is our poolside chat, followed by dinner and dancing at the Chula Vista club."

I had indeed forgotten, and when I hung up, thought of my Saturday night date with Jack. A month ago, he had moved here to spend the winter. Perhaps he may wish to join the group at the pool, and later dance with all the girls; especially Elise.

I waited until evening to call, only to hear an answering machine say, "I'm not at home, you know what to do." Curt! Blunt! Then I got to wondering? It sounded somewhat like Gordon. Had I dialed the wrong number? Hopefully not. I left the following message: "If this is you, Jack, will you please call Bootsy, at 753-0881, in regards to tomorrow night? It's our scheduled Singles Mingle, with a pool side chat, dinner and dancing at the Chula Vista Club." I hung up, somewhat stupefied. Lordy! Lordy! Supposing I had erred, and did indeed, phone the rascal down around the corner? I checked the list of phone numbers. His appeared directly beneath Jack's.

I recalled the day Gordon first showed up unexpectedly at my door, and I told him no one does this without first calling. Now, he has started all over again, to appear weekly, or every other. It's exasperating. Though, I sort of like the attention, I must be careful not to encourage him in any way. Admittedly, he does turn me on, yet I shall never submit to his wishes, mentally nor physically. My phone is ringing. Jack or the rascal?

"I just got your message, and can't go tomorrow. Something came up and I must leave for Venice in the morning."

"This is Jack, right?"

"Right. I can't attend the club's poolside chat, etcetera."

I breathed a huge sigh of relief in learning it wasn't cutie pie's. "That's Okay. Did you make a date with Elise?"

"Yes. I'll get back to you."

I hung up with mixed emotions, happy he called, yet sad when I pictured him, and possibly Elise, taking off together and heading for Venice. I had no idea where Venice was, except the one in Italy, and felt for certain, this Venice may be a posh and elegant spot in Elise's own corner of the world. But that's okay. It would make up for my grabbing Jack away from her on Saturday evening.

The following morning, my phone rang crazily. The rascal, Gordon, from down the street was indeed on the phone. The blunt answering machine message had been his. The call from Jack, last night, was in response to one made earlier in the day. Totally forgotten, but made in haste. Am I losing it? Sometimes I've begun to wonder. Gordon was saying, "It sounds like a grand time at the Club. Have fun. I'm not sorry you called by mistake. Feel free to call anytime. I'd love hearing from you."

Saturday evening, neither Jack nor Elise showed up at the club house. I learned later, she did have a date with Jack, and I never saw nor heard from him again. The next time I saw Elise, I asked how she was. She smiled, gave me a gentle hug, and quietly said, "Fine, thank you." Then I became busy entertaining out-of- town guests, and didn't see her again, until the following weekend. I arrived at the club house somewhat late, and while she chatted with the gentleman next to her, I sat on the opposite side of the table, next to Don, a member who doesn't attend club meetings too often. The three were engrossed in heavy conversation when suddenly it dawned on me. *I'm not supposed to be sitting here.* I noticed the table next to us, empty, except for two ladies, and I told the girl to my right, "I'm going to move to the other table. Those two ladies are all alone over there."

"They're talking to each other. They're not alone," she said.

I stayed, and Don turned to me and asked, "Would you like to dance. It's a slow fox trot. I can handle that."

"Me, too, and I'd be delighted." A nice quiet man, I had seen him only once before. Later, a gentleman named Ken, tapped me on the shoulder, and soon we were out swaying on the dance floor. I liked Ken, with the nice head of hair, and his slow, easy smile. We were near to dancing cheek to cheek, when he surprised me with, "Poor Elise. Look at her, sitting over there, alone."

I followed his glance, and in a fit of compassion, said, "Ken, go ask her to dance. If she asks where I went, tell her to the powder room."

"Are you sure?"

"Yes. You can catch me later." I left the building, but not before I glanced over my shoulder, to see Ken lead Elise out onto the dance floor. As I made my way through the parking lot, now enshrouded in moonlight, I found myself humming my favorite song, "Somewhere out there, someone waits for me." Then I wondered where he could be, and how much longer I'd be waiting?

# Chapter 42
# Douglas

A rainy Monday morning, and I lay in bed thinking about a potpourri of many things: About yesterday, and the pure white, three-inch cocoon found on a branch I had severed while trimming bushes. Neighbor Jo had been as excited as I about it, while her husband, Lu, said, "Spray it with Raid and tramp on it."

Never! I could not do such a thing. Admittedly, curiosity had gotten the better of me, and to protect it from the cold, I brought it indoors, and placed it in a Cool Whip container in my lanai. If it came loose from the branch I wondered if that would matter. Was the branch its source of food? I had no idea about such things, nor what the cocoon would eventually turn out to be.

One lady I shared this with in Publix, told me, "Probably it'll be an ugly green snake." Still another said, "Maybe a big Palmetto bug?"

Thoughts turned to Doug. Whatever became of him? Doug, the handsome blue-eyed dancer, with the bronze dance certificate. Doug, whom I first met at Mulberry Grove, and at first monopolized all of my dances. Doug, who later became my escort for the Ballroom Dance at the lovely Savannah Center, my first time to attend such an elegant affair. I felt terrific, in my favorite dress, royal blue velvet, with a v-neckline edged in rhinestones, but now, while thinking about it, I shouldn't have worn those black panty hose. Off-black would have looked better. Though, when Doug picked me up, he did say, "You look nice." At the dance, he walked before me, in a peacock fashion, and in my mind I called him "my Napoleon." Even when a lovely waltz began to play, he didn't lean across the table, gently touch my hand, and ask, "Would you care to waltz?" Instead, he stood, raised his hand, snapped fingers, motioned to the dance floor, and took off without me. A good dancer, he whirled me this way and that, swung me around, turned me under arms which brushed the top of my seventy-three dollar coiffure. Yes, I had done something silly. Splurged. After my doctor's appointment, I stopped off at Arco, and there, stylist, Dianne, ran fingers through my hair, and said, "The color needs brightening. Your hair is too thin, and needs a build-up." So my hair was colored Vanilla Creme, trimmed, and blow-dried. Yes, I felt pretty.

But Doug, at the end of the evening, hadn't even kissed my cheek. He left me at my villa door, with a simple, "If I find time, I'll call you. My two sisters who live here, keep me quite busy. And I'll be leaving in a week and be gone for three."

Nice looking, and yes, with those blue eyes, like my father's, he was as cute as...a bug in a rug...and I pictured him as rather pampered, having been the only boy raised amidst eight sisters. No, I hadn't taken advantage of his kindness. I paid my own way at the Savannah Center, just in case my knee wouldn't keep up. It had, remarkably well, though, tired near the end.

Doug did tell me he is not looking for love right now. He's been widowed for two years, his villa is being constructed, and he then wants to hire a housekeeper to clean and care for it while he travels. In my summation, he needs a dance partner, a young someone without knee problems, and that excludes me.

# Chapter 43
# A Pain in the Neck

Health-wise, my most important concern is periodically keeping a check on nodules on both sides of my neck. Mother and Dad both had them, and they caused little concern during their lives. So far, I, too, am fortunate to be able to say the same.

When I moved to The Villages, though Dr. Binder, my Camp Hill physician, faxed my records to my new doctor here, I was informed doctors in Florida prefer their own tests and records. Consequently, over the past two months, along with everything else, I've been running back and forth for test after test, usually twice a week.

And so came orders for an ultra sound. After two ten-minute sessions of lying completely still with a rolled towel beneath my head, and pressing on three severely narrowed disks, never have I been troubled with such severe and excruciating pain. I don't know how much longer I can cope. It's difficult to move my head, to look this way and that. Particularly, while driving both the golf cart and my car. Bending over to gargle, and tilting my head to put in eye-drops will throw my neck into a fit of anguish.

We've tried different medicines to curb the pain, and the latest caused a thirteen day bout with diarrhea. My doctor was out of town and couldn't be reached, and I ended placing an SOS to Eckerd's local pharmacist, Bill, who, thankfully, recommended Imodium, ending that problem.

The neck pain still continues, and upset with the complete scenario, one day while waiting at the checkout counter in Eckerd's and chatting with a lady customer, she told me,"There's a new doctor in town. He's good. Go to him." So I gathered together my reports, drove to the Imaging Center, picked up my X-rays and took them along to the new physician.

"I'll take good care of you," he said, and sat down to study the film and my records. "Here, it says you have an overactive thyroid."

"No one ever informed me of this."

He, in turn, ended sending me to a Dr. Madonna, who said, "You shouldn't have been sent here. You should be seeing a different type doctor." So, my new doctor, sent me to still another, who sent me to still another, and on and on. Eight doctors in eight months.

Then, came the phone call from my first and original physician. I was due for a follow up. I took all the forms along, only to have her ask, "Why did you go to other doctors?"

I sensed disappointment, but had to speak frankly. "Because I wanted to know what's going on. I'm alone, and must take good care of myself. If I don't soon get help with this neck problem, I'm either going to die of pain, or end up having to wear a neck brace the rest of my life. I've been thinking, with this continuing pain, perhaps I may have cancer in my body, and should have a C125 test, pay for it myself, just to make certain I'll be alright."

"We can do that. Did we do any blood work to check the thyroid?"

"I don't recall. You have my records there."

A rifle of paper work and, "Yes, we did . Five months ago. I'll schedule a time next week and have it done again."

I told her, "There's something else I would like you to do."

A young miss, who had interrupted twice before, bounced into the room with a paper in hand. She and the doctor conversed a few minutes, and when she left, I again received the doctor's attention. "What were you saying?"

"I forgot. Whatever it was, it slipped out the window when she waltzed in. Right now, I need to get rid of this neck pain."

She arose from her chair, came over to the examining table where

I sat, felt the taut muscles, and said, "Yes, you're in bad shape. I'd suggest injections."

"Acupuncture? I'm game for anything to get rid of this pain. Even bedtime sleep is painful. With each turn, I must use both hands to lift my head. I never knew a head could be so heavy."

"I understand. No, not acupuncture, though similar. It's a procedure of three injections in the troublesome area. A doctor is here this morning, and he can do this for you, if you don't mind waiting."

She mentioned his name. Two months ago, he had performed my stress test, and four weeks later I received a phone call from a foreign miss, telling me of a congenital problem, which I was aware of. Yes, I liked this male doctor. A fine young man, so like my twin sons.

The wait was approximately forty-five minutes, but I didn't mind. Anything, anything, to feel good again.

During the procedure, I lay stomach down on the examining table, with a person standing on each side of me. One, was a strapping, young foreign lad, in green garb, the another, a petite lady, in white. The lady, I presumed to be a physician, because the doctor carefully informed her as to what he was doing, and she anxiously drank it all in.

When the first needle entered the back of my neck, I simply moaned. Then screamed, and it was then he told her, "Now, we're hitting the bone."

During the second injection, he said "Now we can't put this one too close, as it will hit the lungs." Another scream, and he again told her, "We're hitting the bone."

Near the end of the last injection, I felt a twinge of pain around my heart, screamed again, and said, "I think I'm going to pass out."

"That's okay. You can go ahead."

My immediate and cocky thoughts were, Buddy, I'm not coming back to you again. If I told you I think I'm dying, you just might say, "alright, go ahead," and I don't want to die yet.

Finished with the injections, he told me, "Now, when you first stand, your head will seem all wobbly. It will take about thirty minutes until it wears off. This should get rid of the pain. If it just mellows a bit, come back next week."

I was accompanied to my feet. My head felt fine, but my left knee buckled. Two arms grabbed me. "I'll be alright." I said. Only, as I broke away and began to walk, my left knee gave out again. I stood still, inhaled big gulps of air and tried again, but ended with a nurse's assistance as we walked out into the waiting room.

"Are you sure you'll be able to drive home?" she asked.

"In a few minutes." She left me sitting by the glass door. I felt whoozy. To pull myself together and hide my feelings from those seated around me, I donned sun glasses, rested my head against the wall and peacefully closed my eyes. Shortly, the young nurse returned and informed me I must wait another fifteen minutes before going off by myself.

Later, once on the road, I did manage to keep a steady head and steady hands on the steering wheel, and arrived home in one piece. There, though I tried to sleep, I seemed to only go off for a second into a weird world, and then my eyes would fly open. Bedtime, that night, also proved quite restless. Sleep absolutely refused to come. Finally at 4:45 AM, I crawled out of bed, went to the kitchen, heated some milk, drank it, returned to bed and slept four sound hours. I had been a mite concerned, because I once spoke to someone who could never sleep following some kind of treatment, and thoughts were, this may possibly be happening to me.

We all know, sleep is a marvelous escape from all worries of the world and personal, as well. I smile as I now write, remembering my dear departed husband, always telling me I was a sleep worshiper. Perhaps! Regardless, I now recall what I wanted to ask the lady doctor. "Could you please listen to my heart?"

Yes, for three wonderful days, I had been without pain. Truly, a blessing. However, since spending yesterday shopping in Ocala with friends, Janie and Suzanne, my neck has begun to hurt again. Not nearly as much as before. Yet, I must keep going. Keep my mind sharp and feet steady.

I sense things are beginning to look up, and I'm going to be better in no time. Through all of this, with Thanksgiving just around the corner, and December not too far away, I can't help wondering. Will I be well enough to travel home and be with my children during the most beautiful time of the year? With rooms trimmed in pine and holly, glistening trees covered with snow, and the laughter of the children, like songs, setting my heart aglow? Ah, yes, Christmas and the beginning of a new year.

# Chapter 44
## Meeting Delbert's Julie

This has been the busiest day in my life. I had been warned, here in The Villages one will become rattled if they allow themselves to become too involved in too many activities. But, what does one do, when everything seems to crop up at one time? In one day?

It began with the jangling phone, and Jake on the line. "Are we still on for lunch?"

Though we'll be together at Savannah Center's matinee performance from six to eight this evening, I said, "Yes." How could I say otherwise, since we hadn't seen each other for over a month?

"I'm calling to tell you, I now have four tickets. If you want, you can invite two of your friends."

"Married? Single?"

"Single. It will be nice being escorted by three pretty girls."

"I'll check around and see what I can do."

I hung up, a mite perturbed, having to add bothersome calls, to the tail end of my 'do' list: giving my villa a once over lightly, and buying groceries. My friend Del, in Connecticut, my Hawaiian hostess for the month of January, would be arriving at the Orlando Airport, at 5:30

this afternoon, to spend Thanksgiving week with me, as she had last year, when I lived in Ron's rental.

With some finagling, I figured a plan on how to achieve all I wished to accomplish. The Village Shuttle would pick Del up at 6:30 PM, at the Orlando Airport, and drop her off at our Spanish Springs Station around eight. The show at the Savannah Center would be over at eight. If Jake and I left immediately, and allowed ten minutes to reach my villa, everything would be fine.

I called five friends. No one could use the tickets. However, later, when Jake dropped me off at the Savannah Center, and went to park his car, a young couple stepped up on the sidewalk, and were headed in my direction. They were grateful to have the tickets and I gave them numbers four and five. Jake was pleased to hear this. Yet, later, we discovered we gave away the best seats. Ours were positioned in such a manner *our* view was somewhat obstructed by chairs on stage.

House lights were dimmed, and lovely Nadia, wife of Larry Peddrick, the shows' producer, all aglitter in a gown of red sequins, opened with a rendition of America the Beautiful. During intermission, Jake and I found two vacant seats in the middle of the auditorium, and the view proved excellent. At the finale I whispered, "Before the mob breaks loose, let's head for the parking lot."

Soon, we stepped out into a star studded night. A clean, sweet breeze caressed my cheeks, and spellbound, I slowly lifted my face and said, "Jake, look at that lovely moon."

Suddenly a lady's lilting voice filled the night air. It came from the area where Jake had parked his car. She was saying, "I never make mistakes. I never really do." Now laughter.

We were soon beside her, and Jake asked, "You never make mistakes?"

She turned to face us. "No, I never do."

Trim and elegant in a black sheath with long open lace sleeves, her jet black hair was styled into a smooth page-boy. Her date, tall, distinguished, an elderly gent with snow-white hair, stood on the other side of his car, and also appeared to be in an amiable mood.

We four laughed together, and I extended my hand to her, "I don't talk to strangers," I teased.

She hurriedly gave my hand a gentle squeeze. "My name is Julie Haines. What's yours?"

I quietly gulped a breath. Here was the lady handsome Delbert, whom I dated three times last year, spoke about plans to marry. Yet, he had called two months ago, to ask if I had ever run into Julie at Katie Belles, where she sometimes goes dancing. I never had. I now hoped she was sort of hung up on this handsome dude she was with, so I would have a chance in dating handsome Delbert. Ironic. Truly ironic, that of all the people I should meet this night, would be this lovely, upbeat lady, whom I couldn't dislike, and one whose dibs I would like to have on her man.

Jake and I made it to the shuttle bus station a few minutes prior to Del's arrival. When she disembarked, we rushed into each other's outstretched arms. As usual, this pert, petite miss bubbled over with enthusiasm, as she told us about her trip. "It was smooth and fantastic. No, I had no trouble at all. It was great, and fun talking to the friendly people on the bus. It was as if we knew each other for a long time."

She loved my villa. "This is all you need. You don't want a place any larger. Too much work." She helped shift pictures around, and cut some silk peach flowers off my artificial tree branches which extended too close to the sliding glass door leading into my lanai. "There! That looks much better," she stated, and I agreed.

For our Thanksgiving dinner, we dined on the upper floor of Katie Belles. She ordered salmon, and I chose turkey with all the trimmings, including pumpkin pie. Later, we bounced down the steps, and crossed the street to join the mob watching the dancing going on in The Square. A couple of dances, Del and I got up and wiggled around a bit, too, and I imagined, usually serene, sophisticated Del, was surprised with herself as we filled the night air with our giddy laughter.

We crowded in so much in those seven days, and yes, now and then talked about the men in my life, and wondered a lot about Delbert. The few times Delbert and I were able to spend together, he nearly set my heart to dancing. My bod, too, the last I saw him, and actually shoved him, and his grinning mug out the door. Would I ever hear from him again? Would he be returning to the Villages? Would he call? The last we spoke on the phone, he told me, "I'm standing here in my green robe, and I think of you each night when I climb into bed. And perhaps I should write to you." I told him it wasn't necessary. When our call ended, he said, "I love you," and I quickly replied, "Likewise." Del and I both thought this sounded cold, unfeeling, yet, I didn't know him that well. That would come later. God be willing, I would look forward to it. As I write, I can see his dear, gentle face, hear his Jimmy Stewart voice, and feel his warm breath as his lips come down to capture mine. "Whew", is all I can say at this tender age of 78, when it comes to thoughts of being with this man I call Delbert.

# Chapter 45
## Visiting Our New Hospital

Here I am again, feeling miserable with severe neck pain, following a thyroid CAT scan. Dr. B consulted Dr. Lowell, a satellite doctor from Ocala, who agreed to see me. Rather young, with a self-confident aura, I felt comfortable the moment I saw him walk through the doorway. "Your problem is, again, that rolled up towel pressing against severely narrowed disks, during the tests. Incidentally, you do not have cancer, so don't worry about that. Tests of neck and spine show severe narrowing of three disks, and acute arthritis has set in."

"I'm aware of the narrowed disks, but never had arthritis before. Only in my wrist and fingers, and it's mainly bothersome when I type excessively."

"Well, now you have acute arthritis, arthritis in full bloom."

Samples of Celebrex for pain, were given to me, and a beginning of therapy sessions set for the following day. His last words had me smiling. "Yes, I feel you'll be up to traveling home to see your family by the time Christmas rolls around."

My first day of therapy was more or less an examination, with a delicate massage. "We're going easy, to begin with," the therapist stated." My second, yesterday, we went a little further, and I was put in traction, to take pressure off the nerves in my neck. It felt wonderful.

The next evening, a Friday, I decided I would finish addressing Christmas cards, scribble off a personal note with each, and get that out of the way. Five hours later, with pen in hand, my mind went blank. Totally! Thoughts refused to come. There were none. Puzzled, I placed the card to the side, and using the address book, continued on, addressing envelopes. Eleven forty-five. Quick, consecutive, shock-like pain hit mid-center in my chest. Lordy, Lordy, was I having a heart attack? Now? When I'm so close to nearly being ready to pack my bag and fly off to Pennsylvania on the nineteenth? My very first doctor had prescribed ten nitroglycerin tablets, in case I ran into trouble. I'd take one. It helped, and I decided to hang up the pen, and go to bed. I dilly dallied, and wondered if I should keep my clothes on before slipping under the covers? No! Think positively. Everything will be alright. Yet? Would it? I called the hospital, in hopes someone there would tell me what to do. The emergency room gent, would put a nurse on the line. I remembered three other times when taken to the hospital via ambulance, back home, my problem proved to be my hiatal hernia which became troublesome only approximately every three to four years.

"Only you can make the decision as to whether you should come in," the nurse was telling me. "I would wait a bit."

The pain seemed to subside. Definitely a good sign. I zonked off the moment my head hit the pillow. At 4:21 AM, the exact sharp pain, again like an electric shock, shot through me. Wearily, I climbed out of bed, and slowly dressed. If the pain became worse I would be ready to leave. I made my way to the kitchen, cleared the table, of cards, stamps, etcetera in case whoever came into my villa, wouldn't be greeted with such a mess, and think me a slob. The pain kept coming, but didn't last long. Still? This, alone, could be a warning. I called the hospital, and the nurse agreed. "Sometimes you can prevent heart attacks, and I would recommend coming in and have it checked out. No, if I were you, and sound so calm, I would try and drive to the hospital rather than call the ambulance."

On my way, mentally, I could hear my Pennsylvania doctor's scolding. "Don't you *ever* drive in by yourself again. Supposing you black out on your way over here?" I turned on the radio, but didn't sing along as I'm inclined to do. During this Christmas rush, the hustle and bustle of shopping, wrapping gifts and driving to the Fed Ex building to mail packages, at times, on the busiest days, I had noted a shortness of breath. I would save all I had.

Streets in The Villages were brightly lit, but quiet. Not like in PA, where traffic over on the highway seldom stands still. Thoughts now were, *here I am all alone, in the solemn night*. No cars...and. . .yes. . .as I pull into the hospital parking lot...I've safely arrived!

The Village Hospital's physician seemed more concerned about my heart. While the heart doctor appeared more puzzled about the terrible neck pain. Two days later, after every heart test imaginable, I departed from my beautiful and well-furnished room, similar to a motel with a report my heart was fine, with the exception of the congenital defect. Discharge papers advised me to see my cardiac man in a week, and the orthopedic physician in three. The heart doctor's thoughts were, the spasms of chest pain were more than likely caused by the neck traction during therapy. They should be continued. So, today, that's where I'm off to. Also tomorrow. Will report in then.

The therapist refused to put me in traction today, following a phone conversation with my doctor. Instead, an MRI was scheduled. So goes life, it seems, with a conglomeration of tests after tests. Though I sense through time, trial and error, I'm slowly improving.

I've discovered, in trying to keep fit, when I attempt to swim and keep my face and head out of water, it further irritates the damaged nerves in my neck. Floating, and swimming on my back, using the water as a pillow, is rather comforting. Also, I now no longer need to lift my head with my hands to get out of bed. Instead, if I lie on my back, with chin on chest, and elbows out to the side, using them to push off the bed, there's no neck pain. I feel the latter discovery is actually tightening and strengthening my neck muscles.

Regarding tests, this will be the last for me, for a long, long time. I must not dwell on anything now, except getting ready to fly home to my children. My perfectly wonderful, wonderful kids.

# Chapter 46
# A Shaded Christmas

With my villa clean, sparkling in every sense, my bag packed, and my neck pain quieted, I hurried out into the lanai, picked up my cocoon, and said "Goodbye. I'm sorry, I've been so busy, with little time to talk of late, and I'll be gone for awhile. If you should decide to come out before I return, you'll have a lot of room to fly around and do your own thing."

My doorbell rang, and there stood friend, Jake, ready to take me to the S\shuttle bus station. Bless his heart!

When I boarded the bus, I threw him one last kiss, and soon was off, heading for the Orlando Airport, on the first trek of my journey to PA. A smooth beginning. However, while we were first seated on the plane, we passengers became somewhat edgy as the captain repeatedly kept us up to date as to why we were not yet airborne. The fuel gauge was not functioning. First, they had to go through security, then drain the center tank, measure the fuel and return it. After two hours, he said, "I'm sorry it's taking so long. There's a plane next to us that's going to Philadelphia. If anyone wishes, they may transfer, but I'd prefer you wouldn't, as it will cause a luggage problem."

Only one couple left.

I spent another hour reading and chatting with those around me. Now and then, thoughts drifted to my children, My first seven days would be spent in the country, where I would bunk down in Keith's and Marsha's home, with my two littlest grandkids, Caralie Elizabeth, 12, and Aaron, 11. When the children were at school and their parents at other schools teaching, would I, without a car and so far away from everything, feel isolated?

Four hours late, our plane landed at the Middletown Airport, and I nearly fell into handsome son, Keith's arms. Seeing him was sheer joy. "We worried about you, Mom," he said, and I choked on happy tears, thinking he was one sweet, sensitive guy, and my kids still loved me, despite my living so far away.

"I worried about you, too, but there was no way to contact you," and I told him about the problem. Ironically, for some unknown reason, my luggage was not on my plane, but, the airlines delivered it the next day.

Things seemed to be running smoothly at Keith's and Marsha's for awhile, until Saturday morning, when I heard Keith conversing on the phone with his brother, Kevin. "Marsha said you told her I could have it for nothing. And now, because I didn't pick it up, you're charging?"

At first I thought it might be something they needed, and at the moment their budget couldn't afford, and interrupted. "What's that all about?"

Quite sharply he said, "It's a family matter, and you shouldn't interfere." Later, I told him my feelings were hurt, and I felt an apology was due, and he actually told me, "I'm sorry, Mom. But you interrupted, just like my children do when I'm on the phone." Then he added, "Our conversation pertained to health equipment Kevin was giving to me."

Next, came my trip to daughter Dianne's and her husband Eric's home, in Womelsdorf, an hour away. I would stay with them four days. Everything seemed to be running smoothly. One day, it snowed, not too heavily. Though Dianne was supposed to be off from work, she decided to go into her office and sort of have an "operation head-start" for the new year. She invited me to come along.

I did, and while she worked at her desk, speaking to customers on the phone, answering inquiries, and filling orders for valve and pump companies, and military contracts, I worked at the desk to the right, cleaning out old files. I removed folders, separated the crowded, neatly marked the tops and filed them in a different cabinet, making room for the new correspondence. It proved fun, taking me way back to my first job as a filing clerk. We worked until five, and I was up to the letter 'S' when she said, "Let's call it a day, Mom." We did, and soon were traveling down the highway on our way home. Then suddenly, up ahead on the left, appeared a building with a big sign advertising ICE CREAM. "It's homemade, Mom, and we're deserving." I told her it was a grand idea, so we stopped in, and I ordered two scoops of butter pecan, and she chose strawberry and vanilla.

I enjoy being with Dianne. She's a happy person, always on the go, and helping others. I also relish time spent in their 150-year-old home, and enjoy the quaint old-fashion Christmas trimmings, as well as unusual food I have never tasted.

The following morning, for breakfast, we had beer toast, made by her Eric. We ate in her dining room, and were seated at a long table clothed in hunter green, and for a centerpiece, she had made an attractive topiary tree of fresh fruit. As I drank in the quaint surroundings, my glance took me down a dark corridor. Rather dismal.

"Honey," I said, "You should remove the snow from the transient outside. It would allow sunlight to filter in and make the hallway bright and cheerful to the eye."

"What snow?"

"Over the doorway." I nodded.

"Mom, if you went outside, you would see that's not snow. It's a Williamsburg, Virginia painting of colorful fruit."

"Oh! But, if it were me, I wouldn't block out the sunshine."

"Mom! I'm not you. You always go around telling people what to do."

"Do I? Really?"

"Yes, Mom."

I was under the impression I suggest what to do and what not to do.

The room was quiet a moment and she continued, "There you go again, with your 'shoulds', and 'woulds', Mom. When you do this, and Eric is around, he'll say, 'Here comes another *should.*' Then he does the exact opposite."

So, I had stuck my foot in my mouth, again. In an attempt to remove it, I said, "Oh! That's okay."

She continued: "You're always telling people what they should do. 'You should do this. Or should do that. You wouldn't do this, or wouldn't do that.' It's a habit you have. You don't stop and think everyone has their own ideas of what to do, and what not to do. Watch it, Mom, because people take it as criticism. Think before you speak."

"Well, I'm speaking, and that at least tells me I'm alive." Why I said that, I have no idea. Probably because I was stunned with hurt. I thought a bit, and said, "You just may be right. I remember when your father was in college and he wrote to me, I'd correct his spelling."

"Yes, Mom. You did the same to me when I was in college, and that's why I didn't write as often as I could have."

Later that day, during the evening dinner hour, I remained quiet. Thoughts were, *I don't need this. Why should I make a long trip and then have to put up with the sleet, snow, and this? Next year I won't do it. I won't! Let them come to me, for once.*

Then thoughts shifted, and before I realized it, I said, "Dianne, this is your home, you and Eric do whatever you wish."

"We do, Mom. You just have this habit and don't stop to think everyone's idea isn't like yours."

And that was that. At least I didn't dwell on the hurt, but let it slip away as fast as my mind would scurry.

My last two days in PA, due to weather conditions, I opted to stay with friend Norma, in the Hershey area, closer to the Harrisburg, Middletown Airport. During that time, not once could we step out her door, because of ice-covered walks.

When my departure time came, I wouldn't allow Norma to take me to the airport. Instead, I called the Hershey Limousine Service. My jovial driver, who cautiously walked ahead, pulled my luggage over ice-filled footprints, and called orders over his shoulder, "Wrap your arms around my waste and hold on so you won't fall." Together as we trudged along, we laughed all the way to his van.

I had only an hour and twenty-five minute wait at this airport. I sat on the plane and watched, while a crew of men hosed down the plane, with water and chemicals to prevent the wings from freezing. The flight to Orlando went smoothly, as did the Shuttle bus to The Villages, where Jake waited for me. In five minutes, I heaved a sigh of relief as I stepped over the doorsill into the cozy warmth of my villa, away from the north winds and the freezing cold. . .and somewhat biting tongues.

In my lanai, my cocoon still quietly rested in the Cool-whip container. I picked him up and brought him close to my face. "Hi, there. It's me," I said. "Are you okay? I'm home now. I'm home."

# Chapter 47
## Dianne's Heartwarming Letter

I'm pretty well caught up, since my return home here in this retirement community. There's no let-down and I'm not bored. Never! Though one could say I'm back in my happy rut. These were my thoughts, as I pulled away from the mail-station in my golf cart, and the basket in back held a conglomeration of magazines, newspapers, bills and letters.

One envelope in particular had caught my eye. I would recognize Dianne's handwriting anywhere. This was the first letter I received from any of my children, since I left over the holidays. I wondered what Dianne had to say. The tiff we had while at her place came to mind. Yet, upon my departure, the air had been cleared one hundred percent.

Back in my villa, I tossed all the mail on the kitchen counter. All with the exception of Dianne's letter. I pressed it to my cheek as I slowly walked into the living room and curled up on the sofa. There, I kissed the envelope, gingerly tore open the flap and sniffed happy tears, sighed, and gleefully laughed, as I read:

Dear Mom,

Just a quick note to check in and say "Hi". It gives me a warm fuzzy when I look through the filing cabinets and see your writing. Thanks again for your assistance. You are now a part of Precision Technology, the company which employs me.

After talking to some of the people I work with, and seeing and hearing how happy you are in The Villages, Florida, I need to admit, you made the right decision. So many of my friends and co-worker's mothers spent their lives catering to their husbands and children, and when their husbands passed on and the children had their own lives, they retreated into a shell of depression. To the point where they have no outside interest and just sit at home and feel sorry for themselves.

Even though you catered to Dad and us, you always had outside activities that kept you well-rounded. Good job, lady!!! You knew what was best for you. Don't let anyone, not even your kids hold you back.

As a side note, I've been thinking about our discussions where I told you that you are always telling people what to do and correcting them. After thinking about it, you have always done it. I'm not saying it's a bad thing, because I know your suggestions and corrections are meant to help, not hurt people. I'm just trying to put it all into perspective, when thinking about it, and remembered the times I would send you letters from college and then receive them back with the spelling corrected. I know this was meant to help me, but what it did was stop me from sending letters, (oh, yes, I am a stubborn little brat.) I love spell check. I just did it on this note and had five misspelled words. I'll never get this spelling challenge...perfect-classy lady, Mother of mine.

I close with much love and bunches of hugs.
Your daughter, Dianne

More than ever, I knew for certain Dianne cared and loved me. I couldn't help myself. I sat down and wrote right back to her:

Hey there, you beautiful, understanding daughter, with the brilliant, sensible mind. Guess you got it naturally. (Giggle.)

Yes, I received your latest and it had me sniffling and laughing at the same time. It was the most important and meaningful letter I have ever received. I mean this sincerely and thank you from the bottom of my heart.

Regarding transferring your files, I'm happy I could help and know that you now think of me when you go to your filing cabinets.

Yes, all along, I've tried to give my best, and guess it's become habitual when it came to tossing thoughts to others. However, since your scolding, during my last visit with you, I've been doing remarkably well in changing. Really, honestly I have.

Only last night, friend Jake, claimed I sulk. Not so! I told him I remain quiet, and try to analyze as to what I should have said, what I should not have, while mentally slipping off in an attempt to be discrete and not open my mouth before my brain is in gear.

Still, here in the Villages, life nicely continues on. At the moment I'm sitting in my lanai and my toes are cold. We've had a cold front for the past weeks. It's supposed to go into the high 60s today. I've been reading my e-mail, deleting all the advertisements . *The Young and the Restless* and *The Bold and the Beautiful* will soon be on TV, during my lunchtime. So, honey, who made my day, I'll close with much love and many hugs from me, your content Mom, who has been there, done than and now this, here in this retire community in sunny Florida. Always and forever, Much love and many hugs, from Mom

# Chapter 48
## The Mardi Gras

Today's paper mentioned The Villages Mardi Gras festivities going on in the square tonight and I thought of my friend, another named Jane, whom I met one day when I was seeing off sis, Kathy, and cousin, Betty, at the bus station. Jane, an artist, and busy with the theater group, and I, in furnishing my new dwelling, had never gotten together again, until several months ago, when I happened to read it was Italian Day, and they were celebrating with a big parade in town. Jane, too, had no commitments that day, so off we went to town in her golf cart.

Like back then, would she happen to be at loose ends, today? I looked back on that festive day when we found the big tent set up in the area where the Sales Office is now. There were many people congregated under the rooftop. Some, seated at tables, enjoyed an afternoon meal, some played Bingo, and directly beyond, at the opposite end, many danced to the peppy music played by a band. Jane and I had stood at the one entrance, and clapped our hands to toe-tapping music. It stopped. The band director called out, "Anyone here from Pennsylvania?"

"Me! Me!" I squealed, as I flung arms skyward, and bounced up and down to get his attention. Immediately, his rendition of The Pennsylvania Polka had Jane and I whirling around on the edge of the dance floor, while a photographer followed us, in an attempt to snap our picture. When the dance ended, he asked our names, for the newspaper. No, our pictures never appeared in our local, undoubtedly because we were living it up so much, with our hair flying as wildly as our feet.

Now, perhaps Jane may want to go into town and see the Mardi Gras Parade, and whatever else would be going on? I reached for the phone, dialed her number, spoke of the festivities and asked, "Want to come along with me? I'll pick you up. Say in about twenty minutes."

"That sounds like fun. I'll give you directions to our house and leave the light on."

This proved pleasing to my ears as she's quite involved, sketching portraits for friends and neighbors, or for one activity or another, and here she was, on the spur of the hour, ready to find time to goof off again with me. Later, seated in my golf cart, we both worried about finding a parking spot. "Since the snow-birds are here it will be rather difficult, I'm sure," Jane said.

"Maybe not. We'll think positively."

In town, we passed streets jammed with six people deep on both sides. "I'll try behind the church where I always park on Sundays." No success there, either. "Jane!" I pointed. "Look straight ahead, at those two Job Johnny's parked over there. My car will easily fit between, leaving room for doors to be opened. But...supposing I get a ticket for illegal parking?"

Jane's eyes twinkled. "Bootsy, don't you worry even a little bit. I'll pay for the ticket, if we get one. I think this is perfect and was reserved just for us."

I smiled at this *one positive-thinking gal.*

Music from the three bands in the square drifted on the clean night air, as we marched through parking lots and made our way out to Main Street. Mobs of street people in a festive mood, awaiting the parade to begin, were dressed in bright colors. Some wore masks, peacock feathers, you name it.

"Come, let's go this way, and see if we can find a good viewing spot to stand." I grabbed her arm and we eased through the crowd on a street not so crowded. "Maybe here?" We inched our way toward the curb.

"You can stand here," a man said, and moved to the side, closer to a lady we learned was his wife. Only one problem. The tall, rather hefty woman with long dark hair, standing in front of me, lit a cigarette.

Jane and I coughed and the gentleman said, "She should know better. Evidently, she doesn't think of other people."

We all growled about the smoke, not too quietly, and she turned around and said, "We were here first. If you don't like it, move."

Jane and I put our heads together, and decided she had to be an outsider, a visitor, and we did move down the street a bit. We ended amongst a group of nice people who, like we, were bubbling over with excitement, awaiting that first drum beat or siren to announce the beginning.

On tip-toes, I turned to Jane, behind me. "Can you see?"

"Yes, pretty good. Can you?"

"Not too well."

The words were no sooner out of my mouth when the air broke loose with sirens, drums beating and the mob's happy uproar, and the young gent in front of me moved back and shoved us in front near the curb. "Take my place. You'll be able to see better."

It proved to be in an ideal spot, beside his mother, and younger brother. As numerous floats passed by with platforms of gaily dressed participants, we chanted "Beads! Beads!" and greedily stretched out hands to grab those tossed our way.

There came a float with a lady from the Singles Club, our Social Chairperson, slinky, petite Dianne Bolton, swathed in coral silk, and dressed as a Hindu maiden. "Beads! Beads! Beads!" I yelled, and received a handful.

Someone on the right, slipped a larger purple pair over my head, and I turned to find the young man's mother, Gale. "It's a strand you don't have," she laughingly stated. I ended with fifteen.

Though the parade was over, an air of exuberance and gala excitement hung over the crowd which hadn't thinned a bit. Only now, people were lined all the way up the street in front of the food counters.

"Hungry?" I asked Jane.

"I could go for a sausage sandwich."

"Me, too. Regular, Greek or Italian?"

She chose regular, I chose Italian, and we had them cut in two, swapped one half and downed them with a soda.

Later, as we hiked through the parking lot, we peppered the night air with our gleeful giggles. And yes, we found my car with no trouble, and no we didn't receive a parking ticket. I dropped Jane off at her home, and when we gave each other a sisterly hug and she told me, "I had such fun, we'll have to do this more often," I agreed. It had been one of the most frivolous, yet most meaningful nights; one never to forget.

# Chapter 49
## Curiosity, My Cocoon and Me

Throughout the week ahead, periodically I picked up my little cocoon, placed it in the palm of my hand, and with face close to it, I would gently say, "Good morning. It's me. I'm here. Are you okay, today?"

Of course he would say, "Sure I am, you silly lady." No he wouldn't. Not really. But one day he moved back and forth, inside his protected home, and I felt a gentle pulsating in my hand. One cannot imagine the thrill which coursed through my complete body, and of course I had to report this to all my friends.

Friend, Karen Schultz, came to see it that morning, and excitedly exclaimed, "Oh, my gosh! I wonder what it is? It's fluttering."

"Yes! Isn't it exciting? It's alive and feels like the first fluttering of an unborn child." We huddled together, and with ears close to it, could actually hear a gentle buzzing.

Friend, Marti Rowland, arrived in the afternoon and also felt the gentle pulsating in her hand, and became excited about its upcoming birth. Daphine, next door, checked in periodically to see how "my baby" was doing.

I laughed about all of this, but, still held the good faith I could help bring him into this world. I found myself telling him, "You're doing fine. Whatever you are, whether you're pretty or ugly, we've come this far, and I will love you."

Silly? I knew this, but couldn't help myself.

On mornings when it wouldn't move, slowly I rolled it from one side to the other. Then, there it was! Just a gentle movement, to tell me it still lived. The last week of February, thoughts were, *it's time to place it outside in my courtyard where it might awaken in its natural habitat.* February 27 and the 28 it rained. Actually it poured, leaving one think it might never let up.

Two days later, I hurried outside to find the poor thing not white, but tan, and floating in five inches of water. I scooped it out, brought him indoors, and as I walked across the room, said, "I'm sorry! I hope you're okay. Give me a sign you are." There was none. Still, I wouldn't give up hope. "I'll just put you over here on the sea-mist green carpet in the sunshine, by the sliding glass door. You'll be able to dry out." No, he didn't say, "Lordy, Lordy, lady, what do you expect of me after what you put me through?"

The following day, I went to check on him, and was shocked to find it had somehow rolled over next to the metal frame of the glass door. I placed him back on the carpet, and called friend, Jane.

"Oh, I'm so thrilled for you. I'm so anxious to find out what it is. Tell me, why do you keep calling it 'he'?"

I laughed. "Truly, I have no idea. Sometimes it's a 'he', sometimes it's an 'it'. This is the first I've handled a situation like this."

"It's simply marvelous that you should take the time. Not everyone would do this."

March 1, come morning I checked to find he hadn't moved from where I last left him. In the early afternoon, I picked him up, and was shocked to find a hole at the one end. Had he escaped, or could he still be inside? Hurriedly, I rushed over to show Jo and Lu. While Lu sat before the TV, enjoying a ballgame, Jo removed a magnifying glass from a drawer, and we both scrutinized the inside, only to see what appeared to be the outer part of a brown shell.

"Look, Jo! There's a piece of the shell knocked off. Could that be his head? And are those marks on the side, his eyes?"

"Nah! It's only a piece of the shell. I think he escaped."

"I'm curious to see what he was, or is."

"Me, too!" I returned home, found a pair of cuticle scissors, and cautiously opened the somewhat white casing, to find only brown shell. In no time, Jo came over, and together we searched my villa. Finally, on hands and knees she called over her shoulder,"I give up! It's not under the skirts of the sofa and love seat. I wonder where that bugger could be?"

"I have no idea, but thank God it's not a little green snake, or something similar." I swallowed hard, then added, "I hope it's not a Palmetto bug." We both agreed it would probably come out from his hiding place one time or another, when it was good and ready.

Later, when I returned from watering five red Hibiscus shoots I had rooted and planted along the garden wall, I stepped over the sliding glass door frame, and paused. Something, directly ahead, about five inches long, straight as a vertical stick, dark brown and ugly, from where I stood, clung to the rung of a dining room chair. I cautiously approached, and wondered if *he* would be something of which I may be afraid? Then I gasped when I bent to stare.

"You finally made it. Good for you. Truly, you are beautiful."

I rushed to the phone and called all of my lady friends to let them know *my baby* had arrived. They were as excited as I. "He just hangs there. I'm wondering if he is, indeed, still alive? With closed wings, he looks like a butterfly."

Four hours later, there he remained, in the same position. Three more hours, and yet he hadn't moved. I gently touched him, and it didn't faze him in the least. He still clung to the chair when I retired for the night. The following morning he sat prettily on the floor, wings beautifully spread, showing off his colors. I went outdoors, snipped off a stem of flowering white Rose Vinca, brought it in and placed it beside him on the floor. Thoughts were he may enjoy the sweet nectar. Humming birds in Pa do.

Later, I returned from a shopping trip and found him on the dining room curtain, wings fully spread. I gasped! "You are one magnificent sight." And I'm sure he smiled at me. His top side was camel brown with wings edged in grey blue and mauve pink. Inner wings had an unusual black circle resembling an eye, with the inside shaded in grey, and a bright yellow dot in the middle.

He vanished again. I didn't see him until much later that evening when I exited from my office and snapped on the living room light.

Then there he came, zooming toward me, crazily flitting up and down, back and forth on his first solo flight across the ceiling, wings making a steady clicking sound.

I became half afraid, fearful he'd land on my head, and yelled at him. "Don't do that! You'll hurt your wings." To make sure he'd listen, I turned off the lights and went to bed. Come morning, I found him, wings frayed, on the marble window sill in the kitchen. "You poor thing. Now look at what you've done to yourself," I scolded. Evidently, he had tried to escape, but the metal edges of the Venetian blind which covered the window, had played havoc to his delicate wings. I pictured a treadmill on which one attempted to get off and couldn't.

Friend, Natalie, my decorator, said butterflies like sugar water. I placed a saucer full in the sink. She had also advised me to drive over to Porters and get a Butterfly bush and plant it outside for him. I would do that later, since those in my garden were not yet in bloom. Now I wondered what to do with my poor baby with the frayed wings? I imagined he read my thoughts. He dropped into the sink, and seemed rather weak, so I placed him on the edge of the saucer. Fearful he would fall in and drown, I tilted the saucer until some water ran off. No, he didn't eat a bit, instead, he simply got the front of himself saturated, then chose to fly back to his station, the window sill, but now landed on a leaf of pink Rose Vinca I was rooting. Could I pick him up and carry him out into the lanai? No, I would take the vase and all, and place the saucer beneath it. That night, I checked in on him and he lay so still on the saucer's edge. I touched him. He moved a little, and I retired that night, with a prayer on my lips the poor critter would live until morning. My prayers were answered. When I stepped over the doorsill into my lanai, for the very first, I picked him up bodily, in my hand, and carried him outdoors into my courtyard.

The sun shone beautifully. Hawthorne bushes in their delicate white blooms, lightly scented the gentle breeze. "You'll do fine out here," I told him. "You'll be okay." I didn't tell him how Jane's husband and the men at the Sunday breakfast at Café Ole' on the square, told me he would make a dainty morsel for bats and owls which flew by night.

Instead, I gently sat him on a leaf of a Azalea bush, full of red blooms, and simply said, "Goodbye now. I must go grocery shopping," and wondered if he would be there upon my return.

He wasn't. I looked inside and under the bush and couldn't find him anywhere. In my mind's eye, I pictured him as he flew over the garden wall, off into the wide blue yonder, and couldn't help thinking we were similar. He had come bursting from his cocoon, and me, from mine, when I uprooted and moved away from Pennsylvania where I had lived for so long. And here we both were, spreading our wings and starting anew in a beautiful place. I also thought of how it hadn't been too long ago when stores sold rocks and people bought them as pets. At least my pet was alive. No, he wasn't a butterfly as I had at first imagined. Instead, he was one of Florida's Eye Moths with a wing-span of five and a half inches, and because of curiosity, for a short while, he was mine.

# Chapter 50
# The Red Hat Society

After thirteen months residency here, where one day melts into another, and people enjoy living life to the fullest, I'm still wrapped up, going with the flow, and not afraid to venture into paths of newness. I have now become a member of that national honorary society called the Red Hat Ladies. It all started when Elizabeth Lucas, 84, an English lady, attended a garage sale and fell in love with a red hat. She purchased one for herself and decided to buy one for her lady friend, who, on down the line, continued the trend. How true this is I'm not certain, but I do know it was Elizabeth who shared her thoughts on aging in the following sonnet:

When I am
an Old Women
I shall wear purple
with a red hat which doesn't go, and doesn't suit me,
And I shall spend my pension on brandy and summer
gloves
And satin sandals, and say we've no money for butter.
I shall sit down on the pavement when I'm tired
And gobble up samples in shops, and press alarm bells
And run my stick along the public railings

And make up for the sobriety of my youth,
And pick the flowers in other people's gardens
And learn to spit.
You can wear terrible shirts and grow more fat
And eat three pounds of sausages at a go,
Or only bread and pickle for a week,
And hoard pens and pencils and beermats and things
in boxes.
But now we must have clothes that keep us dry
And pay our rent and not swear in the street
And set a good example for the children.
We will have friends to dinner and read the papers.
But maybe I ought to practice a little now?
So people who know me are not too shocked and surprised
When suddenly I am old and start to wear purple.

On April 21, my friend, Jane, a member of The Crimson Gem, Red Hat Lady's Society, invited me, a member of the Les'Dames aux Bonnets Rouges, to tag along with her group. We would be attending The Red Hat Society's Spring Fling at the Geneva Camp in Fruitland Park. My phone jangled and Jane was on the line.

"I'm nearly ready," I told her. "I'm attired for the day in purple dress and you ought to see my red hat. It's simply smashing."

"I'll bet you look simply marvelous. You look great in hats."

"I know you will, too. I feel giddy, like a schoolgirl."

"Isn't this fun?" asked Jane.

"Yes, it is. Gotta hurry, I'm having difficulty fastening my red hat pin to my red satin scarf, but I'll be over shortly. There! It's fastened!"

Even though we didn't drink brandy nor wear summer gloves, we, along with Jane's friends and neighbors, Mary and Peggy, traveled down the highway and gathered in the campsite's main building, with a group of seven hundred fifty other Red Hat Society members from The Villages, Water Oak and Spruce Creek, South. There, we would eat lunch and enjoy what we hoped would be our yearly spring affair. It proved to be one fun-tastic day, with the delirium of Spring Fever winning over spring cleaning, as we vented our time and energy, dining, line-dancing and doing *our own thing* in tune to the band music which echoed throughout the auditorium. Of course, being women, we also enjoyed the shopping. Vendors from around the state tempted us with titillating Red Hat-related merchandise such as purple dresses, red rhinestone encrusted lapel pins, hand-painted red on purple shirts, red hats, satin garters, Red Hat bean-bag dolls, and license plates with the motto, "You only think we're old."

Every woman present had let her imagination run wild in assembling her own crowning creations, hats of every sort. There were tennis visors ornamented with purple satin scarves, a picture hat with life-size cascading wisteria blossoms, a red prairie sunbonnet, trimmed in purple braid, wine-bottle corks, plastic grapes, and ribbons and lace galore. My red-brimmed hat was circled with a red sequin belt, never worn, which I attempted to sell at a garage sale, and too, purple plastic flowers removed from a flower pot in my courtyard.

Belonging to the Red Hat Society is great fun. On November 10, of this year, the Red Hat Queen from California, Sue Ellen Cooper, will be coming to The Villages. The Queen's Council has planned a "Queens Only", reception on that day.

I reiterate. In this retirement community there are numerous activities and many clubs offered for all of us to join. Not only for men, but for the tender sex. I'm one of them, and happy to be...a Red Hat Lady.

**Showing off my red hat at the Red Hat Society's
Spring Fling in Fruitland Park**

# Chapter 51
## Steve, Doug and Woody

As I look back, I blink in amazement at the unusual events, the fun times, the full life one can experience in a retirement community. Each day is met with anticipation. Yesterday, the Red Hat Society picnic so happily consumed the complete day. *What would today bring?* I wondered when I answered the phone this morning, to hear an unfamiliar man's voice on my line.

His name was Steve. Last Christmas, we first met in PA, when he arrived at my son Keith's home, and invited me to dinner. We spent the entire evening reminiscing about our departed friend, Ginny, his greatest love, and my cruising buddy. Over the past four years, up until her death, I knew Steve only through reading his many love letters she shared with me. I also enjoyed his humorous, and downright silly greeting cards. Then, last week, while traveling across the states, he made a brief call. He was heading this way to visit relatives. He may drop by.

"Where are you now, Steve?"

"Just outside The Villages."

"On a cell phone?"

"Yes, how do I find your villa?"

I gave directions and it wasn't more than five minutes when I opened the door and there he stood, in white shorts, tan top, a smile and a "Hello" on his lips. We embraced, and while seated in the living room, caught each other up to date.

"Time has to be cut short for me," he said. "Recently I purchased a boat. It's now anchored in the Chesapeake Bay, and I must hurry home, attend two more classes, and learn how to man it." Excitement shone in his eyes. "I've always dreamed of this." Later, over lunch in my courtyard, our chat continued regarding our mutual friend, Ginny, and how terribly we missed her.

In the evening, we drove to town to listen to the Village Christian Coraleeres sing at The Church in the Square. Amongst the sixty, would be two of my sorority sisters, Maureen Nash, and Mary O'Donnell. Because this was the Coraleeres first performance, and outside in the square, the band already filled the air with peppy music, and villagers and visitors were swinging away, I couldn't imagine the church being even half full. Wrong! We found it nearly jammed packed, and had to sit up front on the far right, behind the organ, piano and a wooden railing adorned with high plants. We couldn't see any of the singers garbed in their long black robes.

When a draft from the air-conditioner proved annoying, and I reached to remove my pink, cotton jacket from the back of my chair, Steve helped me slip into it. Blue eyes twinkling, he asked, "Is that alright?" A dear, kind man, as Ginny had always said. Midway through the program, during a standing ovation for a piano duet, I whispered, "Steve, look, over there, at the end of that one front pew, there's a place still left for two. Evidently, reserved for a couple who didn't show up. I'm going to try to sneak over, want to come along?"

He chose not to, so for the last twenty minutes I had a splendid ringside seat. Even gave a little wave to Maureen, and she reciprocated with a smile, and a hand raised slightly mid-air. A fabulous beginning of Steve's and my evening together. Following the delightful performance, we hiked down the street to where we parked, and decided to drive closer to the square, and see what was going on there.

When the band switched to a slow number, Steve said, "It's a Fox Trot. Let's try it." He proved light on his feet, and easy to follow. After two dances we decided to sit it out, and like many others, occupy two of the green chairs on the outside perimeter, and "people watch." We enjoyed the antics of five little ones who put on a show of their own.

From the square, we drove to Applebee's, where we chatted and reminisced some more about our Ginny, and we both ordered my favorite dish, chicken quesadilla, with vegetables. While dining with him, it was jolly fun to watch his moves, to study him, his manners and everything about him. I had noticed he holds your hand when walking down the street, insists on helping you off the curbs, and now he seats a lady before seating himself. . Politeness personified. Long ago, Ginny had said Steve was one polite and grand guy; a perfect gentleman, and I could readily see this.

We returned to my villa, close to ten o'clock. Because he had traveled ten hours with still a ways to go, when I showed him through my villa, and we reached the guest room, I told him, "I trust you, Steve. If you wish, you are welcomed to stay overnight in here."

"Thank you, Bootsy," he said. "That's very kind of you. It's been a long, tiring day, and I thought of checking into a local motel."

It seemed strange to have a man sleep over. At ten thirty, he retired early, and shut his door. Since I usually am up until twelve, I straightened the kitchen, and sat in the living room where I perused the morning paper. When I did retire, in order to make certain of a sound night's sleep, without concern of any kind, I locked my bedroom door.

The following morning, Steve arose at seven. I slept until 8:30, dressed, put on my face, and came out to find him reading the morning paper. It was a pleasant feeling, seeing him there. Like old times with my Bill. Over breakfast of egg omelet, coffee and toast, he said, "I slept soundly, more so here, than back home."

"I knew you would. I sleep more fitfully here, too.

Breakfast finished and he helped clean off the table when the doorbell rang. There stood blue eyes, Doug.

"I'm back!" he said, grinning.

I had wondered about him, and was pleased to see him, and asked, "How were things in Michigan."

"We were without electricity and running water for awhile, because of a snowstorm."

'Poor baby," I said, because I knew what would be coming next out of my mouth. "Didn't I tell you I always request visitors to call first?"

A sheepish grin. "I was in this village, saw a car in your drive so knew you were home, and I stopped for my dance tapes."

"Oh, that's alright then. "

Steve took this opportunity to say, "I'm due to meet my sister and her daughter in Orlando at noon, Bootsy. I'll be leaving. You two have a good time."

"But, Steve, don't you want to travel over The Village golf-cart bridge, to the post office with me, and mail my package, liked we planned?"

"No, I don't want to be late."

"I'll take you to the post office." Doug said, smiling that winning smile of his.

I explained to Steve, Doug had moved here in December, escorted me to the Christmas Ball at the Savannah Center, and last month returned to his hometown for awhile.

Doug piped up, "I just got back. I'll go out and move my car, Steve, so you can back out."

While Doug was outside moving his red Corvette, inside my opened front door, Steve was kissing me lightly on the lips.

"I had a fine time, it was fun, thanks," he said. "I'll see you again." And together we walked out to his car. He brushed lips to my cheek, climbed behind the wheel and with a wave, drove away.

Doug pulled his car into the drive, and with one hand still on the steering wheel and the other holding his cell phone, he asked me, "Wanna come to Ocala with me, I have to pick up a video. First, we'll mail your package."

Finally, I agreed. "Come inside while I lock up, and get my sunglasses and purse." He followed me, shut the door, and stood in my kitchen. "I really hate to leave this in such a mess, Doug. Rarely, do I, but time flies, here. By the way, I haven't had a chance to view your dance tapes. My knee has been acting up. I've been thinking, you might want to find a sweet young thing, with no leg problem. I'm really not interested in furthering my dance knowledge. I'm happy where I am. Except, maybe with the Latin dances."

"I'm not looking for a sweet young thing. I can still take you to dinner, and a dance now and then. It's not necessary to be able to dance every dance. We can sit one out and watch others."

"I just don't want to hold you back."

248

"You're not."

We were in his car when I said, "I forgot my sunglasses. Wait! I'll be right out."

"Don't forget a bonnet," he tossed after me. I thought this quaint. It took a little longer than I expected, as a little Gecko scooted inside when I went to close the sliding glass door in the dining room. "Hey, you, bugger! Get out." I chased him around the table, but where he went, I had no idea. He was at the other end of the door and vanished.

Our trip to Ocala was the greatest. I felt like a teenager on a date, with my hat now off and the wind teasing my hair we sang along with Elvis on tapes. When we pulled into Sam's parking lot, and parked, Doug said, "Here, you may use my card and take advantage of their discounts."

Just then, a young male clerk showed up.

"Man! That's some car. May I look at it? Every time I see a picture like this, I tell myself, one day, I'm going to have a red Corvette, just like this. But it will be nineteen years before I'll be able to afford one."

When he left, I told Doug, "If I won the lottery, I'd buy one for him."

Doug was so sweet in Sam's store. He pushed the cart, lifted a heavy carton of orange soda for me, and we scooted along, and at the end of aisles, sampled the venders enticing samples. Next, it was off to Circuit City for Doug's tape. He hurried in, while I waited in his car, and drank in the afternoon sun, hoping to get a little tan, when a sexy, voluptuous blonde, climbed out of her car, and began walking over. "Your car is wonderful. I love it," she said.

"It's not mine. It's my friend's."

"Hey, Shannah, come here," she called to a girl passenger, seated in her car. "Look at this! Isn't it the neatest?"

I had never seen anyone go ga-ga over a car, as they had over Doug's, his pride and joy.

They left, heading for the store. I just then remembered my eye doctor said not only to take Maxi eye vitamins, I was, at all times, to keep my eyes covered while in the sun. So, I pulled my lime green knit hat over my face, and slid down to comfortably finish my wait for Doug.

The trip home was also enjoyable.

"Go swimming with me," Doug was saying.

"Sure."

"I'll buy you a bikini."

"Can't wear them."

"Why not?"

"Too many battle scars."

A laugh, then, "We'll get one to show off most important parts."

"Where would you like to go, Doug? The family swimming pool near my villa, or the sea?"

"I prefer the sea shore, walking the beach, but not to swim out far, because of sharks."

"Yes, I saw on TV, six people were bitten this week. But all were on surfboards. Theory has it the sharks went after them, thinking they were food."

We were on a long stretch of highway, in nearly bumper to bumper afternoon traffic, and forty minutes away from Doug's home. I sensed his hopes in finding an opening to be able to pass the truck directly in front of us.

"I shouldn't have spent so much time in Sam's. I'm sorry," I said.

"That's okay. Not to worry. We got everything you needed, and it was fun."

When we arrived at his home, Doug found a business card left by a repairman he had been expecting. He immediately phoned, and was informed the repairman would soon return.

We waited, and we waited, while seated on the sofa, absorbed in television and listening to President Bush speak.

"Would you like a dish of ice cream?" Doug asked.

I hesitated at first, as I was due home at two o'clock. My friend, Jake, had promised to pick me up and treat me to an ice cream cone at one of the local parlors.

"That would be nice, but may I first use your telephone?"

I phoned Jake. "I'm on my way home from Ocala and will be late. I'll call you."

In realizing Jake had caller ID, I felt naughty in not really telling the truth. I called back. "A friend took me shopping and I'm at his house." I explained the circumstance at not being able to leave until a man arrived to repair a blind. Jake simply chuckled.

Doug came in, handed me a dish of Dolly Madison nut crunch ice cream, and said, "After you eat your ice cream, if you must, you can take the Corvette, and go home, and I'll bring my Thunderbird later, and you can follow me back."

"Are you kidding? I wouldn't know how to drive your wonderful car. What's more, I'd become lost a million times, and never find my way home."

While I swirled my spoon around, finding the yummy soft masses of ice-cream, I felt comfortable with Doug seated at the far side of the sofa. Together, we read the captions beneath the TV screen as President Bush spoke. Finished with my ice cream, I leaned over and placed the empty dish on the coffee table. Then, I settled back in a comfortable position, and became utterly surprised to look down and find Doug's head in my lap.

I laughed. "This is a new one for me. Of all the men I've dated, no one has done this." He grinned up at me, and I reached down and brushed back his silver and white hair, from his forehead. "It's nice, especially the white sideburns."

He just chuckled. Then blue eyes flashed. "Want to see my sunburn?" Without awaiting a reply, he lifted his knit shirt, and exposed his belly. "See?" He pulled his shirt higher, and showed the scar left from open heart surgery he had spoken about earlier. He patted his belly. "This is my elephant."

"Really?" I laughed.

"Wanna see my trunk?"

"You're bad! A gentleman doesn't talk like that to a lady."

"Would you consider sex?"

"Never. Not unless there was a ring on my finger, I was in love and there was a future in it. I tell everyone this. I want to be loved, adored and respected."

"You're a nice lady and I respect you." He then commenced to tell me, "I'll never marry. At least I don't think so, now. But I can take you to dinner and to dances."

His shirt had already been pulled down in its proper place, and his fingers caressed the top of my hand. I was being *turned on* by this simple act, by this cute, smart -alec, Napoleon-type fellow.

Just then, the man arrived to fix the blind, which took all of five minutes and soon he was gone. Doug turned to me and grinned.

"I better take you home, now, before I molest you." I knew he was kidding, but soon we were out the door, seated in his red Corvette with the roof down, winging our way down the highway, laughing, and again, singing along with the radio. The cool breeze felt wonderful on my face, and again teased my hair in a frenzy, but I didn't care, we were two happy, carefree people, enjoying a lovely day together.

When I stepped over the doorsill into my villa, three messages awaited me. One, from friend Del, in Hawaii. I had told Doug about her, and when I returned her call, he spoke with her briefly, asking if, when I'm spending next January there with her in Waikiki, could he come over and visit? She told him "Yes, that would be nice."

That out of my way, and Doug on his, I got back to calling dear Jake. He was laughing, and saying, "You sure get yourself in a fix, running here, there, and everywhere."

"I couldn't help it. Things crop up and I have to weasel them into my day." Dear man that he is, said, he wouldn't be taking me out for ice cream this evening, instead, I should rest. Tomorrow would be a better day for him, too.

Rest, I did, two hours, when the phone rang. Woody from down around the corner. "Hello, babe. I called earlier. Are you going to be home?"

"Yes, but I'm busy, about to shampoo my hair."

"I just made some fruit salad for you."

"You did? You didn't have to do that."

"The other evening, you made dinner for me, babe, and brought over flowers from your garden."

"Would you like some more Gardenias? Hundreds are in bloom."

"No, that's alright. I didn't go for my walk, and I'm going now, and will just drop off the salad, but won't stay."

In a short while, my doorbell rang, and there he was, smiling in at me.

I accepted the salad, thanked him, and said, "It's dark out, Woody, do you want me to walk you home?"

"No, I have my walker, here."

"Are you sure?"

"Yes, I'll be fine."

"I'll leave the light on for you, until you reach the street."

"Okay, thanks, babe," he smiled, and I stood there and watched as he wheeled the walker down the sidewalk.

My last conversation spent with someone from the outside world came next. I closed the door on Woody, to answer a phone call from friend, Jane, my best friend here in The Villages. When I shared my day, she asked, "How long have you been a resident?"

"Since April the first, of last year."

"Look at all the men parading around you. You have made more friends in that short time. And you'll have many more down the road."

Now, it was me who laughed, with thoughts what would I do with many more? I do realize my hair never got shampooed, it was now 11:45 PM, and there were clothes in the dryer to be folded. I'd shower, shampoo, towel-dry my hair, fold clothes, hit the sack, set my hair in the early morning, and get that out of the way before Sid arrived at 9:00 with my mantel clock he repaired. Yes, each day seems to become busier, and more interesting. On this happy, I'll sign off with, "Goodnight, World."

# Chapter 52
# Caring and Sharing with New Friends

April 22. Today, off and on, rambling through my mind came that ever popular slogan which I first heard when our twin sons were in cub scouts:

Make new friends, and keep the old.
One is silver, one is gold.

It began with my first phone call this morning. My next door neighbor, Jo, was asking, "Are you alright, Bootsy?"

"Yes, I'm fine. Why?"

"Daphine called and told me to phone you, because she was concerned at not seeing you about." A warm feeling of contentment swept through me. Though new to the area, I belonged.

Circumstances differed somewhat. When I lived in PA my neighbors were fine people, but all of them worked during the day. I remembered the time I fell backward off the edge of my patio, and lay stunned on the ground. I reiterate. High bushes and sloping lawn would have prevented anyone from seeing me there, and for a short while, I had sensed a gut-feeling of helplessness.

This would not happen here. Neighbors check upon neighbors. My friends, the Stems, bless them, though not neighbors, go a step further by shoving me out of the house and getting me involved. Through them, I've met other wonderful friends. It's not unusual to pick up two or more, following Sunday services in the Church on The Square, and invite them to tag along with our 'lunch bunch', which meets at Café Ole', a popular restaurant close by. Two weeks ago, I added a few of my own friends, Carol Joseph, my house guest from Trinidad, Polly Irwin, a Singles member, and also Veronica Koenigsbauger. Like family, we seat ourselves around the table, and with hands clasped and heads bowed, our leader, Bob, gives thanks to our dear Lord for blessings of food, friendship, and voices concern for our troops, our government and all the needy.

This past Sunday, our newest added friend happened to be Angelika McCarthy. Carol and I were hurrying across the church parking lot, when I spied her three car lengths in front of us, as she climbed out of her car, and began briskly walking toward the church. She looked like a breath of summer, in her soft yellow, sheer floral dress, with golden hair pulled back in a wind-free fashion.

"Let's hurry," I suggested to Carol. "I want to compliment her on her dress, a copy of a favorite I once owned." Soon we caught up and introduced ourselves. Like Veronica, Angelika also had grown up in Germany.

I excitedly told her, "My twin's Godmother, Waltraut, Ann Louise, Ellen, Grossgebaur, Jelsma, in Pennsylvania, is also from Germany. Speaking of Germany, we'll be meeting another German lady, Veronica, in front of the church. Perhaps we can all sit together."

Enough seats weren't available. So, Angelika, scooted into a pew behind us, smiled, and ordered, "Now, don't forget to wait for me, later".

The Stems happened to be on vacation, but following the church service, we five ladies paraded down the street to the Café Ole's Restaurant. It was a sunny breezy afternoon, and with little discussion, we chose to sit outside on the lanai. There, following grace, we not only enjoyed a delightful lunch, we had one spectacular gabfest. Three hours later, Angelika exuberantly said, "It's amazing. Here we are, still sitting here, having such fun, and we covered every subject imaginable, and we've just met, today. It's *unbelievable*." We ended the afternoon, exchanging names and telephone numbers, because Veronica would soon be leaving for her home in Vermont, Angelika for Ohio, and Carol, Trinidad. Veronica and Angelika, both Snow-birds would be returning in the fall. Angelika turned to me and said, "I'll call you the first minute my husband and I get back."

A week slipped by, and on Monday, when the phone rang, I was surprised to find Bob, Jane's husband, on the line. "Bootsy, we're home. Don't forget, May first."

"Pray tell, what's happening on May the first?"

"How could you forget? The Village Idiot's will meet."

I laughed. The Village Idiots came about one day, when the two of them were seated under the Golf Cart Bridge and came up with a fun idea. Yes, I am not only a member of The Singles' Club, The Pennsylvania, Beta Sigma Phi Sorority, The Red Hat Society, but I became a full-fledged member of The Village Idiots during our first breakfast at the Café Ole' restaurant on April Fool's Day. We consist of a group of forty five or more, happy-go-lucky, fun-loving, men and women alike. We dress in night clothes, with street clothes beneath, and meet the first of every month for breakfast at a popular club or restaurant. To be a member, one must simply wear a dunce-hat made out of our local Daily Sun.

So, on May 1, May Day, I was all ready to leave when Bob and Jane picked me up in their golf cart and whisked me off to the Village Idiots' second breakfast, this time at the El Santiago Club. There, The Village photographer snapped us in our hats adorned in items pertaining to spring. Mostly flowers. Some hats were topped with potted plants, some contained flowers picked from fields, and gardens. Leader, Bob's hat was graced with twigs, and a bird's nest. Mine? Purple flowers, Gardenias from my courtyard, and topped with a *Worry Bird,* purchased several years ago, at Kathy's Christmas in Harrisburg. A *Worry Bird* is a bright red and silver, little glass bird, approximately three inches long, including a tail of straight, clear nylon bristles. If you clip him to a Christmas tree, he listens to your troubles, then flies away with them. No, I would never part with my *Worry Bird.* He's an integral part of my past, and a colorful figure of happiness for all of my Christmas seasons ahead.

# Chapter 53
## The Man on the Park Bench

What another glorious Sunday! How could I think otherwise? There I stood, bathed in morning sunlight, admiring my four breast-high Gardenia bushes bordering the pathway leading to my courtyard. Prolifically speckled with hundreds of white blooms, I inhaled their sweet heady fragrance, and silently thanked God. Because He so graciously shares with me, I, too, must share, and last week, you could find my Gardenias at tellers' booths in the Citizen's Bank, the Sales Office, mailing station, a dress shop, or two, and the radio station. Wherever I went, my flowers reaped a smile, and this Sunday, I ached to share again. I would pick a handful, and pass them around to ushers in the Church on The Square.

Later, as I zipped down the golf cart path, whizzed on through the Del Mar Gate, heading for town, I wondered, since some Snow-birds were still here, would I have difficulty in finding a parking spot? I circled around Main Street, only once, and half a block down the street from the church was an empty golf cart space, waiting just for me. I eased in, parked, turned off the ignition and looked straight ahead to see a smiling, middle-aged gent seated on the bench near the fish pond. He had been watching me.

I gathered my flowers, inhaled a breathe of fragrance, stepped out of the golf cart onto the sidewalk, and standing before him, asked "Would you like one of my Gardenias?"

"I sure would. That's very kind of you. I think they smell wonderful." Following church services, I noticed the bench was vacant. However, the message he left on the steering wheel of my golf cart not only brought a smile to my lips, but in my heart. "Thank you for the Gardenia. You are a kind and lovely lady, more beautiful than the flower." He had signed his name, simply, as "Fred."

That afternoon, friend Jane agreed to come along with me and help distribute even more flowers. Dressed in spring frocks and brimmed spring hats, we admired each other's attire. She in her floor-length turquoise, and me in my sunshine yellow. Chuckling, she exclaimed, "This is such fun, Bootsy, and my! Don't we make a jolly looking pair?" Between us, we carried a large white wicker basket, filled with one hundred and fifty Gardenias to share with the residents at Homeward Bound, and also the Summerfield Assisted Living quarters. The exuberant thanks we received from the management, and the residents at both places was most meaningful to both Jane and me. Basket now empty, as we exited into the afternoon sunshine, and hurried to my car, I agreed with Jane when she grinned, and said, "My! Doesn't that make one feel great? This is our good deed for the day."

The following Sunday morning, before breakfast, still in turquoise nightie and slippers, I again stood outside in my courtyard and inhaled the lovely fragrance of the remaining Gardenias. It seemed a shame they were appreciated only by me. It was Mothers Day, and I recalled how homesick I had been last year when far away from my family. Perhaps other mothers were feeling that way, and one of my flowers would brighten their day? Yes, I would snip off all of them and share. Before leaving for church, I rang the Lady Lake Care Center, and spoke to the Sunday manager.

"Why, yes! We'd be delighted to give all the lady residents a Gardenia for this special day. When you pull into our parking lot, two lady employees will be waiting there for you." They were, and we quickly transferred a tray of forty-nine flowers from my car into their hands. Then I hurriedly made it back across the highway, and arrived breathlessly in The Church on The Square, and on time.

The exotic and fragrant Gardenias are gone now, but their memory still lingers in the hearts of the more than five hundred forty-six who enjoyed them. Because Gardenias represent *Unspoken Love*, and God's love grew so prolifically in my garden, I shall look forward with anticipation to next years blooms, and, again experiencing the joy in sharing His love.

**Carol Coggin, Business Manager, and TJ Wroblewski, Marketing Manager of The Summerfied Assisted Living Quarters and Memory Care, accepting my Gardenias to be distributed amongst their residents.**

# Chapter 54
# A Bird-Day Party

One never knows what to expect here in this retirement community. This evening, while busy at the computer, my phone jangled my attention to the outside world. Bob Stem on the line.

"Bootsy, hurry, and jump in your golf cart and meet Jane and me down here on the corner of Almedia and Rio Grande."

"Why?"

"'Never mind, just hurry."

"Why?"

"There's something phenomenal we want you to see."

"What?"

"Flocks and flocks of all kinds of birds in a field over on Morris Boulevard. Hurry!"

In bedroom slippers, I ran into the bedroom, grabbed a pair of sandals, tore out into the garage, tossed sandals in the golf cart basket and was on my way, sailing through the golf cart gate, and there, coming up the street toward me, were Jane and Bob in their golf cart. I pulled along-side, reached for my sandals, Bob yelled, "Forget them, Hurry! Park your golf cart there in that driveway, with the 'for sale' sign." I did, and he ordered, "Hop in." And soon, we three were on our way.

On Morse Boulevard, he pulled to a smooth stop, pointed, and said, "There! That's what we want you to see."

With hands clasped, I stared. "Oh, my gosh, Bob. this is truly amazing. I've never seen anything like it. Look! More are flying in. It reminds me of a big wedding party. What are they? I'm familiar with the Egrets."

"They're all different kinds," he said. "Look at the dark gray, and the tall black, how they stand out amongst the white."

Another couple, in a golf cart pulled up in front. They climbed out and the man told us, "I was here before, and by this little strip of water, amongst the grass, lay a big alligator. I'll bet he was eight feet long. He's gone now. I don't see him."

He and Bob stepped over the water, and I attempted to. Jane warned, "Bootsy! Don't, it's muddy in there. You'll get your nice white bedroom slippers all dirty." At the time I thought it would be worth it to see an alligator. My grandson, Aaron, 12, when I talk to him via phone, always asks, "Grandmom! Did you see an alligator, yet?" The next time I'll tell him no, but I did attend a bird-day party."

# Chapter 55
# My Day, My Dream

This morning, I lay in bed and told myself, *No one is going to take this day away from me. I'm going to goof off a bit. I have no worries.* In looking back, I was naive when it came to buying property, and I had learned the hard way. Yet, now my villa was in ship-shape. Everything was in working order. I replaced the torn outside screen, installed steps to the attic, added a screen door to the kitchen, front door and garage. The washer, which died in August, had been replaced, as had been its mate, the clothes dryer, and the new air-conditioner still works, my flowers were watered last night, and I was going to simply lay here and daydream awhile longer about my prince, Delbert.

Two weeks ago, Thursday, he surprised me with a phone call. Since we parted, he had been extremely busy doing volunteer work in his neighborhood. He dreamed about me, and now fell asleep with me on his mind. He had just showered, was standing there again, in his green robe, and wanted to hear my voice. Then I received a "Just a little hug" card which said:

A hug can say I'll miss you or, I'll be thinking of you. It can say, You're someone special, or best of all, I love you. It can soothe a hurt, or calm a fear or cheer us when we're blue, It almost seems a miracle all the things a hug can do.

PS: Just a warm little hug and a smile to cheer you, my sweet and dear Bootsy. From your Prince Delbert Hilling. xoxoxoxo.

Short on time, I had hurriedly responded with a quick note. I know I thanked him for the dear card and mentioned he was special to me, but what else I wrote, I had no idea. This past week, I have been so busy with Village activities, club meetings, etcetera, and only quick gobbled moments of him had time to skip across my mind. Ah, yes, dear Delbert. Then his last letter arrived, having me wondering. Did he have marriage on his mind or a simple frolic in the bedroom? I reached over on the night-stand, picked up his letter, and read:

My Dearest Bootsy,
    I received your love card and yes, you may have my love. My recent thoughts of you have been many. How we held each other so close and found a great desire.
    My hope is we will one day reunite and fulfill this desire. Enclosed are two pictures. One is an early morning bedroom snapshot. Look closely, the sun is reflecting on me.

With love,
your Delbert

I wondered what card had I sent to prompt such a letter. Was it one of my Expressions of Love, collection, by Arbutus? Years ago, the company my husband worked for over the past thirty-eight years had threatened bankruptcy. On the side, I joined the work force with a greeting card business. Stores, pharmacies, and college libraries carried my sweet sentiments. I recalled a "thank you" letter written by one college student, now married. Through my cards, he had won his girlfriend's heart. I had also received a "thank you" from Nancy Reagan, for one sent to her to give to the president. It simply said, "It's Easter, and I'll gladly swap my jelly beans, for some of your kisses." I had given up the greeting card business when my husband died.

Now, for the life of me, I had no idea which greeting I had sent to Delbert. One said, "May I love you from afar, if I behave when you're near?" The trouble with that specific card is, though I had shoved Delbert out the door when our eyes spoke of desire, I didn't know if I could do this, again. So I certainly wouldn't send that one. Now, if it were summer, I could have sent the one which said, "It's summer, and on a quiet peaceful day such as this, I'd like to put my cheek next to yours and...whisper, 'I love you.'" Summer was over, and I didn't love him. Not yet! He was nice, and down the road I would like him to be mine, alone. I knew we would be good for each other. Our goals and religious beliefs were the same, and of all I've dated, he was the only man who attended church on Sundays. It would be nice to have a man sit beside me, like old times with my Bill.

Enough, wasting the day away. I stretched, climbed out of bed, and headed for my office. Though I was aching to be loved again, to be in his arms once more, the response to this letter should be sort of toned down. Seated at my computer, my fingers flew across the keys:

> My darling Prince, Delbert,
>
> Now you've gone and done it! Transplanted yourself in my mind and I can think of nothing else. Oh, my! You do look handsome in your Italian white linen suit, with blue shirt and tie.
>
> Yes, there is definitely chemistry between us, but can we write, become better acquainted, learn each other's likes, dislikes, hobbies and what we want from life? I'm a one man woman, yet, you said you and the neighbor lady connected, and I wondered if you are going with her, and also the lady, named Julie, here in The Villages? Please let me know your thoughts.
>
> I close with Love and a hug, from Princess, Bootsy

I slipped the letter into an envelope in which I enclosed two pictures. Yes, in my heart, Delbert could very well be the prince I have been waiting for. I thought this just yesterday at a garage sale when I spied the pastel blue picture frame with cream colored matting and its meaningful printed message. Immediate thoughts had been, as sure as God made little green apples, I must buy it for my Delbert. When I brought it home, I stored it out of the way, in my guest room. Now, I hurried to bring it out. It was rather heavy. I propped it against the coffee table, stood back and read the writings which spoke of my true feelings about life in general, and yes, what I dream the future would hold for Delbert and me:

> To Walk
> And talk
> Or just
> To Stand
> To Watch
> The trees
> and see
> The land.
> To see
> A bird
> A twig
> A branch
> To watch
> A brook
> And see
> No distance
> To have
> The things
> Given
> By God
> To love
> Them all
> To love
> Them hard
> To love
> And be loved
> By Someone
> True
> To love
> and be...
> Just loved
> By you.

I sighed, worked at wrapping it in bubble packing, placed it in a sturdy addressed box, and hurried off to the mailing station. Now, I would sit back and anxiously wait to hear from him…my prince, Delbert.

Later, when I picked up his picture, my eyes flew wide open. Shocked, I stared at something completely overlooked before. He stood tall, beside his dresser, and there on the top, in plain view, was a small, golden framed picture of a lady. I squinted. Even with a large magnifying glass, I couldn't tell who she was, but…I recognized the black dress with the long open lace sleeves. Julie's! Lordy! Lordy! Was Delbert writing love letters, and exchanging pictures to us both?

Friend Irene, back home in Pennyslvania would say I was out of their league. Both Delbert and Julie had worked in high government positions. I simply had worked in a payroll department, then later as a corresponding secretary in a credit office. Both Delbert and Julie were into horseback riding, while, years ago, I had difficulty keeping my balance on a pair of ice skates. No, I wasn't heartsick over this recent discovery. Our relationship hadn't progressed that far, only in dreams, and our imaginations. I returned the picture with the smiling face, back on my dresser. So, he still desires my body? A nice thought, to be put on the back burner of my mind, until it's time to light the flame. But it certainly would be wonderful, if we found in each other what we have been searching for since the death of our spouses.

A week passed. Another letter from Delbert arrived.

> My Dear Bootsy,
>
> I received your picture letter of love. Such a thoughtful gift, my precious. Also, the card, letter and snapshots of you. I absolutely love each one. You look so gorgeous. I cannot decide which I like best. However, the one titled, "Dreamin'", with musical notes beside it is so romantic of you lounging on your bed, with my picture beside you. I want this dream to come true!"
>
> *(Golly Moses! I had forgotten this.)*
>
> You write such interesting letters. Question? What am I looking for? Someone to relate with, share same interests, to be helpful and supportive to our needs. Let's find out where our relationship will take us as we become more acquainted.

You have made me very comfortable in your cozy and beautiful Villa home, with your excellent decorative tastes.

Presently, I have obligations I must fulfill here in Huntington, W.Va. before I return to the Villages. Remodeling two properties. I am my own contractor from start to finish. Being a widower in recent years, I occupied myself with a work schedule, which has been good therapy for both mind and body.

After completing my work, I decided to come to The Villages for the winter. At The Singles' Club meeting, Julie and I were matched at the same table. We are still friends. She is cheerful, pleasant, a remarkable lady with many friends. Our relationship was casual, not sexual.

I do intend to return to The Villages. I want you to welcome my return and save yourself for me. I am eager to see you and hold you close in my arms.

With Love and Hugs,
Your Prince, Delbert

In reading this letter, I nearly swooned, with just the thought of being together with him once more. Plans were to write soon, but Tuesday rolled around, and during my lunch hour, the phone jangled and Delbert was on the line.

"I wrote to you, but wanted to thank you personally for your lovely picture, Bootsy. Thank you. I'm going to hang it in my bedroom. My friend, Beatrice, thought it unusual and meaningful. And the lady who delivered it wanted to see who the prince was, since that's how you addressed the package.

Also, thanks for your photos. You look terrific in your purple dress and red hat. I like to see ladies in hats. Mother always wore one to church. And the one of you in your black and white flowered dress is great, too. You look pretty. You're wearing a white necklace and white earrings, and you're sitting on the loveseat in your living room. And, you're smiling."

"Oh," I said. "Yes, I remember. It was taken the day I first entertained the new sorority here. Delbert, may I ask a personal question?" I didn't wait for a response. "Is that Julie in the picture on your dresser?"

"You're very observant. Yes, that's Julie."

"The one you were thinking of marrying?"

"I was thinking of marrying?"

"Last year, you told me she was your golf partner, you palled around with her group, and were going to marry her."

"I said that?"

"Umhm, she said she was saving herself for you on your wedding night."

A chuckle and, "I don't recall that."

I dropped the subject, and asked, "Would you like to tag along with me, my family and friends, and go Tubing Down the Shawnee on the Delaware over Labor Day weekend?"

"That sounds like a fantastic and fun idea, my princess. But it would be a six hour drive, for me, and after such a long trip, due to the holiday, there may be no room for me in the local hotel."

I told him, "I never gave that a thought." So we dropped the idea of seeing each other that weekend.

He was saying, "Right now I have some commitments, but we'll be together soon. I'll see you there in The Villages. I'm anxious to hold you in my arms again. I should have stayed with you that night, instead of walking out the door."

Hearing this, my heart skipped a beat. "I'm looking forward to being together, too." But was I? If Julie was still in the picture, I couldn't call him my prince. So I asked, "Delbert, just what are you expecting of me? I refuse to be a 'one night stand.'"

"I'm looking for a long-term relationship."

I didn't wish to push the issue, but couldn't help wondering if that possibly meant marriage? We closed with kisses over the phone, and Delbert's, "Goodbye, for now, my little sweetheart."

I swallowed hard, remembering the doctor, a longtime friend, calling me "my little sweetheart." Funny, though his lips were always cool, and tasted of sweet cherry tobacco from smoking his pipe, his kisses were always magical. As were Delbert's, when his warm, sensuous lips captured mine. I shivered, and tossed such thoughts from mind. Now, I'd simply remain neutral, cruise on through life, and see what the future would bring. Though I wouldn't sit around and wait for anyone, I would allow Delbert's picture to remain on top of my dresser. Ah, yes, dear, handsome, and sweet Delbert.

The following morning it rained as I drove into town and he remained constantly on my mind. That evening, sis Kathy called, and then I remembered the card I had sent Delbert. "You're a tease," she said.

"I didn't really mean to be. It just said, 'It's Autumn, and every little leaf that falls is whispering 'I love you, I love you, I love you. May I?'"

"See what I mean? Even Dick, back in PA claimed you were a tease."

"Only because, during the three and a half years I dated him, I allowed him to kiss me, but wouldn't permit a frolic in the bedroom."

"Why not? For Heaven's sake."

"Because, one evening we were sitting on my patio swing, and he said, "Bootsy, whisper sweet nothings in my ear."

"Did you?"

"I whispered, 'Richard Hayden, I think I'm falling madly in love with you. Now, you whisper in mine."

"What did he say to that?"

"Though I knew he loved me, he said, 'I have nothing to say.'"

"So tell me, how's Carl?"

"Fine. He's such a dear."

"I think you should marry him. Look how he took you shopping when your car wasn't there, how he assembled your bedroom furniture when it finally arrived, and loaned you some of his clothing when you were cold. No man can do all he's done for you and not care."

"I know , he's such a dear, and keeps telling me 'a friend in need is a friend indeed.'"

"So, marry him."

"No. He's playing the field, and I think of him as a dear, dear friend, and nothing more. But should I tell you something strange?"

"Yes! Tell me."

"When he was lying on the floor, putting casters on the twin beds in the guest room, he wore shorts and his nice husky legs looked exactly like my Bill's and for a brief moment I itched to run my hands all the way up."

"You should have."

"No, it could lead to something which would get me involved, and I must save myself for Delbert. Should I tell you something else?"

"Yes! What!"

"The men here who are capable of sexually functioning wear no protection."

"Then forget it!

"I will. I have."

When Kathy hung up, I sat there a moment, drifting back to Delbert and his last letter. He addressed me as "My precious one." Whether it would be considered a tease or not, I threw caution to the wind, and sat down and jotted off another note to him. I told him, "It rained this morning, and as I drove down the highway into town, I thought of you, and my windshield wipers were singing, 'I am his...He is mine...He is mine...and I am his,' and I felt good about this."

# Chapter 56
## Doing What Comes Naturally

This Sunday morning, it rained. I would leave my villa earlier, and perhaps find a parking spot close to the church. No problem! At 11:35, I was already seated, and since the service didn't begin until 12:00, I had time to scan the hundreds of early-birds, and discovered only a few ladies wore hats. Mine, purchased at the Harrisburg Farm Show, a white brimmed straw, with hand painted rose pink peonies and a turquoise bow, matched my turquoise short sleeve linen suit, and rose colored blouse. Over the years, wherever our family was transferred, I was always known as the "Hat Lady." I thought about yesterday, when Jane said her Bob feels hats make me look older, and if I continue to wear them, men will think me unapproachable, too sophisticated. Would they, really?

Church was about to begin. Mary Ann Rockenbach, at her organ keyboard began to softly play. Bill Doherty, director of music, and Ministry at the piano, and Marten Adams, in charge of percussion were all set, ready to fill the auditorium with soulful music. Now came the Celebration Choir, robed in royal blue, and next, the Celebration Singers, provided by the courtesy of Central Florida Lyric Opera.

I was surprised when, instead of Bill Doherty, Sam Reynolds, one of the singers, welcomed us and also led us in prayer. A strapping big fellow with a jolly face, and simply a magnificent booming voice, with his aura of happiness shining through his demeanor, he reminded me of my husband. Especially the times my Bill would look at me with that silly, goofy grin on his mug, and in his deepest voice, sing "Oh, Lord, It's Hard to be Humble, When You're Perfect in Every Way." Oh, yes, I still miss that sweet, silly, wonderful man.

Thinking of my Bill and listening to Sam, a feeling of joy swept over me, even before we were asked to join in singing, "When the Holy Ghost shows up, we'll have church." And did we ever. Another song, "Come Holy Spirit, Still My Heart" sung by the group, came next, followed by the singing of The Lord's Prayer, with all holding hands. I always found this quite moving. Then we enjoyed more singing, arranged by Bill Doherty, and the songs he had chosen were "Blessed Assurance," "In the Garden," "Great is Thy Faithfulness," "What a Friend We Have in Jesus," with all joining in singing "Amazing Grace."

Next came the sermon, by Pastor Barry Hunteman, a favorite of mine, from the Hope Lutheran Church. He preached on "Jesus' Joy in You," and I mentally gobbled it up. "Joy," he said, "is the spirit of well being that stays with you. Joy is the inner peace during outward turmoil." How true. He had us all laughing, when he asked, "I'm sure you all have heard one song, and he began to gustily sing, "I've got Joy, Joy, Joy, where?" he pointed to the congregation, and we all called out, "Down in my heart." Then he spoke of new versions of footsteps in the sand. When footsteps turned into one, we were dancing with Jesus.

He told us, he, himself was a happy man, who loves to attend weddings. "Kay, my dear wife, does, also. She loves to dance at all the weddings, and insists I get my feet to moving. Now, my singing's not great, I know that. But my dancing is worse." He laughed. "I just stand there and do this, the box step. Back and forth, back and forth, back and forth."

Church ended, and as I eased my way toward the door I did so with a smile on my face. Everything learned regarding my Lord, the calmness of soul, the sweetness of His spirit seemed to be rejuvenated, tied up in a bundle of love, and I looked forward to next

Sunday and another dose of spiritual uplifting. While in line, four ladies told me they loved hats, and I looked spectacular. One said, "I thought you were a designer."

I laughed. "Only of my hats."

"Every Sunday, I notice you are color coordinated, and this got me to wondering," she said.

I spoke of Jane's husband's thoughts. "Because of my hats, do you feel men will think me unapproachable?"

One said, "No, I don't think men will turn away because of your hats. If so, would you even want them?" Never had I thought about that. Outside, I strolled across the courtyard on my way to my golf cart, passed the waterfall, and for one moment, felt giddy with thoughts of 'good luck,' in finding a nice man, and tossed a coin into the sparkling waters. I wished the man to be my prince, Delbert. He liked to see ladies wear hats, didn't he?

A pleasant looking gentleman, in passing, touched my shoulder. "Nice outfit. You look great." I noticed his wedding band, and continued on.

On my way home, while zipping through the golf cart gate, I thought of Woody Wilkins. Last evening he called and said I should stop by for a box of strawberries. I would do that now, and get that out of the way. I found him stretched out in his lounge chair, swollen feet propped. Still, he grinned up at me. "I'm lazy, today. Had a rough night. Couldn't get to sleep until three. My legs froze on me."

I still wished with all of my heart, I could heal this nice man who exudes kindness. All I could do for him was dress his bed, leave with my box of strawberries, and a pile of his clothing to take home and iron. Clothing he had laundered and left on a dining room chair.

Later, in my villa, the direct opposite of the proud lady in her chapeau, I chuckled to myself and wondered what men would think of me now, a barefooted bohemian, in shorts, standing over an ironing board? Ironing can be quite enjoyable. It gives one a lot of time to think. Eight shirts hung on hangers, and I was on the last of six pairs of shorts, when the radio blared…"God is Watching Us." Yes, I truly feel the dear Lord is looking after me. He's watching over all of us, and isn't this great?

# Chapter 57
# Prince Delbert Hilling's Letters

Each time I find a letter from Delbert in my mail box, I clasp it to my breast, and think, *Oh, be still my heart!* Today's read:

My Dear Bootsy,

I wanted to get this card to you sooner, however I have been so preoccupied. Currently, I still have obligations I must fulfill here in West Virginia before a return to The Villages.

As I said before, being a widower in recent years, I have occupied myself with a busy work schedule. My most recent, and enjoyable, is this do-it-yourself project of building on a sundeck, and it is coming along near completion.

The weather has been extremely humid for West Virginia. We had a break in the rain for the past week, with evenings and mornings cooler. Thank goodness.

My dear Bootsy, my thoughts of you are often. I'm anxious to see you again and bring back nice memories of times we shared.

With love,
Your Prince, Delbert

His card read, "Dear friend, though we are miles apart, you will always remain close in my heart." Every letter I receive draws me closer to wanting to snuggle in his arms. Last Christmas, near the end of time spent in PA he had phoned while I was at my son, Keith's home, and expressed disappointment in my not letting him know I had been there, so he could drive over and see me. I would again be in PA on October third for my sixtieth class reunion. Why not write and ask if he would consent to tag along with me? Yes! Yes, I would do this.

During the next two weeks, I awaited his reply. When the letter arrived, I smiled as I read:

Ms. Arbutus E. Focht
My dearest Bootsy
The Villages, Fl. 32159

My Dearest Bootsy,

I am so delighted that you would have me escort you to your class reunion. Also that we may reacquaint ourselves with each other again, if only for a few days. I can hardly wait.

Let's find out where our relationship will take us as we become more acquainted. During our few dates, you have made me very comfortable in your cozy and lovely villa in which you decorated so tastefully. I so enjoyed sitting out on your swing, in your charming courtyard, and drinking pink lemonade.

Regarding Julie, when you and I spoke on the phone that one time, about her picture in the photo which I mailed to you, I neglected to tell you, I met her there at a Singles meeting. We talk on the phone from time to time. We're still friends. She is a remarkable lady with many friends. Our relationship was casual...not sexual.

I intend to return to the Villages. I want you to welcome my return, and save yourself for me. I am eager to see you and hold you close in my arms.

With love, hugs and kisses,
Your Prince Delbert Hilling

Dear Prince Delbert,

My, how time flies. Here I am again. Today, I went down to the 3 A's and picked up some maps for you. Oh, my dear friend, I can barely wait to see your smiling face again, and feel your arms around me. I will get a big hug, won't I?

I'll be flying to Harrisburg on Delta, leaving Orlando October 3, Friday, and arriving at 6:30 PM. I'll stay with my dear C.H. friend, Peggy DeStephano, for a few days, then travel on to Montoursville, to spend time with a wonderful couple, Jack and Dolla Barbour, friends of 42 years. Jack and my husband worked together. I would like you to meet them, and perhaps some of my relatives. Also, if possible, another dear, dear old-time couple, Wally, from Germany, (Waltraut Anne Louise Ellen Grossgebaur Jelsma) and husband, Wiebe Jelsma, from Holland. Wally was maid-of-honor at Bill's and my wedding, and she and Wiebe, to this day, are our twin son's Godparents. They're also good friends of the Barbours. Dolla used to work with Wally, before Wally came to work in the office at The Narrow Fabric Company in Williamsport, in 1945, where I was employed. Can you believe this? Where has the time flown? We worked together in the payroll department. Because our children are pretty much the same age, naturally, WE ARE FAMILY, and I'm known as their "Aunt Bootsy." It's a terrific and nice feeling of belonging.

Now, that you are caught up to date, I must confess, the real Bootsy may be somewhat different than how she comes across, and I do hope and pray you won't be disappointed in "yours truly." I've been classified as classy, upbeat, fun to be with…and *moralistic*. Did you guess?

To put it simply, down the road ahead, I'm searching for someone to love, someone to love and adore me, and someone to laugh with when things go wrong.

We'll build a deep, meaningful relationship and see where it leads. Please, my darling Prince, be patient with me? Strangely, Orlando is having a singing contest on TV right now. Last week they chose 6 out of 800 contestants, and a male is now singing…"You Gotta Let Somebody Love You, Before it's Too Late."

I don't think it's too late for us, and we both realize love is what makes the world go around. And…you're nobody til somebody loves you. Ah! My, yes! I'm breathless in merely thinking of the possibility of falling in love again. Are you? Your thoughts, please? Bye for now…7 more days…XXXOOOXXX

Love and some hugs,
from your Bootsy

Delbert's next letter thanked me for the trip ticks, and said I write interesting letters. Also included was a greeting card with Pooh Bear and it said, "Thinking of you turns a bothering sort of day …into a Happy, Humming sort of Day!

He closed with: To my Dear Bootsy, Just to let you know my thoughts are of you.

Love, from your Prince, Delbert

My Darling Prince, Delbert,

Every day I look at your handsome face in this picture you mailed to me some months ago, and I smile. More-so, since your Pooh Expressions from Hallmark arrived. I could hear your sigh, and this morning I've been catching myself humming…'You sigh, the song begins and I hear violins, it's magic. The stars dessert the sky and rush to nestle in your eyes, it's magic.'

Will this magic continue and end as that popular song Doris Day was known for? Oh, my! The very thought of you has me sighing and wondering, and I can barely wait to see you, again. Ah, yes Prince of mine, I sigh with thoughts of being in your arms. Even for a minute. Do you think me bold? Hugs and kisses,

From Your Princess, Bootsy

I thought of Delbert's kisses, warm and magical. Then I looked back on the past, and friend, DJ, how I had longed to show him life wasn't over simply because it had been for our spouses. Could I be successful with my Delbert?

# Chapter 58
## Bruce Jenner's Advice

The day arrived for my trip to Pennsylvania, where, on the weekend, I would be attending my class reunion in my hometown, Williamsport. With a lot of scurrying around, I managed to arrive at the Village shuttle bus station on time at 5:15 AM, surprisingly wide awake. I boarded the bus, greeted the passengers with, "Good morning. No, I'm not your tour guide," and this brought laughter, a nice beginning for our one hour and fifteen minute trip to Orlando's airport. During it, I had time to meditate. Delta airlines would fly into Atlanta, where I would transfer on Delta 29, which would take me to Harrisburg. I would stay four days in Camp Hill with my dear friend, Peggy DeStephano, visit friends and relatives in close-by areas, then head for my hometown.

My flight into Atlanta went smoothly. Here, my waiting section was not crowded. Here, I would have a two hour and twenty-nine minute lay-over, plenty of time to enjoy people-watching, and pay attention to the periodic intercom message, not to leave my luggage unattended. During my travels I'm keenly aware of all that is going on around me. This time, now and then, I chose to spend some time over by the large plate glass window and watch flights arriving, and people disembarking. I still maintain an everlasting hope of one day seeing a recognizable face. Undoubtedly, I'd end wildly jumping up and down with glee. For my favorite past time, I chatted with those seated nearby, and also kept my ears finely tuned to other's conversations. Now, a man and lady, seated behind me, were excitedly chatting. My ears perked up on a higher level, like their voices. Did I hear correctly? I turned to face them. "Peter Jennings? Where is he?"

Both smiled, and told me, "No. Not Jennings. It's Bruce Jenner." The woman added, "He's the US Olympic winner. His picture is on the Wheaties box. He's standing over there, across the next waiting section, and is wearing a white sweatsuit, with a splash of red on his top pullover, and is leaning against the wall. I wish I could get his autograph for my husband."

I looked to where she pointed, and asked, "Why not go ask him for one?"

"No." She shook her head. "I can't."

I bounced off my seat, and told her, "I'll go, then."

Brows raised. "You would do this for me?"

"Surely. No problem!" As I took off, I laughed to myself, realizing, of late, I'm picking up on that 'no problem' habit. It proved quite a jaunt to the other side, but there I stood before this famous person, and smiled up into his tallness. Eyes covered in sunglasses, he smiled down at me.

"You are Bruce Jenner, and the lady over there, who pointed you out, would like an autograph for her husband. At first, I thought she and her husband said you were Peter Jennings."

"Others have also been mistaken. Do you have a piece of paper I can write on?"

I rifled through my purse, came up with a Guidepost, ripped out a page, handed it to him, and he told me, "That will do."

"We chatted a bit, and I said, "Bruce, I have a fourteen-year-old granddaughter who is having a rough time in school this year. Could you write something for her?"

"No problem." So on another sheet of the Guide Post, he wrote, "Christina Takach, Dream Big and Work Hard." He signed his name and handed it to me. "I tell everyone this."

"Would you also write one for my son Keith's son, Aaron, my only grandson?" I tore another sheet from the Guide Post, and the same message was written to both, Keith and Aaron, and I watched as he signed it. Then he looked at me. "So tell me, what are you doing here?"

"I'm on my way to attend my sixtieth class reunion in Williamsport, Pennsylvania. I'm excited. A gentleman friend whom I dated last year in my retirement village is driving six and a half hours to be my escort."

"Fantastic. That's sweet." He patted me on the back.

"Better yet, Bruce, could I have a hug?"

"You sure may," he said.

In the next moment, with face pressed to his chest, I softly murmured, "You hug like my twin son, Keith." I broke away and grinned. "I also have to look waaay up at him, too. He's six feet four inches tall."

We parted with Bruce telling me, "Have fun at your reunion. Remember, you only live once, so, live it up. You have my permission."

# Chapter 59
# The Class Reunion

My plane arrived in Harrisburg an hour late. Because of a trailer accident and traffic tie-up over on the Eisenhower Exchange, Bill Wenfindale, my former faithful handy-man, who would again be picking me up, arrived on time. Amidst the crowd, I recognized his straight-as-a-soldier gait, and there came that comical twitch to his white mustache, accompanied with a welcoming smile of relief when he found me at baggage claim. We stopped along the way for dinner, before traveling on to the home of my dear friend, Peggy DeStephano, in Camp Hill.

There, as always, she greeted me at her front door with a smile, a big hug, and "You are always welcomed here, Bootsy. It's a pleasure to have you visit." On my second day, I was fortunate to have both of my daughters, Dianne, from Womelsdorf, and Debra, from Duncanon, drive in to join us. Sorority sis, Betty Kublic, from Mechanicsburg, and Marian Trone, in New Cumberland, other special friends, also dropped by. It proved a day of excitement as we noisily piled into cars and headed out for dinner at a favorite restaurant of mine in Mechanicsburg.

The next day, friend, Norma Dubinsky, from Hershey, called with good news.

"I enjoy driving, and it will be no trouble taking you to your Montoursville friend's home. Peggy will come along and keep me company on my return trip."

The two and a half hours didn't seem long at all. We chatted like always, stopped along the roadside for lunch at a quaint little restaurant, and took time for me to snap pictures of that grand Susquehanna River, with its banks embraced with trees brilliantly colored in autumn's foliage. "You will have this to remember, until you come back," Norma stated.

Later, she surprised me even more when we pulled into the Barbour's drive and, not only did she remove my luggage from her car, but a large bag containing a rose and white colored afghan she had made to match my rose colored rocker in my villa. After many parting sighs and hugs, they left almost immediately.

So here I was, settling comfortably in my room at the Barbours, while Dolla, seated in the nearby chair, and I chatted like old times while I hung my clothes in the closet. She was telling me, "Always remember, our home is your home, Bootsy, and feel free to use the phone anytime you wish." I took her at her word, finished my job, and hurried to the kitchen to call my best childhood friend, Jo Fila Williams. She wouldn't be attending the reunion. We would meet for lunch tomorrow at the Bird Nest Restaurant, there in Montoursville, PA. I could barely wait to see Jo. It had been over thirty years since the last time.

When Dolla dropped me off at the restaurant on her way to the hairdressers, I sat outside on a bench and enjoyed people watching, and also traffic as it whizzed by. Then there came Jo. I stood, she greeted me with, "Hello, Arbutus," and I greeted her with, "Hello there, Jo." We embraced, grinned, gave each other the *once over*, and agreed we each looked pretty good. She wore glasses, and I, contacts, and over lunch, we sat there talked about our growing-up years.At one point, I leaned over the table and asked, "Jo, do you remember in the third grade, when the school bus dropped us off in front of the Lincoln School in Newberry, how we would scamper into the girl's room and swap dresses for the day. Then before the bus picked us up, we would hurry and change clothes again?"

She grinned, showing her forever white and even teeth. "I remember."

"It was during the depression. Times were rough. Your dad was employed, mine wasn't. I wore hand-me-downs, my stepmother's nieces, some from our principal, Ms. McKillop's niece, and some from the Salvation Army. Yours were brand new Shirley Temple dresses, and it was so sweet of you to let me wear them."

Her smile broadened. "Arbutus, what you didn't realize was your dresses were also new to me." I chuckled deep upon hearing this, and with foreheads pressed together, we ended laughing ourselves silly, like the schoolgirls we once were.

She dropped me off at the Barbours, where introductions were made, and we stayed to chat awhile, before heading for the Genetti hotel, where our class reunion would be held, and where Delbert had reserved our rooms. We found them in the motel section, on the second floor, overlooking an empty swimming pool. Neither Jo nor I were impressed. When we exited the last, there, straight ahead, on the walkway, an athletic-type man leaned on the banister railing.

"I don't think that is Delbert. But I'm not certain."

As we approached, my heart fluttered at just the sight of him. He stood, smiled, and said, "Hello, there, my Bootsy. It's so good to see you again. I'm really disappointed in our rooms. Later, I'll see if we can change them."

Jo left and together, Delbert and I returned to the Barbour's home in his car. Following introductions, we all amiably agreed with Dolla, a dish of ice cream would taste just great. While Jack and Delbert camped down at the dining room table, Dolla and I, busy in the kitchen, chatted a mile a minute. "Of all the men I've dated, he's the closest to my Bill. He's kind, considerate, and the only one who has all the qualities in a man that I've been looking for. So, tell me, Dolla, what do you think? Isn't he a dear?"

She touched finger to lips, and with a contemplative smile, said, "Why, yes. He seems nice." A giggle, and, "He has nice blue eyes, a nice smile, he and Jack are hitting it off, and it's easy to see he's fond of you." Later, Dolla gave directions to Wal-Mart, and with my afghan in the back seat, Delbert and I took off in search of something in which to carry it home.

We were no sooner inside the door, when Delbert said, "I'm thirsty and could really go for a cup of coffee." The dining area was unoccupied, except for Delbert and me, and there, over his coffee and my lemonade, we chatted for two hours. We covered every subject imaginable. When we spoke of our departed spouses, and our lives since their departure, I was totally surprised to see his eyes suddenly mirror pain, and he soulfully asked, "Tell me, my Bootsy, will the hurt ever go away?"

His tears were about to brim over. Mine were, too. I reached over and covered his hands with mine. "Yes, Delbert. More, with each passing day."

"I'll always love my Bonnie."

"And I'll always love my Bill. At times, I still cry when I place flowers on his grave, yet I'm able to go on, without hurting. Do you have a picture of your wife?"

"Yes." He reached in his pocket, removed his wallet, slipped out the picture and handed it to me. "I've never shown it to anyone else. You are the first."

"She's lovely," I said, and handed it back to him. "Just continue to carry her with you and, in time, the hurt will vanish and all that will remain will be happy memories. Believe me, Delbert. One day, this will happen." We talked about our children, his three, my four, and finally, got around to finding a case for my afghan.

Then it was back to the hotel, where we discovered all the single rooms were occupied, and we opted to take the only rooms available...Bob Hope's suite. It proved comfortable, delightfully homey. Like a honeymoon suite. Though his bedroom was way on the other-side of French glass doors, clothed in sheer white curtains. After our tour, while entwined in each other's arms in the living room, I looked up into his smiling face, and now in a pensive mood, quietly told him, "I've never done anything like this before."

He kissed my nose. "This will be the first, since my Bonnie died."

"I feel uncomfortable, Delbert. Will you do something for me?"

"Sure!"

"Let's marry ourselves."

A sparkle lit his blue eyes, and he leaned over and captured my lips with his, which I found tantalizing sweet. "Okay!" he said.

We broke away, held hands, and I said, "I'll go first. I, Bootsy Focht, take thee, my Prince Delbert Hilling, as my lawful wedded husband." In my mind's eye, down the road I pictured him as my husband, but fearful of frightening him away, before we even became close, I paused, then quickly added..."For this weekend."

He, in turn, reciprocated with, "I, Delbert Hilling, take thee my Princess Bootsy, as my lawful wedded wife, for this weekend."

Later, while I viewed television, he disappeared, and upon his return, I was surprised to see him across the room at the bar, and pouring ruby red wine into crystal goblets. "I thought this would be nice, and you would enjoy it," he said. "I also brought up some crackers from the kitchen."

When it was about time to retire, I teased, "Do you plan to shack up."

Brows furled a moment. "Shack up?"

The funny expression on his dear face made me laugh. "Yes. I was eighteen, on my first date and he had asked me this. I didn't know what it meant either, until someone said he wanted me to spend the night with him in his cabin."

"Oh. We're married so we're allowed." That dear man actually blushed.

The following morning, I rolled over in bed to see him quietly enter my room.

"I was here earlier, and sat awhile in the chair, and watched you sleeping so peacefully, but didn't want to disturb you, and tiptoed away. I've been awake for quite some time now, and lay there thinking it would be much nicer being over here with you. Do you mind if I hold you in my arms, again?"

"No." I lifted the covers, and feeling quite giddy, softly sang "Lay your head...upon...my shoulder,"

"And hold your warm and tender body close to mine," he sang along with me, and the room rocked with the merriment of our laughter.

"Never have I heard you laugh so much, my Bootsy," he murmured against my cheek.

"Never in sixteen years, have I felt such sheer freedom as a woman." I brushed his lips with mine and again snuggled down into the comfort of his arms.

He gently swept back a few strands of my blonde hair, and his hand slowly slid down the full length of my cheek. The room remained wonderingly quiet a moment. "Did you like the way I caressed you?" he asked.

This brought nearly a giggle, but I smiled and told him, "Umhmmmm."

He said, " I would like to make…"

"Shhh." I reached up and placed a finger to his lips. "Not yet. Remember what I told you last night? A lot of men worry because they can't at this stage in life, and they're not even aware seventy-five percent of the women prefer cuddling, being hugged and held closely, like this."

"Tell me, my Bootsy, do you like sex?"

"Love it. My husband and I both agreed, it's the cheapest and most pleasurable source of entertainment."

We lay there quietly, content to be together. After awhile, he said, "Let's disengage, and go check to see if the Continental Breakfast is still on."

Fifteen minutes later, he suggested, "Let's disengage and go check to see if we can still get the Continental Breakfast."

Fifteen more minutes, with my head still peacefully resting on his shoulder, he told me, "That clock is ticking away. Let's disengage and…"

My lips silenced his. "I'm not really hungry."

He pulled me down, kissed my cheek, and whispered, "I'm not hungry, either. This is wonderful, snuggling together like this, like we did last night. You're beautiful early in the day."

"Really?" I kissed the soft nape of his neck, inhaled the manly scent of after shave lotion.

"Really, I mean it."

"That makes me feel warm and fuzzy. Years ago, when our family moved from Maryland back to Pennsylvania, our Dianne was in the seventh grade. When classmates, doctor Clemens' twin sons told their class, 'You should see Dianne's Mom, she's beautiful,' she told them 'You should see her in the mornings.'"

Our class reunion proved to be equally terrific. With my prince Delbert by my side, in meeting old friends and making new, it was all one could ever ask for. After introductions were made at our individual tables of eight, and dinner was over, Delbert stayed and became better acquainted, while I skirted around the room, and chatted with old class mates. Two tables over, sat Doris Starr Wool. She always remained a star in my book. Ever since she parted with her blue silk dress, with a white Peter Pan collar trimmed in pink satin ribbon and flowers, so I would have something to wear to our sixth grade party. And there was her husband, Joe, a likable chap.

He surprised me, when he reached up, grabbed my hand, and said, "Arbutus, you have another twenty-five years to go."

"Thank you, Joe, that's nice of you to tell me that. But, twenty-five years? You're sweet, like your brother, Clyde. I dated him a few times in my tender years."

Astonishment swept his still unlined face. "You did? I didn't know that."

I excused myself, and departed from that table when I spied a favorite classmate, Ruth Armstrong Burkholder, and she me, and with hands flailing mid-air, we rushed to embrace. Her braids were pulled back from her elfish face, and I blurted, "You haven't changed a bit, Ruth. I'd know you anywhere."

Cheek pressed to mine, she said, "Arbutus, I'd know you, too." Breaking away, she grinned, and whispered, "Where's your wrinkles?"

"Don't look too closely. They're there." I learned she still belonged to St. Marks Lutheran church as both our families had fifty years ago, and she continued to sing in the choir. I chatted with class-mates I hadn't seen for ages. I enjoyed seeing Shirley Leidecker Collins, an A student in my Biology class. I remembered there were only five of us who didn't have to take the final exam, and now here she was, one of the reunion planners. And there sat Dick Bower who e-mailed us all in regards to upcoming socials.

All in all, I'd recommend attending class reunions.

However, one never knows what will happen. We missed most of the 6:00 cocktail party. A message had been left at the front desk to call both Delbert's room, and mine. My phone rang, and I answered, but he hadn't heard his, so I trotted over and found him sleeping. "It's not necessary to be one of the first attending," he said. So, I didn't hurry. However, I should have, because the black, pantyhose I recently purchased, were made to be worn with capris, and were minus feet. Then, my black, rayon, half-slip stuck out four inches from beneath my new black dress. Though rolled up at the waist, it unrolled with my first step. In the end, I chose to wear a short petticoat. The secret is to have a trial-run pertaining to even undergarments.

Still, it proved to be a splendid weekend, introducing my

handsome escort to everybody near and dear to me. Included were my 90-year-young stepmom, LaRaine Smith, two brothers, and families, school-chum, Jo, and my longest-time friends, the Barbours, and even the Jelsmas. Through the Barbours, we had learned the Jelsmas were in town for physicals, so Delbert and I drove over to the Williamsport Hospital and sat in the waiting room until they, and their daughter, Barbara, came out. What a reunion that was! Following many hugs, and passing on family news, before we parted, Wiebe turned to me, and in front of Delbert, said, "Bootsy, he's a nice guy. Keep him." In his ear I whispered, "Yes, I would like to."

We left Williamsport that afternoon, and drove to my son Keith's home in Etters. There, Delbert had time to stay for a short visit. When he was about to leave, and we were alone outside, he gently took my hand in his, and led me between the two parked cars. "Let's say goodbye here, where it's more private." Our bodies molded during his last sweet and lingering kiss, and my arms clung to him, not wishing to let go. His last words uttered were, "I have a lump in my throat." I turned, headed for the house, and refused to watch as he drove away.

**Me and my Prince Delbert, dining at the Barbours' home in Montoursville, PA**

# Chapter 60
# Homeward Bound

Here I am again, seated on Delta, ready to head for home, as I take pen in hand and jot off a hurried note.

My darling Prince Delbert Hilling,

Strangely, a touch of nostalgia sweeps over me as our plane cruises down the Harrisburg, Middletown extended runway, constructed years ago by Hempt Brothers construction engineer, my husband, my Bill. From where I sit, our 38 happy years together now seemingly whiz past my window.

But, oh, my dearest one, there you are, as we lift skyward into the air, and again in my heart. My thoughts are, if I should never safely arrive in Orlando, I would die happy for having lingered awhile in your arms this past, alarmingly sweet weekend. I thank you for the time we shared. As I told you before, in my life you are like a ray of sunshine in a cloudy day. I feel we were able to help each other over a roadblock of loneliness. Please know, if you ever run into another, I'll be there, always, to help you hurtle over onto a calm and peaceful pathway.

I wish you were here by my side. I burn with desire to be in your arms once more. Until we meet again, God Bless, keep well, and miss me. I love you,

Only yours, Bootsy

Throughout the day, while busy working around the villa, settling in, my mind now and then would look back on that wonderful weekend. The following morning, when I first awakened in my villa, now totally refreshed after my trip home, I stretched tall, glanced around the room and thought, *I am home. Really home!* I hurried to the window. Directly outside, stood my Holly tree, covered in orange berries. It wouldn't be long until they turned a Christmas red. Beyond, over by the swing, Sweet Williams, planted in my courtyard prior to my departure, were still in bloom. Warm thoughts were, this is my beautiful world. I wondered about Delbert's? Was he also happy to be home? Perhaps, down the road, months or years to come, we would be together and our home and our thoughts would be the same?

The next day, I called him. "Our pictures are developed. You will be pleased. They all turned out and I will send a copy to you."

"Off and on I thought of you, today," he said.

"That's nice. I thought of you, also."

We both ended our conversation with, "Goodbye, I love you." Had I been the first to mention the word "love"? Had I coaxed it out of him? Did the weekend together mean more to me than to him? I would sit back, simply bide my time, and await his next letter and see what he had to say. He would receive the pictures and my note in four days. If he answered immediately, then it would be my turn to wait.

Eight days passed with no response. He undoubtedly was still taking time to settle in. Maybe pay bills, as I was? Nine days. Ten. Eleven. Twelve, Thirteen, and still no letter. By now I began to wonder if he had second thoughts in building a meaningful and lasting relationship. I imagined him to be truthful. Yet, there, in that picture on his dresser…was Julie. Perhaps the lump in his throat was regrets in spending time with me instead of her. Would my world still be beautiful without my Delbert in it? How could I not wonder?

# Chapter 61
# The PA Club's Talent Show

Regarding Delbert? C'est la vie! Such is life. This is what I told Jane when she called this morning. "I'll simply do as my Tennessee friends always advised. 'I won't fret none.'"

"I wouldn't either. You're too nice a person. Perhaps in time he'll still call. Think positively."

"That's easier said than done, Jane. I tossed him far from mind over the past five days, yet his dear face haunted me in dreams, and one night I called out his name in my sleep, and there he was again, making me yearn to hear from him, to see him, be in his arms once more."

"I can imagine how you feel. Probably the way I would if I didn't have my Bob. You just hang in there, hon. What will be, will be, and remember, God knows best."

Over the next two weeks concentration on the upcoming Pennsylvania talent show took precedent. Six months ago, President, Clair Auckey, formerly from Hanover, PA, had urged me to participate again this year. Last year I shared some of my poetry. This year, though I had never sung in public, except as a teenager in the Baptist church choir, I would attempt to sing two songs. One with

Kirk Kirchdoerfer, a Jim Thorpe native, husband of friend Nancy, whom I met two years ago. He volunteered to accompany me on his guitar. Because of my travels, it wasn't until three days ago, when Kirk arrived at my villa for a practice session. The only song we both knew all the words to was an oldie, "When I Grow Too Old to Dream."

"You keep going up too high on that one note," he said, and sang in his deep voice until I blended in with his.

So, the night had finally arrived, and here I was, nervously seated across the table from a group of nice ladies during the club's business meeting, which soon ended.

Talent time, and Clair, on stage, was making an announcement. I leaned forward, expecting to hear him introduce Kirk. I would be next and my part would soon be over. Instead, I was shocked to hear, "This evening our first participant in our talent show will be Betty Ganz, and she'll entertain us with a tap dance." She did remarkably well.

Kirk, with his guitar, came next. I listened as he sang "I Can't Help Loving You," but in the middle of his second song, "I'll Never Forget the Day I Was Born," I excused myself and headed back stage for the dressing room.

Clair soon came looking for me. "Bootsy, are you about ready? You're next."

He left, and I hurriedly switched into my knee-length black and white striped PRISONER OF LOVE night-shirt, with the bright red heart painted over where mine should be. When I scooted down the hall and climbed the stage stairs, there stood Ed Klemmer, our Vice President, and stage-hand. He, like me, was formerly from the Harrisburg area.

"Clair's announcing your number. Are you ready?"

With heart thumping against ribs, I nodded. "Do I look okay?"

"You look fine."

I parted the curtains. Straight ahead, right smack in mid-stage with his guitar, sat a confident and composed Kirk, the total opposite of me. As nervous as a cat on a hot-tin-roof, now before an audience of 212. I needed to gather composure. I could do this! I told myself. First, I feigned sleepiness, stretched my left hand skyward, and with my right, pretended to silence a noisy yawn, and smiled to myself as I slowly crossed the stage to Kirk's side. The message on my shirt not only brought chuckles from the audience, but a confidence which swept over me as I looked down and asked, "Play the number for me, Kirk?"

He plunked a few cords and we began to sing. "When I grow too old to dream, I'll have you to remember, when I grow too old to dream, your kiss..." Whoops! Too high! I had hit that wrong note. A look of puzzlement swept across Kirk's rugged face, and I fought hard to hold back a giggle. He hesitated, looked up at me, and I jumped in, feeling sillier than ever, and continued to sing on alone, at a slower tempo, 'Live...in...my...heart. So...kiss...meeee...my sweet, and sooooo let us part. And when...I grow...toooo old to dream, your kiss will live...in my heart." He relaxed his hold on the strings a moment.

With microphone still clasped in hand, I swung the other mid-air, and Kirk began to strum as I repeated the last line in my highest, and most squeakiest voice, "Your kisssss will live in my...haaa...art." My hand completed the semi-circle and came down with a slap, to rest right smack on the printed red heart on my chest. By now I thought I would die laughing and the crowd would, too.

Clair was saying, "After Ed Klemmer and I entertain you with one of our funny skits, Bootsy will return and put on another for you." While they were busy on stage, in my dressing room I, soon to be a cowgirl, fought buttons on my white silk blouse, and hurriedly tugged into tight blue jeans, donned a denim pink, blue and white floral vest, and silently prayed I wouldn't flub this time. Would I remember the poem that ran through my head during breakfast? Before curtain call, could I get into those white boots in that bag over there? For the past two years, not since my last knee arthroscopy had I worn shoes or boots with heels. I reached for them now. First the left. Tight! There! I wiggled toes and they felt better. Not cramped. Now the right. I stood, donned my white brimmed straw hat, glanced in the mirror, pirouetted, smiled and said, "Here we go, my Lord. Please be with me."

Curtains parted, and with head held high, and the staccato of heels clicking on hardwood floors, I strutted up to the microphone. I once heard it's always good to first obtain audience participation. I would do that.

"Good evening dear Pennsylvanians," I greeted.

"Good evening," the crowd reciprocated.

I felt comfortable and continued, "How many of you yearn to pull those weeds?" Silence. "How many yearn to rake those leaves?" Silence. "How many of you are yearning to go back to Pennsylvania and shovel that snow?" Only chuckles. "Me, neither." I laughed. "Yet, though I'm far, far away, when I think of our PA it's with a 'Hip! Hip! Hurray!' So let's give it three cheers. 'Hip! Hip! Hurray!'" They all joined in, and I was proud of them and our lovely state of Pennsylvania. I continued, "Tonight, I'll sing, in a cappella, a song which comes to mind from sometime ago, when our family moved nine times in fifteen years. I can't recall the name, so I'll simply title it, 'Sometimes.'" With microphone in right hand, and tapping my left thigh to mentally get the rhythm, I slowly began:

> Sometimes...I wonder why I have to roam.
> Somehow...my thoughts are traveling way back home.
> I miss the hills, the old folks and my little sister, Lou,
> And I wonder if they miss me, too.
> Though I'm a long ways from home,
> And that blue Mountain dome,
> Still, I hear the echoes from the hills.
> And there's my sweet Lillie Belle and my Hill-Billy Pal,
> Calling in the echoes from the hills."

Having practiced with a tape, I did my best at yodeling, and then I continued:

> Now, when I left, my father said,
> "Now, don't do nothing wrong."
> And, I recall my Mama saying,
> "Honey, don't be long."
> And I know that one day,
> I'll be wending my way,
> Back among the echoes from the hills.

Again I yodeled. My finale was to have everyone give yodeling a try, mocking me by positioning and warbling their tongues. They were good sports, and I exited the stage with a confident smile. Clair was saying, Bootsy wasn't even going to sing, yet I had coaxed her. She did a fantastic job. Let's give her another hand."

What could I do, but return? I stuck my head out through the curtains, grinned, bowed, and with the sound of clapping hands, drank in contentment at having pleased the audience.

Now, I was able to return to my seat and be entertained by Clair and Ed with the last of their routines. In their first, supposedly as Villagers with noses in newspapers, they tossed news back and forth which got them to wondering about the good old days, and how they ever survived. Coming into the modern age in their second, as Bud Abbot and Lou Costella, the latter wanted a computer for his office and called Abbot at the computer help center. What he received was a humorous play-on-words, pertaining to computer functions which left him more perplexed than ever. Lee Goff, from Scranton, sang two heartwarming songs. "You Were Meant For Me" and "Thank God for Little Girls." Then on his harmonica, Jack Brown, from Wilkes-Barre, inspired us with "God Bless America," and "My Country 'Tis of Thee."

When it came to Dick Mowery from Pittsburgh, at the piano, I became spellbound as he played mine and my husband's favorite tunes, which were sung at his funeral: "How Great Thou Art", and "Amazing Grace." Later, I complimented Mowery, and he grinned and told me, "You're the one who did a fantastic job, holding the crowd's attention. You had them eating out of your hands. Some comedians can't do this."

When I apologized to Kirk, telling him, "I really goofed, when singing, "When I Grow Too Old To Dream." He appeased me with, "You didn't. Not really, Bootsy. You turned it into comedy, and it turned out great. Everyone appreciated it."

Back in my villa, in the darkness of my room, before closing my eyes in slumber, I told myself, if I can successfully handle unsuspected problems like the one which surprised me tonight, I can hurtle over anything. To be happy, a man wasn't necessary in my life. Not even Delbert. If this is the way he wanted it, let him go his way. I'd go mine. Come morning, I looked at everything in a new perspective. Not one to harbor ill feelings toward anyone, I found myself seated at my computer. Words flew from mind onto paper.

Dear Prince, Del,

Please note, though I think of you as mine, I did not address you as such, because by now, I have come to my senses. I realize I may have moved too fast, and shoved you into a situation in which you feel uncomfortable. Don't be. You are at the stage where you must be cautious in selecting whom you wish to walk beside you as you continue on through life. Your happiness is all I wish for.

If I'm not the someone special you have been searching for, and you want to continue on and play the field, feel free to do so. If you wish to choose Julie over me, it's your prerogative. Yet, I want you to know I will forever long for you to be mine, and in my heart and mind, I will always and forever be…only yours,

Bootsy

No, I wouldn't mail it. Instead, I slipped the letter in the top drawer of my desk. It had been written for my own satisfaction, to lighten the burden in my heart. Now, I would start a new day with a new untroubled slate. Since today was Friday, a water aerobic day, I turned on the radio to get the weather report. I would dial my friend and water aerobic partner, Jane. One ring. Two. Jane should soon answer. Mondays, Wednesdays, and Fridays, at 11 AM, we have been attending hour long co-ed sessions, along with eighty to one hundred twenty-five others at our Hacienda Olympic Sports Pool. In water no deeper than four and a half feet, we exercise under the leadership of our wonderful, vivacious, and fun-loving coach, Karen Varletta, who keeps us in stitches, while leading us through body strengthening, and age-defying workouts.

"There you are, Jane. Good morning, it's Friday, temperature 65, with no wind, and the water shouldn't be all that cold. Remember a week ago Monday, only you and I showed up, and it was fun? I can't find Karen's name in the phone book, but I'm sure the monitor on duty will again play her tape for us. It's my turn to drive, and if you want to go, I'll be over at 10:40 and pick you up."

"That will be fine, hon. I'm game if you are. I always feel so good afterwards."

"Me, too. Last week I lost three pounds, with only five more to go. By the way, Dr. Ibrahim, in Dr. Zeini's Eye Care Office, recommends we wear brown Polaroid sunglasses as opposed to my gray. Brown tones down the sun's reflection on water. Also, he says not to use Visine eye drops too frequently."

"Did he say why?"

"It varies from person to person. Too much Visine constricts blood vessels, and oxygen and blood is what nourishes the eyes. He said we receive oxygen from outside air, tears, and blood is last. Man's body naturally tries to get oxygen to the cornea." I took a big breath and said, "See what you learned, today?"

"Yes, hon, one never is too old to learn."

Following our aerobics, I dropped Jane off at her home, and returned to mine, to find the red button blinking on my answering machine.

# Chapter 62
## The Long-Awaited Message

I listened to the voice on the answering machine. "Bootsy, my princess, this is Prince Delbert Hilling. I'm sorry I'm late in getting back to you, but I've been extremely busy. I've finished building my deck and have good news. I'm flying to Chicago to visit my daughter and next Monday will return home, unpack, and pack again. Then I and my 93-year-young lady friend, who lives next door, will drive to the Villiages. So anxious to see you, my love. I'll call you tonight."

Tears sprinkled my eyes. No, he did not call that evening. He called the following, and told me, "Yes, we rented on the historical side of The Villages, for the months of December and January, and I'll soon be seeing you, my Bootsy."

"Just to hear your voice, still gets my heart to singing," I told him. "I shall count the hours."

"Me, too, my little princess. Here's a kiss 'til then."

Monday morning, and I pictured him hurriedly unpacking, packing, hopping into his car and heading my way. If they stopped overnight to rest, it should take two days. Undoubtedly, he would be arriving sometime on Wednesday.

Wednesday came and passed, and I pictured him busy unpacking and settling in. Thursday, he would call me. He didn't. Friday, I fussed a bit. Yet, again, I told myself I must not think unkindly, as there were no commitments made, no engagement ring. Nothing! Only dreams and wishes which entwine my heart with his. Saturday morning, grocery shopping day, and the radio announced a cold front had blown in overnight. I would dress warmly. I pondered what to wear and chose my royal blue knit slack set. I buried my chin in the turtle neck. Soft and warm. I slipped into a royal blue with green trim wool jacket, plopped on a white angora hat, trimmed in gold, and smiled into my bedroom mirror. Pert and perky, I told myself, and was off and out the door.

In Publix super market, I wheeled my grocery cart up to the deli section. Here, I tasted samples of boiled ham, ordered Boars Head, and casually glanced here and there, as I pushed my cart the full length of the building. As I turned the corner, there, straight ahead across the room in mid-aisle at the meat bin, stood a tall, strikingly handsome man. I wondered about him. Who he was? Did I know him? If I didn't, I surely would like to.

No, it wasn't tall handsome Nick, the tugboat captain from Staten Island, whom I dated four years ago when I first arrived in The Villages to begin my search for a new home. Who, then, was he? Casually dressed in tan slacks, jacket, and matching baseball cap, his eyes never wavered from my face. Was he flirting? Our eyes caught and held, and a strange, wondrously sweet, and titillating sensation coursed through my complete body. He was smiling. Spellbound, while the words, 'Throw me a kiss, from across the room' swept through my mind, I shoved my grocery cart in his direction, until I found myself standing beside him. His eyes smiled down into mine. Then, he reached up, and ever...so slowly...removed his baseball cap, and said, "Bootsy, I'm your Prince Delbert Hilling!" I gasped, as he reached out and gathered me close in his arms. "This is fate! I can't believe this is happening," he said, still tightly holding me. From the corner of my eye, I noticed his filled grocery cart. "We just arrived last night. I was going to get settled in and call you."

He held me so tightly, I felt he would never let me go. With my head still resting on his shoulder, I breathed in his manly scent, familiarized myself with the beating of his heart next to mine, now certain this man was indeed, my sweet Prince Delbert Hilling, whom I hadn't seen but only that one weekend in the past two years. Still, how could I have forgotten him? We stood there, cheek to cheek for the longest while, then he turned his face, brushed my lips with his and folded me back into his arms. There were only a smattering of people in the store, and I was glad they were at the far end, going about their own business. I couldn't help but sigh as I looked up into his blue eyes and told him, "Oh, wonders of wonders! I didn't recognize you, dressed like this, and wearing a hat. Did you know it was me?"

"No. But I was going to speak."

"Why? When you didn't know it was me?"

"Because I like what I see." I found this pleasing, and too, when he reached out and swooped me back into his arms again.

With lips pressed against his jacket, I muttered, "I can't believe this. I was going to stop at Winn Dixie, but don't know what caused me to change my mind."

"I'll call you tomorrow morning, he said, as his hand caressed my arm sleeve and he planted another sweet kiss to my lips.

"Promise?" I looked up and grinned.

"Promise," he said, beaming one of his usual sweet smiles down on me.

I left the super market and sang along with the car radio all the way home.

Once inside my villa, with groceries now in their respective places, I again found myself glancing out my bedroom window. Berries on the Holly tree were already Christmas red. Oh wondrous of wonders. The holidays were nearly upon us, just around the corner, and my Delbert was here. I turned away and wondered what the New Year held in store for me?

True to his word, Delbert, my returned Prince, called the following morning. We had a nice chat, and he told me, "I'll call you tonight."The night came and went, and I didn't hear from him until the next morning. By then, a bout of laryngitis set in. Via phone, it was more than a little bothersome trying to get him to hear my whisper. Our conversation ended with his, "I'll call you tomorrow morning, my princess."

A return performance. Morning came and was gone, and my phone jangled in the evening. Somewhat agitated, I whispered, "Why do you keep saying you'll call and I wait, and you don't?"

In quite a nonchalant manner, he told me, "It's neglect."

He was so downright honest, I was near to laughing, but only whispered, "That's okay. I still can't talk, and I'm not supposed to strain my voice."

He would be here for two months, approximately eight weeks. Since our surprised meeting in Publics on that sweet memorable Saturday, I yearned to soon be with him again, to see if the magic was still there.

He spent his first four days becoming acclimated to everything in general…Settling in, caring for the needs of 95-year-old Beatrice, and reacquainting himself with former neighbors. At first, I didn't mind. I was up at nights coughing, and until I discovered Nyquil, and caught up on sleep, I sometimes dragged myself through the days. I began to feel better, and wondered if Delbert and I were to fall in love, would I be content to walk side by side, down through the golden years, with someone so forgetful?

Wednesday, such thoughts diminished like the winds. He called. "Are you busy? I have a breather this afternoon."

When I threw open the door, gazed up at him, and drank in that beautiful smile, there was that same old spark and we nearly fell into each other's arms.

Once inside the door, I asked, "How does a cold glass of lemonade sound?"

"Wonderful, my little princess." He gave my hand a gentle squeeze.

Later, we carried our glasses into the living room, and I asked, "Do me a favor?"

"Sure, anything."

"Lift the first cushion of the loveseat." He placed his glass on the marble topped table, leaned over, did as requested, and gave me a puzzled look. "Okay," I chuckled softly. "You may return your picture to where it had been before. I wasn't going to keep looking at it, wondering what you were up to."

He reached out and pulled me into his arms, and I snuggled deep, resting my head upon his shoulder, and listened as he told me, "Oh, my Bootsy, I've been so busy."

"That's alright. I understand."

He confided, "I told my charge I would be back at four and we would go see her friend and spend time with her. But, she won't mind. I took her to the hair dresser's and for a manicure yesterday, and today, I'd rather be here with you."

During our beautiful and tender moments, I wouldn't permit his lips to touch mine. "My cough still lingers, Delbert. Though the doctor insists I'm no longer contagious, we can't chance it. Years ago, when Keith was twelve and came home from school with staph pneumonia, because there were no rooms available in the Berwick hospital, I cared for him at home, and also came down with staph."

"Were you hospitalized?"

"Umhmm. Four days. Topping that, when my husband brought me home, and went to kiss me, I said, "No, darling. I don't want you to catch this, it's wicked," but he still insisted, saying he would be fine. Then he ended in the hospital with staph pneumonia in both lungs, and remained there for seven days."

Delbert and I were unable to spend Christmas together. Much to my chagrin, his lady friend were invited to spend it with out-of-town friends. I would be alone, but friend, Polly, who lost her husband this year, talked me into tagging along with her bus group to Tennessee. There, we went on a noteworthy boat ride, viewed life-size ice sculptures of the nativity scene, visited the Grande Ole' Oprey Museum and enjoyed a spectacular Christmas show. A different Christmas than ever spent before, still it threw me into the usual gloriously uplifting holiday spirit.

Saturday evening, tired after the bus trip home, when I opened my front door, I was pleased as I glanced around. Over the years, never have I left on a trip without first having my home tidy and in pin-whistle order. More so, since living on one floor. I drank in a sweet feeling of contentment and pulled my luggage through the dining room, the living room, into my bedroom, slipped out of my shoes, stared longingly at my bed, hung my purse on the doorknob, looked right, and left, then nearly fainted. Through the opened doorway of the master closet, I saw clothing heaped in piles on the entire floor. I had been meaning to take another car-load over to Women in Need. I stood there, and stared at the narrow metal shelving which hung precariously from the wall, like limp-thin-white-arms. The clock on the nightstand blinked 10:45. Now what should I do? I did manage to cart half of the garments over into the guest room, and place the other half on the opposite side of my king-size bed, before I totally ran out of steam, and retired for the night.

Sunday morning, I rang Delbert, and told him, "I'm tired, honey, and won't be attending church with you, today. I'm going to stay home and catch up on rest." I shared the upsetting news about the collapsed racks in my closet.

"Don't you worry, my precious. I'll put them back up for you." I was gleeful to hear this. He continued, "I'll be free on Friday, and come over with measuring tape, screw driver and hammer. In the meantime, check around the neighborhood, and see if you can find a drill." Friday came, Friday went, with no Delbert. I knew he was an avid golfer, and had mentioned he was anxious to check out the various villages, with hopes of eventually buying, and settling down here, as I had. Oh, my, I so looked forward to that day. Yet, where was he now?

Saturday morning my doorbell rang, and there stood neighbor, John, with toolbox in hand. I had told him about my predicament the other day when he was out in front of his villa. "Did you get your racks up, yet?" he asked.

"Nope! Not yet." Last month, he had straightened and hung my garage door screen when I accidentally forgot it was closed, and backed into it. Now, he spoke quite quickly, as if out of breath. "I have a golf meet in forty-five minutes, but I think I can get this done for you."

"Have you ever done this before?"

"Numerous times, and it shouldn't take long." He jumped right in, measured racks, figured what hangers and fixtures were needed, then sent me off to Lowe's Hardware. True to his word, he was finished in time for his golf meet.

Monday morning, Delbert called. "Did you get a drill?"

"No." I really wasn't fibbing. "But I know where I can get one."

"Ok, little princess, I'm on my way."

When he showed up at my door, he pulled me close, held me so beautifully in his arms, kissed my cheek, allowed me to nuzzle his soft, warm neck, and drink in the sweetness of just being together. Then he whispered, "We better get to work and get that out of the way."

"Okay." I led him into my bedroom. When he walked inside and could readily see the job had been completed, sheer astonishment swept over his dear face. He beamed the biggest smile and, together, we stepped into the closet, and right back into each other's arms.

Before he left, he did carry all of my Christmas decorations to the attic, and now, I no longer have a cluttered garage.

For New Year's Eve, Delbert and his lady guest stayed home. My neighbor, Daphine, and I would be alone, too. So, I tucked a bottle of black raspberry liquor in a basket, along with some crackers and cheese, then dialed her number. "It's 11:30. I'm coming over."

"That's fine! I was hoping you could make it. The door's open." While we sipped one smooth cocktail, screwed up our noses, because it was a tad strong, and with eyes glued to the TV, we counted quite loudly, as if with the bunch of people who watched the ball drift down in New York's Time Square. Midnight! A new day, a new year!

It was Delbert's and his friend's last Friday here, and I was elated when he phoned and we made plans to dine together. "How do you like barbecued ribs?" he asked.

"Love them. I've had them at Sunnys, and they were delicious."

"Then you will like Denny's. We will pick you up at five-thirty." I recalled the one Sunday when he told Jane and Bob, upon his next return, he would be courting me, and we would be spending more time together. Now, I assumed the *we* would mean him and his guest, the neighbor lady from back home.

In my estimation, when he brought her over to see my villa, last year, I classified her as quiet, though quite charming, a fine woman, a retired school teacher, somewhat stern, who could very well be classified as a straight-as-an-arrow kind of woman, who wouldn't take any guff from anybody. Now, I wondered how things would go tonight? Seated together at Denny's, I imagined she had accepted me as Delbert's girlfriend, and we were sort of like family. Delbert, directly across from me, was smiling, and I was drinking it in, and just at that precise moment, I watched as she reached out, and touched his shoulder. I looked across the room to where she nodded. "Delbert, look at that beautiful lady over there at the bar." My heart dropped through the floor, and I blinked in disbelief. The lady was pretty. Perhaps ten years younger than I, but why call attention to her, while I was present?

Delbert simply nodded his head, while I said, "She is pretty. Why don't you get her name and telephone number?"

"I'm not interested," he said, just as the lady came by and stopped at our table. She had caught our guest's smile, and thought she was someone she knew.

I was hurting, but wouldn't show it. Instead, I took it upon myself to introduce each of us, and we all clasped hands. Later, when we were alone, Delbert told me to dismiss the situation. Nothing had been meant by it. Yet, I couldn't help wondering. Had he told her he was seriously interested in me? Or, hadn't he?

# Chapter 63
## His Promise

Sunday, as usual he showed up so handsome, so sparkling clean, so delightfully all smiles as he kissed me at my door. "Ready for church, little princess?" He asked.

"As soon as I gather my purse and the house keys, I'll be on my way."

Church, as usual, had me sitting there drinking in the sweetness of the inspirational songs, and sometimes tapping toes in time to the more peppy tunes. We even clapped hands, when not hidden beneath Delbert's jacket.

Following the service, Delbert and I joined our friends, nine in number, and hand in hand, hiked over to the Café Ole' Restaurant for lunch. Later, we emerged out into the sunlight, a beautiful afternoon; the last of The Village Craft Fair. "Oh, Delbert, can we walk through and look at the items on display? Do you have time?"

"Anything you want, my afternoon is yours, my Bootsy."

We eased our way through the crowd and, there, coming toward us was a comical sight. "Look straight ahead, Delbert!" I grabbed his arm. "It looks like a walking plant."

From waste up, all that was visible were tall fronds of magenta blooms on a huge plant the young lady carried in her arms. We stopped and chatted, and I told her, "That's positively gorgeous. Is it alive?"

She chuckled, and peeking out said, "No, it's really silk. Feel the petals." Then she motioned, "I got it over there at the stand in front of Katie Belles, where the yellow flowers are sticking out."

I thanked her, and Delbert and I headed in that direction, and soon stood before the loveliest tall plant of miniature yellow orchids, dotted with orange centers. "Oh, Delbert, it's exquisite. Exactly like those growing along the one pathway leading into Hawaii's International Market Place. You wouldn't be able to tell the difference." I turned to the salesman. "And it's just what's needed to brighten a room I'm thinking of."

Only, I couldn't make up my mind. An identical plant on the far end of the counter had the same amount of blooms, only the color of the urn differed. The wife of the salesman, in noting my quandary, came over. "What color is your carpeting."

"Blue."

"Then get the one with the blue urn."

That situation cleared, Delbert and I stood to the side and watched as she and her husband gently eased the potted plant into a tall plastic bag with handles.

Delbert insisted on carrying the plant to his car.

"No," Delbert. It's much too heavy. Lets share the weight. You take one handle, and I'll take the other." His eyes sparkled, his lips turned upward and I could have kissed them, right there.

It proved to be a joyful occasion as the two of us, with that beautiful plant between us, eased our way out to the street, and took off on a short cut across the town square. I imagined the yellow blooms, which bounced up and down over the top of the bag, were as happy as I.

Our last evening together, I was still nestled in his arms when he said, "I want to stay awhile longer with you, my little princess, but I'll have to leave. There's still some packing, and cleaning I must get done tonight. Tomorrow, Beatrice and I want to beat the early morning traffic."

When we parted at my front door, Delbert held me so tenderly, and now kissed my lips so beautifully, long and lingeringly, seemingly to make up for lost time in the past, and the future. Never had any man's lips tasted so sweet, and felt so soft. So much so, when our lips slowly parted, and we broke away, I didn't think I could stand to let him go. A fit of sadness swept through my complete being, and the world, at that very moment, seemed to stand still. Then, as he turned away and sauntered down the sidewalk, he called over his shoulder. "I'll call you the minute I get home. I promise!" And everything was alright again.

While television and radio decried news of the winter storm blanketing the complete east coast in snow and ice, closing main highways and roads, I worried about Delbert traveling under such adverse conditions. Nightly, TV pictured cars and trucks jackknifed, and deaths were reported in abandoned cars with snow-covered roofs. I prayed Delbert and Beatrice weren't in one of them, but were holed up somewhere safe. Monday, if they were able to travel, they should have reached West Virginia. Still, I received no word from him. Could he have been in an accident? How was I to know? Jane's husband was adamant with brotherly advice, "Don't call Delbert. Men don't appreciate being pressured. Sit back and wait, and you'll hear from him." I would try to do this.

A long worrisome week dragged by. My mind clouded over with doubts more than ever, now. Delbert had said we would build a relationship and see where it led. How could one do this alone? Saturday night, following dinner, my doorbell rang. Bob and Jane stood there, with bright smiles on their faces. "We have something for you," Jane said, and handed me a package wrapped in red and white striped paper.

"For me? What?" I gleefully asked.

**Building My Own Man**

"Well, open it and see," Bob ordered.

"I saw it in Atlanta last week, and thought of you," Jane said. I tore open the paper, and stared at a five inch little white man, made out of a composite of some sort, resembling rubber. Enclosed in cellophane, the outside printing read:

. . .Grow your own man.

"Thank you, he's cute, and it was sweet of you two birds to think of me."

"We thought, since you are upset about not hearing from Delbert, you could grow your own man," Jane said. "Put it in water. It will grow. Let's do it now."

I got a kick out of this, and placed him in a glass and filled it to the top with water. "I'll keep an eye on him, and let you know what happens."

At the door we hugged, and Jane said, "Now don't you worry about Delbert. There must be a reason why he hasn't called. You will hear from him."

"Thanks, Jane, for everything. I shall strive to hold the good thought."

This following day, snowbird friend, Angelika, invited a group of us to share lunch with her in her new villa. Polly and I were included. When it comes to men, both Polly and Angelika think differently than I. Polly took a bite of her dainty pizza and was saying, "Men! They don't think like we do. They play you along, then drop you. All except my Ron." Her eyes sparkled a moment. Then she continued, "From the way Delbert is treating you, he's like all the rest. You will never hear from your prince, Bootsy. He's in the past. Forget him."

I sighed, and gave my head a negative shake. I was thinking I could no sooner forget Delbert, than forget how to breathe. Angelika was adding her thoughts. "Listen, Bootsy, even if Delbert says he loves you, don't believe a word he says, until he gets down on his knees and says, 'I love you, Bootsy, will you marry me?'"

"So, forget him," came from Polly.

How? When he was in my heart and in my mind. The week before he left, I told him, "I pledge myself to you, my dear prince, Delbert." He, in turn, took my hands in his, smiled deep into my eyes and told me, "And I pledge myself to you, my sweet princess, Bootsy." How could I tell these ladies this? They would undoubtedly laugh, as would anyone else who heard it. Was I being a silly goose, hanging onto love this way? At my age?

Valentine's Day was fast approaching, with still no word from this man who claimed to be my prince. The week leading up to that important day, I spent shopping, writing twenty-one letters and addressing that amount of valentines. All the time, I anxiously wondered what Delbert would be saying in his? I called Jane and hashed over my thoughts. "It seems he has forgotten me, but I can't forget him. Sometimes I don't think love is worth this worry, this heartache. Yet, I'll continue to do what Bob suggests, not let Delbert know how terribly I miss him; not let him think I care. For awhile I thought of not even sending his valentine. Then, changed my mind."

"Yes, send him one. He's a nice man. And he cares for you."

"He certainly isn't showing it. The card I'm sending him isn't all hearts and flowers. Yet, it's nice, and says, 'Happy Valentine's Day. I miss you. Wish you were here.' I'm simply signing it, 'Always, Love, Bootsy.'"

"That's fine. He'll be pleased."

"Oh, Jane. How I long to hear his voice, and know he's okay. Perhaps he's dead, killed in a horrible car accident, and no longer on this earth. Or else, why hasn't he called as he promised?"

"I don't know, hon. Just hang in there."

"I am! Even growing my own man." I managed a chuckle. "He outgrew the glass and I put him in a big brandy snifter, and he has grown to the top of even it."

"Really?"

"Uhuh! You should see him. He stands straight, and is now three times taller. It's amazing. I can't believe it." As days wore on, I still fretted over Delbert, and wondered how he was. Yes, I sent his valentine. Wednesday, two days before the big day, my daughter, Dianne, called, and when I shared my concern, she surprised me.

"Listen to me, Mom!"

"Okay, I'm listening."

"No one is perfect."

"I am...nearly...according to your brother, Keith." A light giggle.

"What I'm trying to say is at your age, people sometimes become forgetful."

"Guilty! Yet, he promised to call."

"He may have a reason. Mom, You're looking for the perfect man, like Dad. Dad, at this age, if he were alive, wouldn't be perfect. Question? Now, hear this! If it were any other friend you were worried about, man or woman, wouldn't you call and see how they were?"

"Most assuredly! I never thought about it that way. But he promised to call. Maybe he can't. Maybe he's dead; not even here anymore. I don't know of any phone number to call, but his."

"So call!"

Stubborn me, said, "I'll think about it. I just may do that." In pondering over the situation, I certainly didn't want Delbert to feel I was chasing after him. Yet, if we were establishing a relationship to see where it would lead, I shouldn't be wishy washy, floundering around like a fish out of water, wondering which way to go. Perhaps I should break down and check in on him? Thursday, the day before Valentine's Day, and in my golf cart, on my way to the mail-station, I held onto hopes this was the day his valentine would arrive. Valentine's Day, instead of going for my mail, I broke down and called Delbert.

"Oh, Bootsy, it's so good to hear your voice."

He sounded strange. "Am I still your princess?"

"No."

Momentarily, I troubled my bottom lip, as I'm prone to do at times. "Did you hear what I said?"

"No."

"I asked if I'm still your princess."

"Oh, yes! Yes! Always."

"You promised to call, why didn't you?"

"Oh, my princess, Bootsy, when I returned home, I came down with the flu and have been gravely ill. Today, my son brought over a respirator, and after two weeks, I'm feeling somewhat better."

"I'm so sorry to hear this, but I have been sick, worrying about you."

"I was too weak to hold a phone, and was without a voice, like you were."

"You poor dear. It's rough stuff. I still have coughing spells in the mornings. Do you think you caught this from me?"

"No, but it's strange. Over the past fifteen years, I never even had a cold."

"Are you drinking a lot of fluids?"

"Yes, glasses and glasses full. It helps, some."

"Did you get my valentine?"

"Yes, and it was so sweet and nice of you to send it. You made my day. Thank you, my precious. You won't be getting mine until Monday. I couldn't get it out on time."

"That's alright. I'll look forward to receiving it. In the meantime, do get better soon."

"I will. I'm getting there."

"Oh, before I forget, remember the yellow orchid plant I bought at the craft show?"

"It died!"

"No, silly. You know it's artificial. Well, just the other day, I received a letter from the owners of Silk Paradise, in St. Petersburg. At first, I thought it was an advertisement, but instead it contained a nice letter written by Bill O'Neal, the husband of the lady who suggested we buy the one in the blue urn. Enclosed was a check for $5.00. He said, unknown to him, his wife had reduced the price of my plant, and he was reimbursing me for the difference."

"That's great!"

"Yes, now, hear this. Let me tell you something near to unbelievable."

"What? I'm all ears. Tell me."

"It happened two nights ago. I drove over to Wal-Mart for a few items, hoping to return home before darkness set in. But the few items turned into a full grocery cart and, while standing in check-out, I asked the young clerk if she would please put my cart in an out-of-the way place while I ran to the ladies room. She told me to take it over to Service, they would keep an eye on it. At Service, I was informed the ladies rest room was closed. It was being cleaned, and I would have to go way to the back of the store and use that one. I decided not to do this. I would hurry home. But, as I pushed my cart past the two men who were lining up empty carts, and they asked, 'And how are you, this evening?' I blabbed, 'I'm okay, but did you know the ladies room is closed?' One said, 'Yes, you have to go to the other end of the store. But I can take you there in one of the riding carts.'

"Did you take him up on the offer?"

"No, I thanked him, and said I'd head for home, but if by chance they should see a trickle of water running across the Wal-Mart floor, and hear riveting and pounding outside, they would know a bridge was being built." Delbert chuckled, and I continued. "It was dark when I hurried from the store, quickly found my car in aisle six, placed the groceries in the trunk, slid the cart not where it was supposed to go, but close to two others, and jumped into my car and was on my way."

"Question? Did you make it home in time?"

"Yes, but wait until I tell you what happened. I no sooner walked into my villa, when sis, Kathy, called from Manhattan, and I was curled up on the sofa chatting when my doorbell rang. This startled me, Delbert, as no one comes to my villa after dark unless first calling. Then it's usually a neighbor. Kathy told me to hang up and see who it was, so I did . I turned on the outside light and looked through the peephole, at a man I had never seen before. Remember the old-time cowboy show, 'Bonanza,' and the big, strapping, older son, Hoss?"

"Yes."

"Well, there stood his near duplicate, dressed in black cowboy hat, black sleeveless t-shirt, black pants, and black boots. I hesitated a moment, then stepped out and closed the door. He was taller than I imagined. He looked down on me, in a friendly way, and asked, "Did you lose your pocketbook?" I thought of all kinds of ploys people use to take advantage of seniors, and politely told him, 'No, I didn't."

"What did he say to that?"

"Ms. Focht, I have your wallet which was in your purse I found in a shopping cart in the Wal-Mart parking lot."

Delbert gasped. "Oh, my Bootsy! You certainly are one lucky lady."

"Yes, I am. His name was Michael McCleary. I also met his beautiful mother, Rita. When she climbed out of the van, we three stood there talking. They told me, because it was dark out, and my purse was black, they could readily see why it had been missed. I'm so happy he found it."

"Me, too. Someone else, in all probability, would have kept it."

"My thoughts exactly, and I would have found myself in dire financial trouble, as it contained not only my check book, my driver's license, my Village ID, but also my American Express, Visa, and forty-two dollars. He was such a nice man. One any mother would be proud of."

"Any father, too. I know I would be. What a great story. He has proven there are still trusting people, people with integrity, and it certainly gives us hope in this somewhat unraveling world of ours."

As usual, our conversation ended with hugs and kisses. I broke down, with "I love you, my Prince Delbert Hilling." And I smiled with his, "I love you, my princess."

Because of the weekend, and Monday was a holiday, I had a four day wait before Delbert's valentine arrived. When I finally had it in my hands, I ripped open the envelope, and blinked in amazement as I pulled out the loveliest and largest valentine I had ever seen or received. It resembled a folded red napkin edged in scalloped gold, with an enclosure of a red rose and three lavender Petunias. Printed on the front, sweet sentiments read:

> For My One
> and Only
> You've become
> so much
> a part of me
> that I can't imagine
> what I would do, or who I would be
> without you in my life.

I opened the flaps to see another red rose, and a lavender flower. Still, another page, which brought more tears of joy rolling down my cheeks.

> I only hope
> that with each kiss
> each touch
> and each special moment
> we share,
> you will always know
> how very much
> I love you.
> Happy Valentine's Day
> My Princess, Bootsy
>
> With Love,
> Your Prince Delbert Hilling

I read and reread the lovely message, and imagined it came right from his heart. Tiny shivers of joy swept through me as I dialed his number, and envisioned his dear, handsome face when he picked up his phone.

"Good afternoon, my darling," I greeted, and continued in song, "My heart sighs for you. "

He broke in, harmonizing, and together we sang, "Cries for you, dies for you. And my arms long for you, please come back to me," and the phone lines rattled with our outburst of laughter.

"Thank you for your lovely valentine, Delbert. It's so beautiful, and your sentiments are exactly like mine, the wonderful way I feel about you. "

"That makes me happy, my precious princess."

"So please tell me, Delbert, how are you?"

"Much, much better, after a weekend of rest."

We caught each other up to date, and ended with his, "I'm sending hugs and kisses to you, my princess. Here's a hug." I heard a funny noise, and laughed. "Now here's some kisses." Again, more funny noises.

"Thanks, kind sir. Now here are my kisses and hugs. Catch them."

I hung up, and with eyes closed, hugged myself, and was once again in his arms, with beautiful thoughts of...Oh, the perfect joy of being in love, again!

# Chapter 64
# Then Came Charlie and Frances

Over the few months ahead, in between being wrapped up in Village activities and my travels, I still managed to jot off little notes, and sometimes short messages of love to Delbert, in hopes of keeping the fires kindled. Spring and now, this part of summer, because Delbert had gone into a business with his son and grandson, and worked twelve to fourteen hours daily, more and more his responses became like dwindling rain. I remembered friend Polly's thoughts, before she met Ron and fell in love with him. "Men have flings, play with your heart, then bounce on to another." Had Delbert? Was he involved with someone else? Did he consider me a "part-time girl?" Was this customary for male Snow-Birds? Should I write and revoke my pledge to him?

Strangely, my recent horoscope in Holiday Mathis' column stated: Your mind has a conversation with itself. (How true).This doesn't mean you're crazy: (I hope not) It means you are sorting things through. (Right) You will be pressured to make a decision. but should not until you have absolutely no hesitation about doing so. (I definitely won't). I remembered Delbert's plans were to save money, sell his home, and settle here in The Villages. Like me, he, too, had become smitten. I would simply continue on, attend singles' dances, concerts, get out more, and make the most of life.

Intentions were short-lived. I came down with a virus that night, and spent most of it in the bathroom. Come morning, now sicker than a dog with 'dry heaves', I issued an SOS to Carl, my Kentucky farm boy. Soon, we were sailing down the highway to the new EUC, Exceptional Urgent Care, in The Spruce Creek Medical Center in Summerfield. There, in a half hour, I was ushered into the examining room, where Dr. John Im, hooked me up to an IV. Shortly, I departed with a prescription for nausea, and suppositories to fight bacteria. Food wise, I was 'out of it', lost six pounds that week, yet, felt confident in knowing, in case of need, we could count on help from this modern and close-by facility.

Then came Charley and Frances. Neither were lovers or doctors. We were into the hurricane season which hadn't touched Florida for years, yet these two, the worst, were lovers of destruction, bombarding their way across the state, and ripping open the guts of a huge part of Florida, causing tremendous destruction, leaving thousands homeless or without power.

The moment I heard Charlie was on his way, I hopped into my golf cart and scooted down to the Church on the Square. There, in the solemnity of God's great temple, with head bowed, I begged, "Please, dear Lord, save our lovely Villages which Mr. Schwartz worked so hard to develop. Next, I returned home, and in my car, took off for Wal-Mart. Plans were to buy battery operated neon tubular lights for each room. They had sold out of those, and even matches, by noon. So, my purchase consisted of flashlights, batteries, a long-handled Scripto lighter, and a freezer chest.

The following day, on the way to our Public Supermarket, the radio message coming from the local college advised, most importantly, to, "Have enough water and food to last three days. Fill your tubs with water, (good for flushing toilets) turn refrigerators and freezers up on high in case of power failure, food will last longer. Get refills on prescriptions, get your gas tanks filled. I had done all of that. In Publics I wasn't too surprised to find only a smattering of people. There, I bought shelf-stored milk, water, OJ and cran-raspberry juice. A man in the soda section stopped to pass on some enlightening thoughts. "No, the hurricane won't hit us. I've lived here twenty-nine years and none came through." I held onto that peaceful thought, and, indeed, Charley left us nearly unscathed. In checking around, the high winds and rains hadn't done too much damage. The Villages were spared, with some trees felled, and only a minimal damage to rooftops.

Then we were warned another hurricane, Frances, was on his way, and I again took off for the Church on the Square, and asked our dear Lord to keep us safe in His loving care. Daily, everyone's ears were tuned to the TV news. We were in for a hard one, this time. We were to be prepared. Frances was edging closer, and closer to Florida. Thursday evening, my phone jangled. Del, the representative of the American Red Cross, was on the line. "Yesterday, at your monthly Village Idiots' breakfast, you gave your name as a volunteer to help register those seeking shelter at the Village Elementary School. Could you please come in and lend a helping hand tomorrow morning at eight? People from trailer courts all over will be arriving. During Hurricane Charley, we had four hundred sixty-five check in."

"I could do that. Though not a morning person, I'll be there."

"Come anytime, we'll be grateful. The school is on Rolling Acres Road. It's a big red brick building. Drive to the second gate, and when you see a lot of people you're in the right place."

On my drive to the school the following morning, I wondered what had I gotten myself into, now? Any new undertaking tosses me into a mental fret, yet, the day began quite pleasantly, when I found my station in a large room, empty with the exception of two long tables. There I met Del, in person, and Liz, another helper, busy filling out forms. Liz was saying, "We're supposed to print or write the name of the school, and the telephone number." We were finished with one big stack when outside the double doors a long line had already formed. People, tall, short, thin, richly endowed, all ages, men and women, attired in summer wear, carried chairs, bedding and some with little freezers containing food for their pets. Yes, this was a 'pet loving shelter.' Pets would be residing in a special building. As would the handicapped people who needed physical assistance, and nurses' care. Three meals a day would be provided.

What a joy, simply hurrying down that long line with Liz, as we greeted people, passed out smiles, and slipped an admission form into each outstretched hand. Then, to later assist those who needed help to fill them out, and select places where they would reside. One little lady, with a bird perched on her shoulder, grabbed my sleeve and asked, "Do I have to put her in the room with other pets? She'll be in her cage, and she's deathly afraid of cats." I checked with our leader, Larry, and he said the bird had to stay in the pet section. It had been an interesting morning. I returned to my villa with a feeling of self gratification in knowing I had helped the American Red Cross even a little.

The next day, before Frances hit, I flitted around out in the garage, looking for anything I might be able to use during the storm. For a moment, I realized my closest neighbors were probably gone by now, like before. Their plans were to spend the next two days with relatives or friends. I was alone, feeling somewhat sorry for myself as I reached to the top of the white cabinet to remove a heavy red candle. Upon hearing a high screeching sound, I screamed, and swung around to find my friend, Woody, seated there, in his electric car, and wearing a silly grin.

"I'm sorry I frightened you, babe, but I was wondering if you would come spend the night at my home?"

"Why? Are you afraid?"

"No".

"Let me think about this," I said. "Okay, I thought about it, Woody. I worked two days getting everything ready, and would feel more comfortable sleeping here in my own villa. A curfew is now in effect, and we're not to be out. But, later, I'll sneak down to check in on you." When I arrived, I found him standing at his kitchen sink, and eating his dinner. We chatted awhile and when he finished, I said, "Let me tidy your kitchen, while you prepare for bed early, then in case of a power failure, you won't have to climb out of your riding car and flounder around in the dark, looking for things."

"Thank you, babe. That's a fine idea." I watched as he climbed into the seat and took off for the opposite side of his home. Off and on, while busy in his kitchen, I glanced out on a blackening sky, which became blacker by the minute. Mentally, I began to fret. Without lights on my golf cart, I would be a good candidate to be bumped off the road if neighborhood watch, or someone else came barreling around the corner. Eight o'clock, and I called to him. "Woody, I'm sorry, I must leave."

320

"Okay. I had hoped you would wait until I climbed into bed, but go ahead, and thank you, darlin'. Lock the door as you leave." I came away, wishing I could place my hand upon Woody's head, like Jesus would, and say, "Be healed," and he would be free of that dreadful disease called Parkinson's. I returned home, and before I pulled into the garage, I looked at the sky and it appeared normal.

Friday, I shuddered upon hearing the news Hurricane Francis had already battered the main tourist hub in the Bahamas. I became gleeful, in hearing it had weakened to a category two storm, and slowed as it crawled towards Florida. When it finally reached some outlying areas, for some reason, probably to escape the maddening TV news, that night, I didn't listen. Instead I gathered together a short-wave radio, pillow, blanket, toiletries, flashlight, water, a few other items, and prepared the center bathroom, just in case a more secluded and protective area became necessary. At 11 PM, an hour and a half earlier than usual, I slithered between cool sheets, hoping to sleep the night away. At 11:48, high winds, blowing in a frightening fury, awakened me and I sat bolt upright in bed, wondering what I should do.

Relentless noise, resembling a bouncing basketball on my rooftop proved unnerving. I could not sleep. I gathered my pillow and headed for the guest room. There, a repeat performance...the same noise. Finally, I moseyed out into the living room, curled up on the sofa, and there slept soundly until 2:10 AM. Everything was quiet for awhile, and I made a hasty retreat and climbed back into my own bed. I slept until 9:00AM, and the high winds had returned. All morning long, they continued, rattling windows in their fury. At one point, I sat near the sliding double glass doors in the dining room, talking to sis, Naomi, in Altoona, PA, and screamed when four shingles from my neighbor's rooftop, slammed into the window, and ripped a long slash in the screen directly in front of me.

That afternoon, when my phone rang, it happened to be Jane's husband on the line. He was saying, "It's a beautiful day in The Villages."

"And you are full of baloney, too," I told him.

"Are you okay?" he wanted to know.

"Yes, Bob. I tried calling, but couldn't get through. Did you hear the Orange Blossom Hills is without electricity? Just now, my lights flicked off, then on. Did yours?"

"No. We haven't had electricity for a day and a half. Here's our cell phone number. Use it from now on. Wait, Jane's on the line."

"You mean you have power? You are lucky. What are you doing now?"

"Don't laugh! I spend all of my free time keeping some semblance of normalcy. I'm sitting here, ripping apart a favorite gown I wore twenty years ago, when I last danced with my husband. I still love that dress and hopefully will again be able to wiggle into it."

"What color is it?"

"It's black, spaghetti strap, with big red and orange poppies, and white daisies swirling horizontally between narrow white stripes to the bottom. Also while busy at this task, now and then I reach beneath the sofa where I hide candy, and I have now eaten three Hershey's Chocolate Nuggets, and feel right at home. In Camp Hill, I lived only fifteen minutes away from the Hershey Chocolate Factory."

Jane giggled, and said, "I found a piece of Whitman's candy in our bed this morning. I offered some to Bob last night and must have dropped a piece."

"Are you going to fight over it?"

Another giggle, and "No, Bob already ate it."

"What have you two been up to?"

"We're actually having fun. We just had a picnic, ate by candlelight here by the pool, and with the sliding glass doors open in the lanai, a soft breeze is blowing in. It's quite romantic. Don't leave your home," she added. "A curfew is still in effect until Monday at 8 AM. They warn on TV, if you plan to leave your home you may as well head for the police station with your $500 fine."

"I can picture you two love birds. Here I am, alone, and somewhat envious."

# Chapter 65
# The Calm, After the Storm

During the hurricane season, I had thought of nothing else, but saving my house. Not until my phone jangled, and another familiar voice was on the line—Delbert's!

"Oh, my Bootsy, I've been so worried about you. Please tell me you're okay. Whenever I could reach a phone, I tried to get through to you, but couldn't."

"Yes, I know. The lines were tied up. But, oh, darling, yes, I'm fine, and it's so wonderful just to hear your voice. In talking to you I feel a sense of reality, with my feet once more planted on the ground."

"I'm glad for that, and pray you will accept my apology for not responding to your last three notes. I've been so terribly busy. I've missed so many summer picnics and haven't had a golf club in my hands for months."

"I understand, and you're forgiven. Tell me, have you ever gone through a hurricane?"

"No, and I don't care to."

"It's terrible, the devastation they've caused all across most of Florida."

"Yes, I've been reading the papers, and listening to radio and TV."

"Here, The Villages were spared. Some parts were without power for quite awhile, and we've had some felled trees, damaged roofs, and a few twisted lanais in the historical section. "

"Thank the dear Lord, it wasn't worse."

"Yes, I already thanked Him. We, here in the San Pedro Village, feel a Tornado my have swept through, because many of our roofs, including mine, must be replaced due to the loss of so many shingles."

We talked on a bit, and he added, "The money is still coming in, and I'm saving to come down. I must go now, must get back to work, but I'm going to send some hugs and kisses to you, my princess."

"Delbert? Since we've been apart for so long, let's close our eyes and make believe we're together again. Okay? Mine are closed, now close yours."

"Okay! They're closed."

"Good. Now, Delbert, picture me. Here I am, walking towards you."

"I see you, keep coming. My arms are open."

For a fleeting moment I was 21. Our office force at The Narrow Fabric Company had come into town to L L. Stearns and Sons for lunch. Down Pine Street, my Bill's bronze, curly head towered above the crowd in front of The Old City Hotel. With staccato of high heels pounding sidewalk, and echoing in my mind, I ran straight toward his open arms.I trembled, then suddenly, it was Delbert's arms reaching out to me, and as I nearly fell into them, I breathlessly spoke out loud, "Here I am, darling."

"I know, and you feel so...super marvelous," Delbert said.

"Umm. You do, too. As always, you smell and feel so...wonderful. I like to snuggle like this. Now, hug me gently, and we'll kiss goodbye."

We made the usual parting sounds, and laughed. "I love you, my little sweetheart, my Bootsy," he said.

"I love you, too. I'm going now. Goodbye, my love."

"Goodbye, my princess. Goodbye, for now."

When I opened my eyes, I slowly replaced the phone in its cradle, and drank in the sweet feeling which still lingered. It resembled the way I felt during the thirty-eight years of marriage to my Bill, when nightly, before retiring, his last "good night" was like a comfort blanket, covering me with his love.

I stood there a moment, and began to wonder, if down the road, someone asked how I succeeded in wiggling my way into Delbert's heart, what would I say?

First, to all women, I would toss out one of Dr. Phil's philosophical comments. "Men don't think like women. You don't throw a slice of bread to them. You have to throw a lot of little pieces to get them to understand."

Finally, I would quote myself: "Think young, dust your mind in dreams, plant a seed of faith, pull the weeds of distrust, and love may blossom, even in a retirement community. For it is here, where after many years of waiting, I have now awakened to a renewing of life and love, with a prince of a man, my Delbert.

*Been There, Done That, and Now This...*